Don't Be Afraid to Win

Don't Be Afraid to Win

Jim Quinn

Radius Book Group
New York

Distributed by Radius Book Group
A division of Diversion Publishing Corp.
443 Park Avenue South, Suite 1004
New York, NY 10016
www.RadiusBookGroup.com

For more information, email info@radiusbookgroup.com.

First edition: November 5, 2019
Hardcover ISBN: 978-1-63576-678-3
Trade paperback ISBN: 978-1-63576-692-9
eBook ISBN: 978-1-63576-685-1

Library of Congress Control Number: 2019909118

Manufactured in the United States of America

10 9 8 7 6 5 4 3 2 1

Cover design by Charles Hames
Interior design by Scribe Inc.

Contents

Foreword

FOR TYPICAL FANS, KNOWING A TEAM'S WIN-LOSS record or a player's individual stats is more than they need or care to know about sports. Of course, there is more to know—much more. To start, sports is not simply "playing games." Sports is business. Big business. And as in every other American-grown business—especially those that prove lucrative—tension has surrounded the division of power between management and labor. In some instances, that tension has morphed into virtual war. This was certainly the case in the evolution of professional sports in these United States.

In *Don't Be Afraid to Win*, Jim Quinn—a veteran of the sports wars—takes the reader onto the battlefield. In a no-holds-barred style, Quinn introduces combatants from both the leagues' and players' camps. Tons of books have been written about the development of player rights in professional sports. Few, however, were written by someone who not only had a seat at the various tables involved but, indeed, sat at the head of the grown-ups' table. As onetime lead counsel for each professional players' association—the Major League Baseball Players Association, the National Basketball Players Association, the National Football League Players Association, and the National Hockey League Players' Association—Jim Quinn occupied a seat of leadership for over 40 years. Writing from that vantage point, he shares, quite colorfully, the risks, strategies, failures, and triumphs experienced by the players.

An assortment of key participants in the battles between labor and management—both those still living and those long-since dead—is vividly portrayed in this work. Quinn is unsparing in both his praise and criticism of these folks, introducing us to "pricks," "horrible ass-holes," and "pompous fools" in both camps, as well as those he found "charming," "insightful," and "legendary." (President Donald Trump has a role in the book; try guessing how he is characterized!)

From this work, we learn how Quinn and his colleagues—together with the players and their player associations—weathered, fought, and ultimately defeated management efforts to restrict players' free-dom and reduce players' enjoyment of the revenue generated by their games. Quinn outlines owners' efforts to bankrupt player associa-tions, acts of owner collusion, and the leagues' tactic of locking out players from formal competition. He shares the players' decisions to strike, their attempts to locate alternative revenue streams, and their decision—or threat—to commit the ultimate act: union decertifica-tion, a Quinn proposal.

As the current executive director of one of the player associations that Quinn so brilliantly supported and defended, it was a joy to be introduced to those fiery and pugnacious union leaders and to learn about the solidarity and determination exhibited by the players as described in this book. As a litigator and "jury lawyer," I salivated at the stories Quinn shares of the legal maneuvering undertaken by him and his legal team to support the players' efforts. Their—and his—contributions were invaluable.

Jim is truly (if I might borrow the headline of a *Boston Globe* story written about him) *"The Mighty Quinn."*

Michele Roberts
Executive Director, National Basketball Players Association

Prologue

DON'T BE AFRAID TO WIN.

Those were the words Gene Upshaw whispered in my ear as I rose from my chair to deliver the closing argument in our lawsuit against one of the most powerful corporate entities in modern America, the National Football League (NFL).

It was September 8, 1992, and we were at the federal courthouse in Minneapolis. We'd been there for months, fighting over whether professional football players should have the same rights as every other American citizen to receive market value for their work.

It seems almost quaint now, more than 25 years later, to remember pro sports without free agency. It's become part of the game, a spectacle in and of itself. But the battle to achieve free agency in all four major leagues was vicious—and I can tell you that from personal experience because I was there at critical moments for all of them.

I had a very special seat to watch the drama and turmoil unfold as the American sports world underwent these monumental changes. As a lawyer over the last four decades, I represented the players' unions in all four of the major professional North American sports leagues, with an occasional time-out to represent a couple of doomed sports leagues. For a while it amused me to tell people that I was like Zelig, the quiet figure from the Woody Allen movie who was always at the periphery of the story, but that's not quite the case.

In fact, I helped to create and draft the first free agency agreement in professional sports, as well as the first league-wide drug agreement. I participated in the first decertification of a sports union, which felt incredibly risky at the time, and won the first and only jury verdict upholding player free agency. Much to my regret, I also played a key role in bringing about the first salary cap in professional sports. I participated in one way or another in the selection of union leaders in all four of the major team sports and was twice drafted at the 11th hour to settle season-ending lockouts.

Our fights against the NFL were the toughest of all for the simple reason that NFL owners made the most money and were hell-bent on keeping the players from sharing in the wealth. I wouldn't be surprised if there is still an NFL owner or two who agrees with Tex Schramm, the longtime president of the Dallas Cowboys, who once told Gene Upshaw, "The players are just cattle and we're the ranchers. We can always get more cattle."

Beating the NFL would not have been possible without a leader, ally, and friend like Upshaw. Left guard on the dominant Oakland Raiders teams of the 1970s, Upshaw was among the greatest players of all time, a first-ballot Hall of Famer, but his contributions as director of the National Football League Players Association (NFLPA) were greater still. He was nothing less than a hero. The law may have been on our side, but the money and power were on theirs. Upshaw's toughness and fierce commitment to the well-being of players past, present, and future changed the nature of professional sports forever. He was also a truly great guy to hang out with—always knew a good place to eat, no matter where we were, and I could sometimes beat him at poker, though rarely at golf.

I still can't believe that I ended up in the middle of it all. I was a blue-collar kid from the suburbs of New York City. Catholic school, Notre Dame, Fordham Law at night, a fan of all the major New York teams. Growing up, I didn't have a clue about the business of sports, never really gave it much thought. But landing as a junior litigator at an up-and-coming New York law firm, Weil, Gotshal & Manges, in the early 1970s, I heard about the "basketball case" kicking around the office and gravitated naturally toward it. The central figure there was Oscar Robertson, another legendary athlete to whom I grew close, and it was through Oscar, the product of a segregated high school in

Indianapolis and a self-made man in every respect, that I came to understand my work as a calling. Helping athletes get the compensation and rights they deserve is about economic justice—a lesson I learned from a man by the name of Larry Fleisher, a once prominent, now largely forgotten, sports figure. Fleisher was the early leader in this fight, which I later joined.

Economic justice was also very good business for the leagues. I firmly believe that recognizing the primacy of players and compensating them accordingly is a major factor in the explosive growth of professional sports. We would never have gotten where we are today if owners had been able to keep treating players like cattle. Martin Luther King famously said, "The arc of the moral universe is long, but it bends toward justice." Nowhere has this been truer than during the past 75 years in American pro sports, as professional athletes moved from virtual serfdom to relative freedom to often unwanted idolatry, and sometimes even to hatred. More than 70 years ago, Jackie Robinson risked hostility and worse by breaking the color barrier in professional baseball; more than 50 years ago, Muhammad Ali fought a five-year prison term, hatred, and the end of his boxing career by opposing an unjust war; and a half century later, Colin Kaepernick almost certainly ended his NFL career by taking a knee during the playing of the national anthem to protest racial injustice. This book chronicles the deeds of other pro athletes—some famous, most not—who took similar risks to change the face of sports in America forever.

When I began my professional involvement in sports, the teams and the leagues were relatively small businesses run by odd, cranky men. Most of the athletes were so modestly paid that they took second jobs in the off-season. The average salary of a player in the National Basketball Association (NBA) was $16,000 a year. The Baltimore Orioles signed baseball superstar Reggie Jackson, in the prime of his Hall of Fame career, to a one-year deal for $200,000. In 1980, the sixth game of the NBA Finals between the Magic Johnson–led Lakers and the Julius Erving–led 76ers was shown on tape delay after the local news because CBS did not want to preempt an episode of "The Dukes of Hazzard." That same year, the match between the American and Soviet hockey teams at the Olympics in Lake Placid—arguably the most famous single game played in any sport in North America—was also shown on tape delay.

Nowadays, they wouldn't dare show a bowling tournament on tape delay. Professional sports in America are today's version of the bread and circuses of Roman times. Wildly popular and ever-expanding, sports in general and professional team sports in particular have become one of the largest and most profitable segments of our entire entertainment industry.

We now have a 24-hour sports news cycle, ESPN from one to a hundred, Fox Sports (regular and regional), plus the monotony and idiocy of sports talk radio around the clock. The issues that blanket sports media today are a far cry from those that dominated the sports pages in years gone by. They range from the silly, like "Deflategate," to the very serious, such as discussions on domestic violence, long-term head injuries, and even patriotism versus racial justice. Sports dominate America today; to paraphrase Karl Marx, sports may have replaced religion as the opiate of the people.

Even the person who watches no sports whatsoever has to know LeBron James, Peyton Manning, Serena Williams, Tiger Woods, and Derek Jeter in order to be considered culturally literate; a nonsports fan must also understand the stories of Jackie Robinson, Muhammad Ali, Billie Jean King, Lance Armstrong, and Michael Jordan if they are to comprehend the most significant developments of postwar America.

Sports has become the vehicle through which we discuss race, free speech, gender roles, patriotism, sexual orientation, drugs, and violence. Today you can learn more about the hearts and minds of America from ESPN than CNN. And yet athletes continue to occupy a tenuous place in American hearts: they are admired as performers and lauded for their achievements but derided as spoiled millionaires for their desire to earn a fair share of the income their abilities generate.

This baffles me. I have certainly met my own fair share of selfish people, and some of them were athletes. I'll never forget Reggie Jackson insisting on being prepared for a deposition in the pool of a Miami Beach Hotel. Our lawyer actually had to put on swim trunks. But the vast majority of the athletes I've dealt with were genuine role models—bright, inquisitive, hardworking, and committed to a cause larger than themselves. The same cannot be said for many of the team owners I've met.

I want to warn you in advance that Donald Trump does appear in these pages, as does his notorious mentor Roy Cohn. Virtually every big sports star of the past 40 years makes a cameo. You'll read about George Steinbrenner, Howard Cosell, Pete Rozelle, Ken Starr, Bowie Kuhn, and the owner of one hockey franchise who interrupted me at a meeting by yelling, "Who the fuck are you and what the fuck are you doing here?" He then challenged me to take it outside.

The core of this book is based largely on my recollections, some of which are inevitably flawed. Other individual or collective memories may differ, although I spent valuable time checking my memory with colleagues and other participants in these events. For the early history, I relied heavily on published reports as well as what I learned from my extensive experience in handling scores of cases and legal proceedings of all types in the four major sports. So whatever is wrong, blame me.

My hope in setting down this history and telling these stories is to give some insight as to how the current structure of the major team sports in America came to be, with particular emphasis on the central role players and their unions played in shaping that structure. Along the way, I plan to explode a few of the myths about the people and the events critical in getting us where we are with sports in America today. Maybe, just maybe, I'll be able to shed some light on what the future of professional team sports in this country holds for players, owners, and, while largely ignored, the fans who love these games.

CHAPTER 1

The 21-Minute Strike

IN 1964, THE NBA PLANNED TO BROADCAST ITS ALL-Star Game in prime time on national television for the first time. It was a huge coup for an NBA that had only nine teams and was very much the stunted stepchild of the baseball and football leagues. The game was scheduled for January 14, 1964. The day before, a massive snowstorm blanketed the East Coast; all flights into Boston were canceled.

Somehow the players (a group that included 17 future Hall of Famers) and most of the team owners managed to get to Boston Garden by late afternoon of game day. The broadcast was set to begin at eight o'clock that evening on ABC.

The players, however, had a surprise in store for the owners. Led by a 34-year-old lawyer named Larry Fleisher, they had been demanding a pension program, and the negotiations continued right up to game time, with Fleisher shuttling between the players' locker rooms and the suite where most of the NBA owners were huddled. The players decided this was the moment to stand up to their feudal owners. *Unless their demands were met, they would not come out for the game.*

The owners tried calling their bluff and refused to budge.

The players were not unanimous, but when Bob Pettit and Oscar Robertson stood up on benches in the east and west locker rooms and implored them to stand together, they did so. As the clock ticked past eight o'clock, Boston Garden's famous parquet floor was devoid of players.

Emotions ran high; there was a great deal at stake for both sides.

Celtics owner Walter Brown stormed into the east locker room, calling Tommy Heinsohn, his own star player, "the biggest heel in sports."[1] Heinsohn shrugged. Bob Short, the Lakers owner, tried to barge into the west locker room but found his way blocked. He directed a clubhouse attendant to deliver a message to his star Elgin Baylor, saying, "If he doesn't get his ass out here fast, I'm done with him." Baylor's response: "Tell Bob Short to go fuck himself."[2] The players could hear Fleisher and NBA commissioner Walter Kennedy shouting at each other in the hall. Cincinnati Royals center Wayne Embry (later to become professional sports' first black general manager and first black team president) expressed a feeling shared by most of the players: "I was scared shitless."[3]

Fleisher returned to the locker rooms, urging the players to hang tough. Ignore the threats, he told the players—"You have the leverage."[4] Fleisher didn't need to talk about the risks his members were taking. They knew them. For each of those men, there would come a day when his contract expired, and no team was required to re-sign him. It's hard to be a basketball player without a team and without a league.

At 8:12 p.m., Kennedy came into the locker room and said the owners had caved. He could not give the players a pension plan right there and then, but he would give them his word that he would do whatever he could to make it a reality.

Some of the players were reluctant to trust Kennedy, but Wilt Chamberlain said that his word should be good enough for the game to go on. At exactly 8:21 p.m., the players came out on the court and the game was played.

The first player strike in history lasted 21 minutes and changed professional sports forever.

The heroes that day were the players, but they would have been lost without Fleisher. I didn't know him in 1964; I was still at Notre Dame. But later, as a young lawyer, I learned the legend of Larry from the man himself. As general counsel for the NBA's fledgling players' union in the 1960s and 1970s, he not only led the first player strike but also conceived of the first league-wide legal attack on the old reserve system structure that prevented players both from bargaining for their real value and from moving to another team that would recognize that value.

Though Marvin Miller, the leader of the baseball players' union, usually gets the nod as the godfather of sports labor, it was Fleisher who got the first free agency labor contract, negotiated the first league-wide drug agreement, and established the first revenue-sharing system in pro sports. He was also the first union leader to threaten to blow up his union to get a better deal. Along the way, he became the first prominent sports agent in all of professional team sports. Back in the 1960s and 1970s, owners and sportswriters attacked Fleisher and Miller, deeming them the sports equivalents of Sacco and Vanzetti—"anarchists" and "bomb throwers" whose militant leadership would destroy the very fabric of professional team sports. This was slander. In fact, Fleisher's "bomb-throwing" ideas shaped the entire structure of professional sports as it exists today.

Larry Fleisher was born in the Bronx in 1930. His father, Morris, a Russian Jewish immigrant, ran a small print shop in Manhattan and insisted that his dozen employees become union members. Morris was a card-carrying Communist, which may strike some readers as strange but wasn't all that unusual in the 1930s. Fleisher the son was a Jewish agnostic—irreligious and irreverent. He was more comfortable playing stickball or basketball than studying the Torah or learning calculus, perhaps because studying was boring to someone as bright as he was. He graduated from DeWitt Clinton High School in the Bronx at age 16, made it through NYU in three years, and graduated from Harvard Law School at age 22. He was unpredictable, and though the man never told a joke, his stories were often hilarious.

I met Fleisher in the summer of 1973, when I was a young lawyer at Weil, Gotshal & Manges, and I got involved with the "basketball case." I was just two years out of Fordham Law. I remember walking into a conference room and meeting an intense, jovial, rotund, dark-haired man with a cigar. He was 43. I was 28. We became inseparable. Over the years, he would teach me everything I needed to know about the history of sports and labor.

Larry was a flaming liberal both politically and socially. There wasn't a left-wing cause he didn't embrace—from socialism to Darwinism and all the -isms in between. He also possessed an uncanny facility with numbers. He had the capacity to comprehend complex actuarial formulas and do detailed mathematical calculations in his head simultaneously. His negotiation skills were legendary. According to the *New York Times*, Fleisher "was known for his tough-minded negotiations, for his financial acumen and for the wide circle of warm friendships he made on both sides of the labor issue."[5]

Fleisher was both feared and respected by the team owners, general managers, and executives of the NBA. According to one longtime NBA owner, one of the reasons the league had gotten into some trouble was that "Larry did too good a job of negotiating over the years."[6] NBA players, for this and other reasons, would follow him to the ends of the earth, and some of them literally did. In the off-seasons, he organized "NBA player trips" that took players and their wives, as well as the two of us and our wives, to Brazil, the Ivory Coast, Greece, Italy, Yugoslavia, and China.

The number of unforgettable "Fleisher stories" floating out there, told eagerly by friends and player-clients, are legion. There was the time he got a busload of NBA players lost in the south of France looking for a casino in Monte Carlo. Then there was the time he sneaked a trunk full of basketball equipment (uniforms, basketballs, sneakers) onto a flight to Rio because he didn't want the players on the trip to know that they were going to have to play a series of exhibition games in Brazil to pay for what they thought was their "summer vacation."

Fleisher's early career was a mix of precocity and underachievement. He graduated near the bottom of his law class at Harvard—probably because he spent the bulk of his time in Cambridge shooting hoops with classmates like Bob Pitofsky (later FTC chairman), Lee Sarokin (later a US federal judge), and Derek Bok (later president of Harvard).

After a stint in the army, Fleisher got his CPA license and set up shop as a sometime lawyer but mostly tax accountant and financial advisor working in the entertainment and restaurant worlds. He had some prominent clients, including songwriters and musical producers Lerner and Loewe of *My Fair Lady* and *Camelot* fame. During this period, Fleisher also became the vice president and chief financial officer for Restaurant Associates, a holding company that operated a dozen restaurants in New York City, including the Four Seasons, Charley O's, and Mama Leone's.

Fleisher became a union leader more or less by accident. In 1962, a mutual friend introduced Fleisher, an avid basketball fan, to Tommy Heinsohn, star forward of the champion Boston Celtics. Heinsohn had taken over the presidency of the then embryonic NBA Players Association from his Hall of Fame teammate Bob Cousy, who had started what would become the first recognized sports players' union in 1954. Cousy had hoped to get the NBA players a pension but became frustrated by the lack of dues support from many players and the staunch opposition of team owners. Nearing retirement, he ceded leadership to the tough, jovial Heinsohn.

A part-time insurance salesman, Heinsohn came up with the idea of funding a pension for players with insurance. A native of Jersey City, Heinsohn was a no-nonsense guy both on and off the court, but he had a big heart and an even bigger sense of humor. Like Cousy, he was destined to have a Hall of Fame career as both a player and a coach—all for his beloved Boston Celtics.

The Bronx kid and the Jersey City kid hit it off immediately. Heinsohn saw in Fleisher the keen intelligence and willingness to fight for the underdog that would become the hallmark of Larry's career. Neither Fleisher nor Heinsohn had a clue about unions or labor law or the National Labor Relations Act. But when Larry met Tommy in the fall of 1962, the National Basketball Players Association (NBPA) became a real, functioning organization.

They immediately began building up the organization, recruiting the respected All-Star Bob Pettit; the soft-spoken, cerebral Lenny

Wilkens; and the fiery, outspoken Oscar Robertson as vice presidents. The three complemented one another beautifully. Robertson, with his fighter's temperament, would later take the lead in the battle for free agency.

Fleisher began devoting less time to restaurants and more to the union. He would spend the next couple of years meeting with players and getting to know their problems and encouraging them to stick together and fight for what they believed was right. This organizing effort would lead to the showdown at the 1964 All-Star Game, the first real labor confrontation in modern pro sports.

In the early days of these struggles, the goals were very modest, like securing a pension plan. The idea that players were tied to their teams for life, like modern-day serfs, was so ingrained in professional sports that no one seriously sought to challenge it in court or at the bargaining table. Every athlete who wanted to play for a professional team had to sign a player contract that contained a "reserve" or "option" clause, making those contracts automatically renewable at the team's option. These clauses made it impossible to try to move to another team even after the term of the player's contract had ended. Clubs could just keep exercising their "option" to renew for another year in perpetuity. As long as a player couldn't move, he had no leverage to get more money, regardless of his performance. (In a famous example, the Chicago Cubs cut the salary of slugger Ralph Kiner by $15,000 for the 1953 season even though he had just led the league in homers for the seventh consecutive year.)

These clauses were the Holy Grail that the feudal Lords of Sports vowed never to relinquish without a fight to the death. The reserve system was all about power and control and making sure owners could pay players as little as possible, whether the sport be baseball, basketball, football, or hockey. The owners' attitude was "Let's keep the players in their place."

The system had withstood multiple legal challenges in baseball, dating all the way back to the turn of the 20th century. In what became known as the *Federal Baseball* case, the Supreme Court determined—incongruously and erroneously—that professional base-ball was somehow not in interstate commerce and therefore was not subject to the antitrust laws of the United States. This absurd ruling remained in place for nearly a century until it was partially overturned by Congress in the late 1990s. Years later, Lakers Hall of Famer Elgin Baylor told the *Los Angeles Times*, "All of us felt like we were slaves in the sense we had no rights. No one made anything then. You had to work in the summer. It was the stone ages."[7]

In 1957, there was a sliver of light when a professional football player named Bill Radovich sued the NFL. Radovich had been a guard for four seasons with the Detroit Lions. When World War II began, Radovich, like many young men, put his occupation aside to serve his country and enlisted in the US Navy. After the war, he returned to the Lions, but after a year, he asked to be traded to the Los Angeles Rams because he wanted to be able to spend more time with his sick father, who lived near Los Angeles. When the owner of the Lions refused, Radovich signed with the Los Angeles–based team in the All-American Football Conference, which was a competitor of the NFL at the time. A year later, he tried to return, but the NFL had blacklisted him from playing or working in the league in any capacity. Radovich sued, citing the US antitrust laws and claiming an illegal boycott by the NFL and its teams.

The Supreme Court determined that unlike baseball, the NFL (and presumably, other sports leagues) was indeed subject to US anti-trust laws. The NFL quietly settled the case. But despite the *Radovich* ruling, professional athletes did not begin to see the enormous impact competition could have on player salaries until some years later, when the newly formed American Football League (AFL) went after top col-lege players like Heisman Trophy–winner Billy Cannon and other All-American college players like Lance Alworth, John Hadl, and later Joe Namath, the number-one college quarterback in the country in 1964. In its first year alone, in 1960, the AFL signed more than half of the NFL's first-round draft picks. Football players' salaries in both the NFL and AFL grew dramatically, and veteran NFL players like

George Blanda, Len Dawson, Art Powell, and Don Maynard jumped to the AFL.

The football players were happy, but the football owners were not. AFL and NFL owners conspired to put an end to player competition by secretly ramming a merger bill through Congress—what came to be known as the "Midnight Merger." The legislation was approved near midnight on December 31, 1966. It was rumored that two powerful Louisiana politicians—Senator Russell Long and Representative Hale Boggs, the men who had spearheaded this effort for the football owners—had made a deal with then NFL commissioner Pete Rozelle that Louisiana would get the next NFL expansion franchise. The New Orleans Saints became a reality just a few months later.

The NFL-AFL merger succeeded in turning the clock back to what owners in all sports considered the "halcyon days," when players were no better than serfs on the owners' feudal estates.

During the late 1950s and early 1960s, while all this was taking place, I was growing up in a middle-class suburban home in White Plains, some 25 miles north of New York City. Oblivious to the plight of professional athletes who were virtually imprisoned by their owners, I spent my time scouring box scores for my heroes, the baseball Giants' Willie Mays and the Yankees' Mickey Mantle, as well as checking the running and passing stats for Frank Gifford and Y. A. Tittle of the New York Football Giants. After graduating first in my overcrowded class of some 55 eighth graders from Our Lady of Mt. Carmel Parochial School in nearby Elmsford, New York, I began high school in the fall of 1959 at Archbishop Stepinac High School in White Plains. I was one of 250 or so freshmen from the largely blue collar Irish and Italian Catholic stock who came from all over Westchester County. Back then, we spent most of our summers in the caddie yard at Knollwood Country Club in Elmsford arguing over the demise of the New York Yankee dynasty and the arrival of the pathetically inept New York Mets. We were more focused on free baseball tickets than free agency and on new baseball caps than salary caps. My dream was to go to Notre Dame, where my brother already was; my father had graduated from

ND back in 1936. That dream came true when I graduated at the top of my class from Stepinac in June 1963 and joined a dozen other Stepinac graduates entering ND that fall. I was blithely unaware of the formation of nascent player unions and couldn't have cared less about player goals and aspirations.

• • •

Meanwhile, during his first couple of years as general counsel, Fleisher devoted himself to turning the NBPA into a strong union. It wasn't easy; operating on a shoestring budget, the NBPA consisted of a few hours of Fleisher's time, some letterhead, and the part-time contributions of Larry's enigmatic secretary, Curt Parker. In the late 1960s, Larry and Curt moved the NBPA offices to what was then the Gulf and Western Building, located at Columbus Circle and overlooking Central Park. (Years later, the building would become the Trump International Hotel & Tower.) Fleisher had by then drafted the first NBPA bylaws and constitution, which consisted of six pages and had more typos than paragraphs. The new bylaws stipulated that there would be a president and several vice presidents as well as an elected player representative from each team. Dues were $100 per player. The officers and player reps would meet formally twice a year, once during the midwinter All-Star break and again in the summer.

The goals of this fledgling association were, in retrospect, fairly modest: pensions for NBA players, increased meal money, dues checkoff, first-class travel, a shorter preseason schedule, and health insurance for players and their families.

The NBA players' hope for some kind of pension led to a series of meetings that a few players, including Heinsohn, Pettit, and Robertson, held with Commissioner Kennedy and a handful of NBA owners. Fleisher was initially excluded from the meetings because several owners refused to meet with a so-called labor provocateur, a description that hardly fit the soft-spoken Fleisher. On several occasions, he was told to sit outside the meeting room, forcing players to leave the room to consult with him.

It was a frustrating situation. As Robertson described to me years later, "The owners would tell us they were going to do things, and then they'd change their minds." After a year or so, Fleisher, Heinsohn, Pettit, Wilkens, and Robertson came up with a novel tactic—labor stoppage at the 1964 NBA All-Star Game. As Pettit recalled to me, "They wouldn't recognize our union or give us a pension plan, so we told the owners we're not playing the game."

That night, after the 21-minute strike, Robertson was named MVP, with 26 points, 14 rebounds, and 8 assists. The next year, he replaced Heinsohn as the NBPA president. There would be many more fights to come—and indeed, it took another couple of years to hammer out the details—but in 1966, the NBA and the NBPA signed the first formal collective bargaining agreement (CBA) in the history of pro sports. When the NBA owners once again reneged on their promise to fund the pension and provide other benefits, Fleisher and the players threatened to strike the 1967 playoffs, which led to a quick settlement. In January 1968, the players finally got the pension Kennedy had promised. The newly recognized union would sign two more short-term CBAs before open warfare between NBA players and NBA owners broke out in the spring of 1970.

Some years later, Fleisher told me that he never felt more alive than on that snowy night in Boston. That short strike would become a seminal moment in the fight for players' rights. Fleisher told me, "As long as the guys stick together, the owners can't win." I was hooked.

CHAPTER 2

The Agent from Hell

WHEN BILL BRADLEY RETURNED FROM HIS RHODES scholarship at Oxford in 1965, he went to see Marty Glickman, a former Olympic star and the premier New York radio and TV announcer at the time. Glickman did play-by-play for the football Giants, the Knicks, and the Rangers. Bradley, who graduated from Princeton as the top college player in the country, had been a first-round draft pick of the Knicks in 1964.

Glickman advised Bradley to get someone to help him with his contract with the Knicks, suggesting Fleisher because he knew Larry was very good with numbers. Fleisher did in fact negotiate an extraordinary contract for Bradley. The salary numbers made him, as a rookie, the highest-paid player on the Knicks and one of the highest-paid players in the league. Fleisher even got Bradley a so-called "no cut, no trade" contract, which was quite likely another first for that era. That meant Bradley could not be traded without his permission, and if he were cut from the roster, the team still had to pay him. This was what became known as a "guaranteed" contract, something virtually unheard of at the time.

The term "sports agent" was also unheard of, but when word got out about Bradley's contract, players flocked to Fleisher's door. Sensing danger, some NBA owners tried to exclude Fleisher from their face-to-face negotiations with players, but it didn't work. A new era was born.

Eventually, Fleisher would become the premier sports agent in basketball and, for a while, in all of team sports. During the 1970s,

Fleisher's clients included John Havlicek, Oscar Robertson, David Thompson, Ernie DiGregorio, Zelmo Beaty, Billy Cunningham, Paul Silas, Bob Lanier, Jim Paxson, Archie Clark, Marvin Webster, and Maurice Lucas—just to name a few, and all of whom were All-Stars. At one point, Fleisher represented nearly a quarter of all the players in the league. In fact, he represented most of the championship 1970 and 1973 Knicks teams. In addition to Bradley, Fleisher worked for Dave DeBusschere, Willis Reed, Earl Monroe, and Phil Jackson, along with several of the Knicks' backup players. This gave him enormous bargaining power, which drove NBA general managers and owners nuts.

Fleisher was a terrific (if quirky) negotiator with a knack for creating special contract terms in order to get the very most he could for each of his players. He worked his magic in both collective bargaining and negotiating individual contracts for his player clients. Bruce Meyer, my law partner of 30 years, recounted one story of Larry's negotiating style. After hours of frustrating discussions over a particularly complicated contract provision, Larry finally gave in and said, "Fuck it, I agree." When Meyer asked him later why he agreed to such a complex clause that no one would possibly understand, Fleisher replied, "How else do you think we could get around it?"

Fleisher wasn't above playing mind games. I once happened to sit in on a session of contract negotiations for a new client of his, Ernie DiGregorio, an All-American guard from Providence College. "Ernie D," as he was known, had been drafted by the Buffalo Braves in the NBA and the Kentucky Colonels in the American Basketball Association (ABA). When Braves owner Paul Snyder arrived for a meeting with Fleisher to discuss his career in the NBA, Ernie D sat quietly in a corner dribbling a red, white, and blue ABA basketball. Later, when Kentucky's owner John Y. Brown showed up for his negotiating session, Ernie sat in the corner just as quietly dribbling the traditional orange NBA ball. A few days later, DiGregorio signed a multiyear guaranteed deal with Buffalo for what was then the highest amount ever paid to a rookie guard. He went on to win NBA Rookie of the Year honors in 1974 but had a career-ending injury a few years later.

Fleisher had made sure, however, that Ernie D was set for life; they remained good friends to the day Fleisher died.

NBA owners often cried foul and accused Fleisher of having had a conflict of interest because he represented individual players and was also acting as the general counsel of the NBPA. The charge never really stuck because most of the players in the league believed that Fleisher was fighting for all of them. Eventually, his dominance in the agent world of basketball would ebb as more and more people—many lawyers, some not—jumped into the business of representing professional athletes.

During the early NBA collective bargaining negotiations, Fleisher often came in contact with the NBA's lead labor lawyer, Ed Silver, who was perhaps the preeminent management labor lawyer of his time and the father of the current commissioner, Adam Silver. They would eventually become great friends with enormous mutual respect and affection.

Larry and I shared a passion for the underdog, which back then was, believe it or not, the lot of most professional athletes. I had wanted to become a lawyer since the age of 12, when I first read *To Kill a Mockingbird* and so admired Atticus Finch in his gallant but failed defense of Tom Robinson. Larry felt the same way about championing the oppressed.

He loved working with people who were just beginning their careers and enjoyed mentoring the "next generation," whether they were pro athletes or young lawyers. He wasn't into hierarchy; he treated young associates like partners and vice versa.

All of which is not to say that Fleisher was perfect. His work habits were, to say the least, erratic. He regularly took naps in the afternoon. His workday seldom began before 10 in the morning and often ran well past midnight, meeting with players, owners, and general managers before and after Knicks games. Fleisher's Madison Square Garden seats were midcourt, right next to the radio booth, where he would chat with Knicks announcer Marv Albert. In the pre–cell phone era, Fleisher would spend seven or eight hours a day on the telephone talking to his own clients and other NBA players, as well as team owners, league officials, his lawyer friends, and sometimes even his friends' wives. He often called my wife, Katy, or John Havlicek's wife, Beth, "just to chat." After a leisurely lunch and short nap on his office couch, there would always be a bottle of vodka nearby to be enjoyed by whoever stopped by the office. On any given day, you might run into Ted Turner (Atlanta Hawks owner and later TV mogul), Bill Bradley, Governor John Y. Brown (Kentucky Colonels owner), an FTC commissioner or two, and even the Italian ambassador, all swinging by to talk basketball or politics. His opening line, whether in person or on the phone, was invariably "Whatcha doing?" He was one of a kind.

Individual athletes—tennis players and pro golfers—had hired agents, such as Mark McCormack of IMG fame, starting in the early 1960s. But Fleisher was a pioneer in introducing the idea of sports agents to professional team sports. The term has become tarnished over the years by a handful of bad actors. In truth, the role that Fleisher and those who followed him still play today is important in ensuring that players in whatever sport get the best deal possible. Fleisher's so-called conflict of interest was more imagined than real, which is proven by Larry's groundbreaking accomplishments for both his individual clients and his union members at large in a career that spanned three decades. Fleisher would eventually step down as the preeminent sports union leader and continue his agent business, in part to lay to rest any hint of conflict, however misperceived.

CHAPTER 3

TV Changes Everything

IN THE 1950S, BASEBALL WAS THE KING OF SPORTS IN America. Boxing and horse racing, numbers two and three, didn't involve teams at all, and at the time, college football and basketball were far more popular than their professional counterparts. Though sports had a huge hold on the country's imagination, you couldn't really consider it an industry. It was decentralized, dispersed, and very local in nature.

Some baseball owners were wealthy businessmen—like Del Webb (real estate), Augie Busch (beer), Lou Perini (construction), and Bill Wrigley (gum)—who treated their teams as hobbies. But most were conservative businessmen running relatively small enterprises with tight margins, sometimes making a little money, sometimes losing a little. There were no huge bidding wars when franchises came up for sale. In the late 1940s, Del Webb, Dan Topping, and Larry McPhail bought the Yankees, the most successful and glamorous franchise in the history of organized sports, for $2.8 million, the equivalent today of about $29 million, or less than a fifth of their 2018 payroll. Small-market teams were worth a lot less. Bill Veeck, who owned three different teams over the course of his baseball career, bought the St. Louis Browns in 1951 for less than $100,000.

At that time, the pro leagues were East Coast–centric; the only teams west of the Mississippi River were the Los Angeles Rams and San Francisco 49ers in football, and the Los Angeles Lakers and San Francisco Warriors in basketball. This was due largely to the prohibitive cost of air travel. Ownership in the other sports leagues, like the NFL, were small-time, family-run operations, dominated by the Maras in New York, the Rooneys in Pittsburgh, the Bidwills in Chicago (and later St. Louis), and the Halas family in Chicago. Nobody knew or cared who owned the local basketball or hockey teams; in many cases, it was the same guy who owned the arenas where they played, like Ned Irish with Madison Square Garden and Walter Brown with Boston Garden. Teams were often created for the express purpose of increasing bookings at their buildings.

Then television hit the scene.

The first baseball game was televised in its entirety in 1939, though it would be more than a decade before TV had a real impact on the game. By the late 1950s, most baseball teams had local TV deals and were starting to expand their businesses, looking for new stadiums and new markets. They saw what everybody else saw—a country bursting at the seams, spreading south and west. Formerly small regional outposts like Atlanta, Denver, Dallas, Houston, and San Diego were transformed into big, vibrant cities. Baseball franchises began to chase the population boom, notably the heartbreaking departure of the Brooklyn Dodgers for Los Angeles and of my beloved Giants for San Francisco. As baseball became a national industry, the major TV networks took notice. First CBS, and later NBC, agreed to pay baseball owners millions to broadcast exclusively what became known as the "Game of the Week."

Television had perhaps its greatest impact on pro football. On December 28, 1958, the New York Giants played the Baltimore Colts at Yankee Stadium for the NFL championship. It was so cold and snowy that the stands were half full. But millions of television viewers were treated to what has been memorialized in NFL lore as simply "The Game." Quarterback Johnny Unitas rallied the Colts to a game-tying touchdown in the fourth quarter, and fullback Alan Ameche put them over the top in sudden death. I can still remember watching the game on our black-and-white TV in White Plains and becoming a New York Giant football fan from that day on.

Television ratings for the Game were off the charts, inspiring a group of wealthy heirs—including Lamar Hunt, Barron Hilton, and Bud Adams—to start a rival venture called the American Football League, placing franchises in the up-and-coming cities that had no NFL teams. It was a crazy time. The cloistered business of pro football gave way to frenzied bidding wars as the nascent AFL went after NFL stars and top college talent. Out of nowhere, there was real competition, creating all sorts of exciting new opportunities as well as conflicts. I loved watching the flashy AFL of the early 1960s, with the likes of Babe Parelli, Len Dawson, George Blanda, and later Joe Namath lighting it up for 500-plus yards passing and a half-dozen touchdowns on a weekly basis.

A few years later, more or less the same thing happened in basketball, although in this case, the owners were less wealthy and the market for pro basketball was much less developed. The National Basketball Association had been created in 1949 out of two failing leagues, and by the late 1950s, the original 17 teams (which included franchises in major metropolises such as Sheboygan, Illinois, and Tri-Cities, Iowa) had been winnowed down to 9. By 1966, it was back up to 14, with new clubs in Chicago, Seattle, and Phoenix, among others, but business was hardly booming. The launch of a new venture calling itself the "American Basketball Association" and boasting a red, white, and blue ball seemed, at best, impetuous. This was particularly true in the wake of the early demise of the American Basketball League (ABL) a few years earlier. That venture lasted less than two seasons despite the presence of a young George Steinbrenner and some top college stars like Jerry Lucas, Dick Barnett, Bill Bridges, and the controversial yet brilliant Connie Hawkins.

In many respects, the ABA was ahead of its time. Cofounder Gary Davidson, who later had a hand in both the World Hockey Association and the World Football League (more on those later), wanted to make basketball more entertaining. He succeeded. The ABA introduced the three-point shot and the slam-dunk contest and, like the AFL, put teams in thriving new cities, such as Dallas, Denver, and Houston.

The problem was that most ABA owners weren't nearly rich enough to spend money as recklessly as they did. A couple of smart ones (like Angelo Drossos, who would eventually steer his San Antonio Spurs into the NBA) did well, but most lost whatever business acumen they had when it came to basketball. Franchises moved or folded every year like a game of musical chairs, which was confusing and dispiriting for fans. Who wants to invest their passion in a team that might not make it back from their next road trip?

But the ABA had a mission that kept it from drowning in red ink: the goal of these nouveau semi-riche owners, according to Dick Tinkham, another cofounder, was to quickly force a merger with the NBA.

Toward this end, the ABA caused real trouble for the older league. By offering to double and triple the salaries of incoming rookies and luring young stars out of college early, the ABA grabbed Artis Gilmore, George McGinnis, George Gervin, Maurice Lucas, and Julius Erving, all of whom would later become legends in the NBA. The ABA also went after NBA veterans like Billy Cunningham of the 76ers and the Warriors' Rick Barry.

When Barry attempted to sign with the ABA, the Warriors tried to use the reserve clause in Barry's contract to prevent him from leaving. Barry sued. The court agreed with him, sort of, saying that his option could not be renewed perpetually but that Barry would have to sit out a year before he could officially sign with the ABA's Oakland Oaks. This was an early chink in the NBA owners' sacred reserve system and a sign of things to come.

The ABA stabilized a bit in its third year, as the undeniable star quality of its rosters netted a national TV deal, albeit a modest one. Like the AFL, the emergence of the ABA revealed a truth that sports owners had actively suppressed for years and would continue to suppress for years to come—that the players, not the teams, are the essential attraction and the driving force of fan interest.

The ABA was very good for my mentor, Larry Fleisher, and his clients. Fleisher grasped immediately that a stronger ABA would boost

NBA player salaries, and sure enough, after the ABA's first three years, the average salaries in the NBA tripled, going from less than $16,000 a year to nearly $50,000 a year. Competition wasn't always aboveboard; there were rumors that star players like Lew Alcindor (later Kareem Abdul-Jabbar) were recipients of under-the-table offers and cash payments. There was also jockeying over cities. Over the next few years, the NBA would add four more franchises—Buffalo, Portland, Cleveland, and New Orleans—at least in part to prevent ABA expansion into these cities.

Soon the two leagues called a truce. In late 1969, with both sides claiming they were hemorrhaging money, a merger was announced to take effect the following season. The NBA and ABA now had a common cause: to stop the escalation of player salaries and get their finances under control.

Fleisher had other ideas. And soon enough, I'd be in his corner.

CHAPTER 4

"The Big O" Sues the NBA

THROUGH HIS UNIQUE PRISM OF AGENT, BUSINESS-man, and union leader, Larry Fleisher knew exactly what would happen if the NBA and the ABA were allowed to merge—the budding interleague competition that had boosted player salaries and benefits would be squelched. You did not have to look further than the NFL's absorption of the AFL for evidence that this was true.

Fleisher resolved to block the basketball merger.

He began to recruit a legal team, placing his first call to his old basketball-playing classmate from law school Bob Pitofsky, then a professor of competition and antitrust law at Columbia Law School. Pitofsky, who later became chairman of the FTC in the Clinton administration, recommended another member of the Columbia Law faculty—Ira Millstein, a senior partner at the unpronounceable firm of Weil, Gotshal & Manges. Millstein had been a litigation lawyer in the antitrust division of the Justice Department, and after entering private practice at Weil in the early 1950s, he garnered a reputation as an antitrust litigation expert. Pitofsky became an unpaid consultant to his friends Fleisher and Millstein as things progressed.

Antitrust laws had originally been passed by Congress to encourage the government to bust up oil, railroad, and other monopolies existing at the turn of the 20th century. It wasn't until the late 1960s that these laws became powerful tools for private citizens to ensure competition in a wide variety of industries, including sports and entertainment.

Millstein was another character. By the time he was 40, he possessed a head of curly white hair and a high-pitched voice perfect for yelling at partners, opposing lawyers, or anyone else he deemed intellectually deficient. The only people he spared were clients, whom he invariably both charmed and revered. In Millstein's view, clients were never wrong—even when they were dead wrong. Millstein was brilliant, mercurial, perceptive, funny, and the most creative lawyer I have ever known. Some years later, when antitrust litigation was on the wane, he single-handedly created an entirely new area of the law known as "corporate governance," of which he became the leading guru.

After hearing from Pitofsky, Millstein quickly set up a meeting with Fleisher and Oscar Robertson, the president of the NBPA. Fleisher, no antitrust expert, had floated the novel theory that the players could block the merger by arguing that it violated the Constitution's 13th Amendment, which prohibits slavery. Millstein countered that it would be hard to depict men who earned tens of thousands of dollars as slaves. Instead, relying on the Supreme Court's earlier ruling for Bill Radovich in football, Millstein suggested that asserting violations of the US antitrust laws made a lot more sense as a legal argument. Afterward, over dinner, Millstein and another Weil partner, Peter Gruenberger, scratched out on a large linen napkin the outline of a complaint attacking the merger. Millstein came up with the concepts, and Gruenberger filled in the details, spelling out all the merger's anticompetitive effects, especially its impact on competition for player services and the inevitable driving down of player salaries.

As an afterthought, the two lawyers decided to throw additional claims into the lawsuit, attacking the entire NBA player reserve system (including option clauses), compensation rules, and even the NBA college draft. This was a massive shot across the bow, a clear challenge to the business of professional sports as it was then known. Millstein and Gruenberger were declaring war.

By early April 1970, it had become clear that the NBA and the ABA intended to finalize their merger within weeks, if not days. There was no time to lose. The legal team working with Fleisher and Robertson went to the federal courthouse in New York to get a temporary restraining order blocking the merger until there could be a full hearing on its legality. They also decided to file the case as a class action, which was quite unusual for that day.

While any one player could sue (as Curt Flood, the St. Louis Cardinals All-Star centerfielder, had just recently done in baseball), Millstein and Fleisher opted for safety in numbers. The teams' NBPA player reps were the obvious choice, so the plaintiffs would be Oscar Robertson and the other 13 elected team player representatives. These 14 men would stand as the representatives for the entire class of the 200 or so NBA players. The roster of plaintiffs features some of the greatest names ever to play the game, including Robertson (Royals), Bill Bradley (Knicks), John Havlicek (Celtics), Wes Unseld (Bullets), and Chet Walker (Bulls). They were joined by a group of solid pros and a few journeymen: Joe Caldwell (Hawks), Archie Clark (76ers), Mel Counts (Lakers), Don Kojis (Clippers), Jon McGlocklin (Bucks), McCoy McLemore (Pistons), Tom Meschery (Supersonics), Jeff Mullins (Warriors), and Dick Van Arnsdale (Suns). All 14 understood the historic nature of this fight.

The case was filed in Federal Court in the Southern District of New York on April 16, 1970, with a request for an immediate temporary restraining order (TRO) blocking the merger. At the time, I was still in law school, and all I cared about basketball-wise was that the Knicks would win the NBA championship, which they did a few weeks later. It would be a couple of years before I joined the legal team. But this history, told to me firsthand by the participants, is essential to appreciating the importance and severity of the later fights.

The very next day, a hearing on the TRO request was held before Judge Lloyd McMahon, a crusty old judge who had been appointed by Eisenhower in the 1950s. When Millstein got up to argue, McMahon told him to sit down. He only wanted to hear from the NBA's lawyer, George Gallantz, a senior partner at the NBA's law firm, Proskauer Rose Goetz & Mendelsohn, a bigger, more prominent firm than Weil back then. McMahon was not impressed with Gallantz's arguments, and within a matter of minutes, he granted the TRO blocking the merger.

Typically, a TRO remains in place for only a few weeks. So two weeks later, in early May, a hearing was held to determine whether a preliminary injunction to block the merger should be entered until the case could be tried before a jury. After a lengthy hearing, Judge Charles Tenney, a Kennedy appointee and old-line patrician, entered an injunction against the merger, but he did allow the leagues to seek congressional approval. Thus began a six-year battle fought not only in Court but also in Congress and before the National Labor Relations Board (NLRB).

A mere month later, on June 18, 1970, the two leagues formally voted to merge, subject to the approval of Congress. Fleisher and the players were unbowed. Later that same day, Robertson told the *New York Times*, "We're going to fight a merger every way we know how," said Robertson. "We think it's a violation of the antitrust laws, and it clearly eliminates competition."

First, the basketball owners went to the NLRB, arguing that this was just a labor dispute and should be decided by the board and not in an antitrust court. The NLRB demurred. Next, the basketball owners went to Congress, seeking an exemption along the lines of the one the NFL and AFL got in their "Midnight Merger" five years earlier. Their timing was unfortunate. Their bill needed the approval of the Senate Judiciary Committee, and it ended up before the Senate Antitrust Subcommittee, chaired by Senator Samuel J. Ervin, who happened to also be chairing the Watergate hearings. Not surprisingly, Watergate was keeping Ervin quite busy. To his credit, Senator Ervin did hold several hearings in which Fleisher and Millstein—along with Robertson, Bradley, Dave DeBusschere, and others—testified against the merger. Strangely, the only player who testified in favor of the merger was Rick Barry, who had challenged the NBA's reserve clause after signing with the ABA and was forced to sit out a season. Barry's support for the owners earned him the scorn of his peers for the rest of his career.

It was around this time that I got involved in the case. As a young, eager associate at Weil, Gotshal & Manges, I attended several of the hearings at Millstein's direction simply to observe. I watched as Senator Ervin—in his deep North Carolina drawl—gently and patiently questioned the player witnesses as to why the merger would threaten their livelihood and their families' well-being. He dripped with southern charm.

But when the owners got their turn, Ervin switched styles, aggressively questioning the economic motives of the merger. The senator asked owner after owner why they were unwilling to permit competition for players which, according to Ervin's drawl, "is the A m e r i c u n way." The owners and their representatives looked more and more sheepish as the day wore on. It was delicious to watch this patrician North Carolinian turn these arrogant, rich men into mush. This process dragged on for several years, as Ervin made it clear that the owners would have to address the players' concerns if the merger had any chance of going through.

Back in court, the new judge on what was now called the *Robertson* case was a recent Nixon appointee, Judge Robert L. Carter, who just happened to be both black and a basketball fan. Carter had been the chief litigation lawyer and later general counsel for the NAACP and had worked closely with Thurgood Marshall and others in the 1950s and 1960s in the fight for racial justice. The NBA and the team owners were less than pleased to have landed in Judge Carter's courtroom. He was a brilliant, no-nonsense judge with a wry sense of humor, and he clearly relished this case. Over the years, he became known as the "basketball judge," and that twinkle in his eye was well-known to the lawyers from all sides.

Meanwhile, competition between the ABA and NBA intensified. In early July 1973, more than three years after the injunction blocking the NBA-ABA merger had been placed, Judge Carter, the new sheriff in town, scheduled a conference for all parties to the *Robertson* lawsuit, signaling his intention to move the case along to trial.

A few days before the conference, Peter Gruenberger, the Weil partner whom I had worked with on several other cases, formally asked me to join the "basketball case," as it was known around the office. I was excited and immediately said yes. The next day, I walked into Ira Millstein's conference room for a preparation meeting. Sitting around the table were Millstein, Peter Gruenberger, Oscar Robertson, and Larry Fleisher.

Fleisher and Millstein were both colorful men—eager, passionate, idiosyncratic, iconoclastic. Gruenberger was also unique. He had a squint in one eye that made the other eye look so fierce that you thought his stare would drill right through the back of your head. Balding, combative, and highly intelligent, he managed to be mean and funny all at the same time. He was also a cigar-chomping chain-smoker, and I spent many a health-endangering hour in his foul-smelling office as he drafted and redrafted briefs. In today's world, Gruenberger would probably be arrested for creating a hazardous work environment for young lawyers. But in exchange for black lung, I got the legal education of a lifetime.

And then there was Oscar, a big bear of a man, 6'6", all muscle. Nearing retirement as a player, he was still loved, feared, and respected as an all-time great. His eyes were immediately striking—wide and round—and he wore a smile so big that it covered his entire face. In the years that followed that meeting, Oscar and I became friends. He is one of the truly special people in the world: he has a wonderful sense of humor; is part cynic, part joy maker; and meets the world with complete candor. Like Gruenberger, he can be mean and funny at the same time and was tough on people both on and off the court. He has a long memory, particularly about the slights he endured as a young black player growing up in segregated Indiana. It takes a while for Oscar to trust you, but once he does, it is complete.

At that first meeting, we were discussing strategy for the upcoming conference before Judge Carter. As plaintiffs in the case, we wanted to move the case forward, though we also knew that as long as the injunction stayed in place, players in both leagues would continue to benefit from heated NBA-ABA competition for players. We also knew that because of the risk of multimillion-dollar damage claims, the NBA owners would oppose any effort to move the case forward as a class action on behalf of all the players. Their aim was to convince Carter to dismiss the case, arguing, as they had before the NLRB, that this was a labor dispute, not an antitrust issue. The NLRB moved in super slo-mo, in part because it was during the Nixon years and anything to do with labor was a very low priority.

The hearing before Judge Carter took place on July 31, 1973. True to form, Judge Carter took charge immediately. He wanted to get this case ready for trial within a year. This was a tall order. The case was getting huge. New parties were joining on an almost weekly basis. In addition to the NBA and its 17 teams, the ABA and its dozen or so teams joined in, as well as the American Basketball Association Players Association (ABAPA). It was going to be a litigation free-for-all.

Fleisher, Gruenberger, and I added a couple more young lawyers to our team: Irwin Warren (who would spend his entire career at Weil) and Ken Lemberger (who later became general counsel and then president of Columbia Pictures). The NBA's lineup from Proskauer was also young but impressive. Their team was now led by two newly minted Proskauer partners: David Stern (yes, *that* David Stern) and Michael Cardozo, who would later serve as New York City Corporation Counsel for the Bloomberg administration.

There was also another young Proskauer partner, Howard Ganz, who would spend his entire career at the firm representing the NBA, the National Hockey League (NHL), and Major League Baseball (MLB) in a variety of labor-related disputes. They also had two young associates: Betsey Plevan, a dark-haired, quick-witted woman who would go on to become one of the leading employment lawyers in the United States, and Jeff Mishkin, who would eventually follow Stern to the NBA and become his general counsel. Over the many years I fought against them, I would come to both like and respect each of them, though not always so much the commissioner-to-be. We'll get to that later.

The ABA was represented by Bob Carlson and Dick Tinkham, who were affiliated with the ABA's New York Nets and Indiana Pacers, respectively. The ABA also brought in the bombastic Fred Furth and his young acolyte Dan Mason, who would make their own reputations and money as nationally known plaintiffs' antitrust lawyers. It was, to say the least, an eclectic group. While the ABA cried poverty in court, Furth, a giant of a man and a bit of a buffoon, would roll up each day in a maroon Rolls Royce limousine. He was never one to be bothered by optics.

The legal maneuvering went back and forth for more than a year. By this point, Oscar Robertson had retired and been succeeded as NBPA president by Paul Silas. Motions and cross motions and cross–cross motions were filed by everybody under the sun. My task was to research and write, and then re-research and rewrite, the dozens of briefs and responses. Finally, on February 14, 1975—Valentine's Day—Judge Carter issued all his legal rulings. It was a bombshell.

Carter found for the players on almost every point. He ruled that the case could go forward as a class action on behalf of all the players in the NBA. He found that the merger was illegal absent the agreement of the players, and he also said that all the NBA's rules barring free agency—including reserve and option clauses, its compensation rules, and even the college draft—were likely illegal as well. Judge Carter threw the owners one lifeline: if, he said, "the owners could show that these rules were all the product of collective bargaining," then some version of them might be lawful. In other words, the NBA had to prove that the players had previously agreed to the very rules that were preventing them from having a free market. This was going to be an uphill battle for the NBA owners, and they knew it. The owners and their lawyers began referring to it as the "Valentine's Day Massacre."

Making matters worse for the owners, the judge also said that he wanted all discovery completed in six months so that the case could be tried before the end of 1975. This meant that each side had to exchange tens of thousands of documents and records and take scores of pretrial depositions in a matter of a few months—a daunting, if not impossible, undertaking.

Knowing their legal position was shaky, the owners adopted a new strategy: bleed the players and the NBPA to death economically by forcing them to run up huge legal bills. The owners claimed they needed to take testimony from every player in the league, all 200 of them, which we knew would cost the NBPA and players a fortune in legal fees, travel, and other expenses.

We complained, arguing that this was ridiculously burdensome, costly, and unnecessary. The judge compromised on 90 player depositions, including the 14 player plaintiffs. The NBA also wanted to take depositions from a dozen player agents as well as the heads of the other three players' unions. Our side needed to take some testimony as well, both from owners and league officials. In all, more than 150 people would have their sworn testimony taken in less than six months.

This was a herculean task and an extraordinary circumstance. Typically, cases—even complicated ones—involve at most a few dozen depositions spanning several years. Nothing like it has ever been seen, before or since, in the sports world. It also led to some of the funniest, craziest moments of my entire career.

The owners and their lawyers knew that the NBPA had no money to cover this kind of effort. Deposition transcripts and travel costs alone would be in the hundreds of thousands of dollars, and legal fees would be in the millions. Fleisher and the players so far had been getting along on a shoestring, relying on dues and some player licensing fees they had cobbled together. It became clear at this point that we, the lawyers at Weil, were going to have to fund the case if we were going to get it to trial. Millstein and the other senior partners reluctantly decided to go all-in. This was a big deal to a law firm that Millstein once referred to in conversation as "a bunch of guys named Sam." Who knows what would have happened if Weil hadn't agreed? But we knew if we won, the NBA would be required by law to pay the players' legal expenses. It was a crapshoot, but one we thought worth taking.

In the ensuing chaos, there were a few human moments as well. Less than a week after the Valentine's Day Massacre, my father died suddenly. He dropped dead of a heart attack. It was a shock. At Weil, we were in the middle of trying to figure out how we were ever going to get all this work done by the end of the year. I was sitting at my desk eating a sandwich when the phone rang. It was Mike Cardozo from Proskauer, who I barely knew at that time. He called to extend his condolences and to say that if there was anything he could do to help to just ask, an act of graciousness I will never forget. Over the next 30 years, we found ourselves in opposite corners many times, but we always maintained mutual respect and affection.

But back to the chaos.

In taking all these depositions, the owners had a strategy other than just running up the legal bills: the more players they deposed, the more likely one would slip up and admit to being OK with restrictive concepts like the reserve clause. Their argument, such as it was, revolved around the idea of "competitive balance": if players weren't tied to teams and could sign wherever they wished, there'd be no hope for bad teams in smaller markets—they'd stay bad forever. Some people still buy arguments like this, but it's never been true. In the 1960s, with the reserve clause in full effect, the Celtics won 9 out of 10 championships, the very opposite of "competitive balance."

When we deposed the owners, we were simply trying to show that the illegal reserve rules had existed decades before any labor negotiations had taken place, that owners would never voluntarily negotiate them away, and that players had never willingly agreed to these restrictions.

The competition between the lawyers on both sides was fierce. Every deposition was like a mini tennis match, with each side anticipating the other side's next move and taking steps to block it. It was scary, fun, and exhilarating all at once.

One of my major assignments was to prepare and defend the depositions of the 14 player plaintiffs as well as testimony from dozens of other players and a few of the owners too. I was also tasked with preparing the other labor union leaders—Ed Garvey in football, Alan Eagleson in hockey, and Marvin Miller in baseball—for their testimony.

There were a lot of firsts for me in the insanity of all this: the first time I ever flew first class, the first time I traveled to the West Coast, the first time I stayed at the Beverly Wilshire Hotel or saw Century City, and the first time I had lunch at the Bel Air Hotel. The very first day I arrived in Los Angeles, after checking into the hotel, I went for a walk down Wilshire Boulevard and promptly ran into Spencer Haywood, then playing for the Lakers. Spencer himself had successfully sued the NBA for the right to sign with a team before his college eligibility expired, and his case had made it all the way to the Supreme Court. After chatting with Spencer, I walked one block down and bumped into Paul Newman at a bookstore. Wow, Los Angeles definitely lived up to the hype.

But there was little glamor or glitz to most of the job. Depositions took place in cities like Kansas City, Omaha, Cincinnati, Portland, Seattle, San Diego, Boston, and half a dozen more. Back then, I wasn't exactly what you would call a frequent flyer; frankly, I didn't like to fly at all. Somehow the NBA lawyers learned of this, and Jeff Mishkin told me later that, knowing I was on them, they had intentionally plotted some of the field trips to make them as tortuous as possible. It worked. I remember one late night leaving Kansas City and flying to Omaha in the middle of a thunderstorm to defend the testimony of a player by the name of Bob Boozer. It was frightening. I absolutely believed that my fledgling legal career was going to end the same way my Notre Dame hero Knute Rockne's had—in the middle of a Kansas wheat field.

But I was also having the time of my life. To prepare for all this, Fleisher decided we all should fly to Brazil right at the end of the 1974–75 season. This was to be the annual summer NBA player trip, which included all the teams' player reps, a handful of Fleisher's clients, a bunch of wives and girlfriends, and others. He had arranged for the Brazilian government to fund the trip in exchange for our players participating in a few exhibition games against the Brazilian national team. He hadn't told our players about the games for fear some might not want to come. We had to smuggle their athletic gear onto the chartered flight to Rio. As we were waiting to board the plane at JFK, I overheard an older woman, who was gazing at our group with big, wide eyes, turn and say to her husband, "Fred, it must be a convention of tall people." When I told that to Willis Reed, he couldn't stop laughing.

It was winter in Rio but still sunny and warm. That first night at dinner, Fleisher told the players about the exhibition games. There were audible groans. If they didn't play, he warned, we might not be able to get home. The minirevolt was quashed, but the players weren't happy about it.

The first game was to be played in Rio's largest arena before a sellout crowd and a Brazilian national TV network audience. The Brazilian players were big and physical and had nearly won a medal at the 1972 Olympics in Munich. They seriously didn't want to lose to a group of US players on vacation.

Our team, coached by the recently retired Reed, was no All-Star squad—Mel Counts, a career backup, started at center. The game was played under international rules with Brazilian referees. The fix was in. The refs fouled out several of our starters while allowing the Brazilian team to pound on us at will. The Brazilian team won by a single point, 98–97, and Reed and Fleisher were pissed, complaining bitterly to the officials after the game.

We decided to retaliate. The next game was to be played three days later in São Paulo, also on national television. We started John Havlicek, Dave Cowens, Paul Silas, Jo White, and Don Chaney—the Boston Celtics lineup that had won the NBA championship the year before. The score after the first nine minutes was 36–2. The Brazilian coach called time out, walked over to Willis, and literally begged him to make it stop. Reed agreed with the proviso that the refs call the rest of the game fairly.

The final score was 108–62. We were never invited back to play in Brazil.

Of course, we were in Rio, so we had a great time dancing and partying on that trip. We indulged in a lot of what we called "Cookie watching." Walt ("Clyde") Frazier had brought along a stunning young lady named Cookie as his date; many of the players and others commented favorably on Clyde's choice of friends, particularly around the hotel pool and on the dance floor.

Some work did get done. I do vaguely recall an hour or two sitting around the hotel pool with the first two player plaintiffs scheduled to be deposed—Mel Counts and Don Kojis. I think we were talking about their upcoming depositions. The margaritas were excellent.

• • • •

Back in the United States, Counts was the first of 150-odd depositions. Howie Ganz, with a cigarette dangling from his mouth as usual, took the deposition for the NBA. Mel, a member of the 1964 Olympic team, was a journeyman player, 7'1", white, and slow. Ganz had a script, and I had a script. It was a dance, a waltz, and neither of us wanted to trip and neither of us knew exactly what we were doing. I am proud to say that not one of the players ever slipped up and gave the NBA lawyers ammunition to help their case.

Kojis went second. He had been an All-American at Marquette and a very good, if not great, small forward for a number of teams in the NBA. Don was charming and funny and an all-around nice guy. Despite making a couple of All-Star teams and leading his club in scoring several times, Don was never able to get a big raise because, as he testified, he was blocked from testing his bargaining power in a competitive market. The highlight of his testimony was the story he told about being sold by the San Diego Clippers to Seattle for $100,000 in cash shortly after a contract hassle with the Clippers general manager. Kojis testified that when the San Diego coach, Alex Hannum, found out he'd been shipped off to Seattle, he went into the locker room and yelled at Kojis, "Who the hell is this guy Cash and how am I supposed to get 20 points out of him?" That was the NBA in the 1960s.

On our first West Coast swing, we took the depositions of several NBA owners, including Jack Kent Cooke, the owner of the Lakers and one of the most miserable people in all of sports. Cooke also owned the NHL's Kings and the Forum where both teams played as well as a majority interest in the Washington Redskins. At that time, Cooke had his longtime lawyer, Edward Bennett Williams, running the Redskins, himself preferring the sun and young women of Southern California. Peter Gruenberger and Cooke got along famously, yelling at each other back and forth for eight straight hours.

Cooke was too ornery for his own good. He told Gruenberger, "You're an idiot and know nothing about sports." He then testified that the NBA owners would never bargain away their reserve system, thereby eviscerating a central tenet of the league's labor defense—that their illegal system was exempted from antitrust attack by the collective bargaining process. This would happen time and time again over the years—the owners were often their own worst enemies.

Cooke's lawyer, on the other hand, was charming and funny and smart as hell. His name was Alan Rothenberg, and he would later go on to found Major League Soccer and serve as its first commissioner. Twenty years later, I would meet up with him in that capacity, and we would fight the same battles. In the words of Yogi Berra, "déjà vu all over again."

One of the depositions on my plate was the owner of the Phoenix Suns, a Los Angeles real estate entrepreneur by the name of Dick Bloch, to whom I owe a debt of gratitude for educating me in the real world of pro sports. Bloch's deposition was held at the NBA's Century City law offices, and David Stern was defending the deposition on behalf of the NBA. It proceeded uneventfully for several hours until I asked Bloch whether or not the Suns had ever entered into any secret arrangements or oral agreements that were not included in the standard-form NBA contract. The point of the question was to show that the NBA clubs, because of their monopoly power, were able to force all the players to sign the exact same form contract with the only change being the dollar figure.

When I asked the question, I noticed Stern had an odd expression on his face. David asked if we could "go off the record." I agreed. Bloch smiled and said yes, we do have one oral arrangement with a player that was not in his written contract. He said it was with Connie Hawkins. Bloch went on to explain that the team had agreed to supply him with a hooker before each game to give him a blowjob. Everyone in the room burst out laughing. Bloch then added with a deadpan face that, "This was only for home games. Connie was on his own on the road."

The player depositions went on through the summer all over the United States—as many as 10 or more depositions a week. Some got heated. Chet Walker, a great player at the end of his career, was barely able to contain his anger. He believed—correctly—that the NBA's reserve system rules had deprived him of many hundreds of thousands of dollars in income over the years, and he made sure that Jeff Mishkin, who took his deposition for the league, experienced the full force of his bitterness. Walker's unhappiness would rear up again before the case was finally over.

Kareem Abdul-Jabbar (née Lew Alcindor) showed up for his deposition sporting a huge afro and four-inch platform shoes. Jabbar was smart and cooperative, and he made an excellent witness for the players.

I looked up one day to see Wes Unseld filling the doorway of my office. At 6'7", he was also the widest person I had ever seen in my life, at least until I started representing professional football players some years later. Wes was quiet, smart, and very dedicated to the cause. He had grown up in Kentucky and had his heart set on going to the University of Kentucky. The problem, however, was that when he got out of high school in the early 1960s, Kentucky still enforced a color line, so they missed out on one of the great college players of the era. He ended up starring at their major in-state rival, the University of Louisville. Wes told me that every time they played Kentucky, he played extra hard. You didn't want to run into Wes in the lane unless you liked running into stone walls—which was exactly what happened when the NBA took his testimony.

I also defended the depositions of both Lenny Wilkens (who by then was an NBA coach) and Paul Silas (who had succeeded Oscar Robertson as president of the NBPA). They both testified about the infamous Ben Kerner, owner of the St. Louis Hawks, who had drafted both of them a couple of years apart. Kerner was known as the cheapest man in the NBA, and Lenny testified that despite the fact that he was one of the best guards in the league, Kerner had twice threatened to cut his salary. That way, Wilkens said, he could appear to be making a concession merely by keeping his salary the same. What a jerk.

Silas testified that after his rookie year, during which he established himself as one of the top rebounders in the NBA, Kerner reduced his salary from $9,000 to $8,000 a year. Lenny and Oscar Robertson, along with several other players, also testified about the 21-minute All-Star Game strike of 1964. These players all had vivid, detailed memories of that first confrontation with the owners and how they had hung together to get what they deserved. Each of them remembered it with pride.

Because of Oscar's status as a union leader, Stern showed up to take his deposition, and I defended. Those two were not a match made in heaven. Stern, round faced, mustached, and sarcastic, was at his most combative. He kept pressing Robertson over and over on every conceivable detail of earlier collective bargaining negotiations. Oscar didn't like to be pressed either on the court or off the court. He gave as good as he got, those fiery eyes bulging every time Stern asked another impertinent question that Oscar didn't like. There were moments during that deposition that I thought Oscar was going to jump over the table and throttle Stern.

Halfway through that unforgettable summer, I got into an argument with Dave Cowens, the great Celtic center and later coach, trying to convince him that the college draft was an illegal boycott because it forced rookie players to deal with only one team. What kind of negotiating power could you have in that situation? Dave kept telling me why he thought the draft was a good idea, and I was scared that, for the first time, one of our players might inadvertently help the owners' case. I called Fleisher for advice, and he told me, "Don't worry about it," which is what he said about everything. In this case, he was right. During the actual deposition, when Dave was asked about what he thought of the college draft, he replied simply, "It's terribly unfair to all players, it's an illegal boycott." I beamed.

And then there was Bill Bradley. Bill, tall and lanky, always had a half-smile on his face, as if he knew everything about everything, which he pretty much did. You would never know it from the droning speeches he later made as a US Senator and candidate for president, but Bradley was extraordinarily funny, playful, and insightful all at once. Even back then, we all knew Bradley was destined to do more than drain corner jump shots.

Bradley was obsessed with privacy and confidentiality, and for that reason he insisted that all his files be kept under the name of "Floyd Cramer," a popular country and western star. Throughout the case, we only referred to Bradley as Floyd. When the owners asked players to produce any documents they had related to the case, none of the players had anything but a few odd pages—except Floyd. He was a packrat with a half-dozen manila file folders, as he had apparently kept every piece of paper relating to his NBA career.

During his deposition, Bradley and Stern got into long philosophical discussions on the rights and wrongs of free agency, free trade, and possibly even free love. At one point, I yelled at both of them, imploring Stern just to ask questions and Bradley just to answer the questions asked. "We are not here for parlor discussions," I told them. It didn't do a bit of good.

On the morning of his deposition, Bradley handed me an autographed copy of his recently published book, *Life on the Run*, one of the very best books ever written on real-life NBA basketball or any pro sport, for that matter. Only David Halberstam's book *The Breaks of the Game*, about the Portland Trailblazers, even comes close. Floyd was a man of many talents.

The deposition of Wilt Chamberlain was a different kind of adventure. Wilt had recently retired, and he insisted on having his deposition taken at his home in Beverly Hills. I sent Ken Lemberger out to handle this one. He was the tallest member of our team, so it only seemed right. As it happened, the day of Wilt's deposition, we were meeting with a group of our players back in our offices in New York. It was about noon when we got a call from Lemberger, who was in a panic, saying that Wilt was refusing to go forward with his deposition that morning. Chamberlain told Ken that he was "just too tired." I looked around the room at Fleisher and a half-dozen or so players, including Oscar, Silas, Bradley, and DeBusschere.

"OK, guys, who is going to talk to the Big Guy?" I asked the room at large. We passed the phone around, but nobody would get on the line. Finally, I said to Lemberger. "Just get it done somehow, nobody is going to talk to the Big Guy but you."

Later I asked Lemberger how he got Chamberlain to change his mind. "I begged," Ken replied. Even in retirement, the Big Guy intimidated everyone.

There were also bizarre moments of levity and camaraderie between the warring factions. I recall one sake-soaked evening when a bunch of us from both sides had dinner at a sunken table at a Japanese restaurant in the Century Plaza Hotel in Century City. It was the first time I ever ate Japanese food or drank sake. The food I've forgotten, though I do remember the sake.

On another of our West Coast trips, Stern invited me to lunch at the Bel Air Hotel, the playground of the stars back then. The place was filled with starlets, deal-makers, and Hollywood pretenders. I'm sure Stern had an ulterior motive; he always did. He had the unique ability to be a bully and a charmer all at once. I never let my guard down, but I do remember enjoying the lunch, because while Stern certainly had his dark side, he could also be extraordinarily cordial and funny. Who knew that I would end up cross-examining him several times over the years to come? As we parted, I kept wondering what Stern was trying to wheedle out of me. It was a technique he would often employ in our many negotiations and occasional confrontations over the next three decades.

There was also one particularly scary deposition moment that remains etched in my memory. In addition to testimony from multiple owners and players, the parties also deposed player agents and assorted hangers-on. The most dramatic by far was the deposition of Sam Gilbert, a UCLA booster and wealthy construction magnate who acted as the quasi-agent for a number of UCLA stars, including Alcindor (Abdul-Jabbar), Lucius Allen, and Bill Walton, among others. He and another Los Angeles businessman, Ralph Shapiro, had negotiated what was then a huge $1.4 million contract for rookie Lew Alcindor with the Milwaukee Bucks at no charge to Alcindor. Gilbert was of particular interest to the NBA-ABA rivalry because it was rumored that representatives of the ABA had left an envelope with $100,000 in cash for Gilbert to give to Alcindor to convince him to sign with the ABA. Gilbert of course denied this.

The deposition took place in a plush office high above Century City, with the lights of Hollywood and Los Angeles twinkling all around us. Bizarrely, the deposition did not start until almost midnight. Mike Cardozo was to question Gilbert on behalf of the NBA, to be followed by Dan Mason questioning Gilbert on behalf of the ABA. David Feldman, the court reporter, was there along with myself and a couple of other interested observers.

The witness showed up late. Gilbert, a multimillionaire, was in his late 60s, tanned in that Los Angeles way, balding, and bulky, if not downright fat. Gilbert explained that his lawyer would be even later, which was more bizarre given the lateness of the hour already. But he told the opposing lawyers to start the questioning. The NBA's interrogation of Gilbert was largely uneventful and over in less than an hour.

Just as the ABA's Dan Mason was about to begin his questions, in walked Gilbert's lawyer, a large black gentleman who introduced himself gruffly as Fred Slaughter. Slaughter was highly annoyed that the proceedings had started without him, and his ill temper combined with his physical presence—6'5" and easily 300 pounds—was something to behold. (Slaughter had been the pivotman on John Wooden's first national championship team at UCLA, in 1964.)

After a bit of a ruckus, things calmed down, and Mason began his questioning of Gilbert. At first, Slaughter stood directly behind his client as Mason asked his questions. As time went on, we could all see that Slaughter was getting visibly upset with the questions, and particularly with Dan Mason. Obviously, this was meant to intimidate Mason. After 20 or 30 minutes of this, as tension rose for everyone in the room, Slaughter walked menacingly around the desk and now stood directly behind Dan Mason, who continued to ask questions of Gilbert, though he was clearly rattled. At that point in the deposition, Slaughter leaned over Mason and said, "Listen, motherfucker, if you ask one more fucking question like that, I am going to throw you out the fucking window."

We all urged Fred to settle down while Mason put a halfhearted objection on the record. He then stated weakly, "I have no further questions."

Slaughter and I would have more encounters over the years, as he became the first successful black agent in both basketball and football as well as the representative of the NBA referees in their negotiations with the NBA. He was always a gentleman after that night.

Toward the end of that summer, as the deadline approached for trial, the NBA insisted on taking the depositions of the other three sports union leaders—Marvin Miller from baseball, Ed Garvey from football, and Alan Eagleson from hockey. I had been assigned to prepare the three of them for their testimony and defend their depositions. As it turned out, it would be a lucky break for me, as I eventually represented all of these sports unions later in my career.

I remember my first meeting with Marvin Miller and his general counsel, Dick Moss, in the modest offices of the baseball players' union on Park Avenue. Moss would later become one of the leading agents in baseball, but at the time, he was chief labor counsel for the union. The two could not have been more different. Moss, balding and round-faced, was outgoing, boisterous, combative, and very funny. Miller wore a pencil-thin mustache, and his right arm had been deformed since birth. Unlike Moss, he was soft-spoken, intense, thoughtful, and a bit standoffish. With a minimum of preparation, Miller's deposition went off without a hitch. He deftly laid out all the arguments—economic and moral—for allowing players to enjoy the benefits of a competitive marketplace for their services just like every other citizen of this country.

Next was Ed Garvey, a labor lawyer by trade. Garvey was outspoken, sarcastic, acerbic, and, like Moss, outrageously funny. He had a youthful appearance and an in-your-face personality. Rumor had it that he was absolutely hated by the NFL owners. I flew to DC on a Saturday to prepare him, but he was impossible to prepare, and it quickly became obvious that he was going to say whatever he wanted. Luckily, he was also smart, and while he gave the NBA's Jeff Mishkin fits with his sarcasm and wit, we got through the deposition without hurting our legal position, which was all I cared about.

Finally, I flew to Toronto to meet Alan Eagleson, the charming and debonair hockey union leader. He was a patrician figure and very famous in Canada. Like Fleisher, he was also a leading player agent. I had my doubts about him during our preparations, in part because of his strangely muted views on free agency. Fleisher had warned me about Eagleson, saying he wasn't sure Eagleson could be trusted. Nonetheless, his testimony essentially supported our legal position, although it lacked the enthusiasm displayed by Miller and Garvey.

In late October, as we were all frantically trying to finish our work, Judge Carter pushed the trial date back to the second quarter of 1976. By this time, the owners knew they were on shaky legal ground, and they wanted to avoid a public shaming. We had worries of our own. The average NBA salary had just passed the $100,000 mark and was widely noted in the press, making our players much less sympathetic as plaintiffs. The fact that many of them were black would no doubt be subtly—or not so subtly—used against them. Shouldn't they be "grateful" for the opportunity to make so much money for playing a game? That's a word you still hear occasionally today.

Pressure on all sides was enormous, and in early January, informal settlement discussions began in earnest.

I wasn't involved in those early discussions; my job was to get the players' case ready for trial. Finally, over All-Star Weekend in February in Philadelphia, Fleisher, Gruenberger, and Paul Silas (now the NBPA president) met with Stern, new NBA commissioner Larry O'Brien (the former JFK aide), and the Knicks' Mike Burke to hammer out a settlement. Over that weekend, they reached a historic agreement that would allow a form of free agency in the NBA for the first time.

That agreement, which came to be known as the *Oscar Robertson* settlement, was to last for 10 years and bring labor peace to pro basketball for the next decade. Players got what they wanted: free agency, albeit with some restrictions. Fleisher, with his typical inscrutability, agreed to a damages amount of $4,365,000—a number he quite literally pulled out of thin air. When asked later about the unusual number, Fleisher explained, "It was time to get this thing done and I came

up with that precise number to make them believe I was serious."
They believed him.

The NBA was also required to pay the players' legal fees and
expenses, so Weil and its partners breathed a sigh of relief. This
amount alone was several million dollars. In a separate deal, the NBA
and the ABA agreed that four teams—New York Nets, Indiana Pacers, San Antonio Spurs, and Denver Nuggets—would be allowed to
join the NBA, and the other remaining teams—Kentucky Colonels,
Virginia Squires, and St. Louis Spirit—would receive compensation
for going out of business. The deal reached with the St. Louis owners, the Silna brothers and Don Shupak, actually gave them a piece
of the NBA's TV revenue in perpetuity. It was the steal of the century.
Thirty years later, the league would buy them out for several hundred
million dollars.

Gruenberger and I spent night and day, including weekends, with
Stern and Cardozo, drafting and redrafting the hundreds of pages
that made up the actual *Robertson* settlement agreement. That agreement, which crafted the details of a new free agency system for the first
time, became a template for settlements in other sports, and many of
its provisions live on today in various forms in other leagues as well.
The agreement was signed and filed with Judge Carter on April 12,
1976. The next day, NBPA president Paul Silas told the *New York
Times*, "The main thing is we can now concentrate totally on basketball. This puts us ahead of other sports in this country, such as baseball
and football, which are having their problems at the moment in this
area."

Two players raised objections, both of whom were retired: Wilt
Chamberlain and Chet Walker. Wilt because he was Wilt, and Chet
because he was still angry at the NBA. The appeals dragged on for
another year or so. But the deed was done—free agency became real.

The promised decade of labor peace in the NBA was short-lived.
Fights over the meaning of the *Robertson* agreement soon broke out,
plaguing the league for years to come. But the 14 players who stood

up on behalf of all NBA players could stand proud. They had taken a giant step forward not just financially but also in gaining respect and shifting the balance of power toward the players for the first time in the history of sports. Everyone else would now have to play catch-up.

CHAPTER 5

The Free Agency Wars Continue

IN 1965, THE MAJOR LEAGUE BASEBALL PLAYERS Association (MLBPA)—powerless and penniless just like the NBPA had been—hired Marvin Miller as its first executive director. Miller was 48 years old, and in his previous job, he had been the chief economist for United Steelworkers, the strongest union in America. He was selected over several other candidates, including Hall of Famers Bob Feller and Hank Greenberg. Richard M. Nixon, then languishing in political limbo, was considered for the job as the union's general counsel. It's hard to imagine how history would have to be rewritten if Nixon had become the MLBPA chief lawyer—no bombing of Hanoi, no Watergate, and no impeachment. But what the hell would have happened to baseball?

Miller, like Fleisher, immediately focused on what now looks like small ball—increasing player benefits and improving the paltry pension for baseball players. Miller, an ardent trade unionist, pushed hard, and by the late 1960s, he had won major concessions, including a vastly improved pension. Miller was the first to raise the possibility of a real in-season player strike, an idea most Americans considered tantamount to treason. Some baseball owners openly referred to Miller as "that Communist." The owners hated Miller's guts.

Miller soon turned his attention toward baseball's reserve clause, which bound every player to his team in perpetuity going back nearly a century. In 1969, St. Louis Cardinals star centerfielder Curt Flood, whose contract had expired, was traded to the Philadelphia Phillies.

Flood, a smart and tough-minded player, refused to report to Phila-delphia and asked to be released. He told the new MLB commis-sioner Bowie Kuhn that he was "not a piece of property." The Lords of Baseball disagreed, citing the reserve clause. Flood, initially against Miller's advice, insisted that since his contract had expired, he was free to sign with whatever team he wanted. The winds of change turned into the winds of war.

In January 1970, with funding and legal assistance from Miller and the baseball union, Flood filed an antitrust lawsuit against the MLB, charging all 16 teams with conspiracy in restraint of trade. The case, known as *Flood v. Kuhn*, would go all the way to the US Supreme Court. In June 1972, the Supreme Court—in what is consid-ered by legal scholars to be among its worst decisions in history (*Dred Scott* also comes to mind)—ruled against Flood. They stuck with their decades-old rulings on interstate commerce and said that it was up to Congress to change their prior decisions with regard to baseball play-ers, which didn't happen for another 25 years. Better late than never.

As it turned out, Fleisher and Miller simultaneously fought the same fight for player freedom, dignity, higher salaries, and real competition—not just on the playing field but in the business of sports as well. The football players waged a similar battle during this period, though theirs ended with far different results.

Although Fleisher and Miller had a lot in common—New York City working-class roots, degrees from NYU—the two never particu-larly liked one another. Miller found Fleisher's dual role as labor leader and prominent sports agent unseemly in the context of trade union-ism. Fleisher, in turn, found Miller's holier-than-thou attitude hard to take. Working at the same moment in history, the two greatest sports union labor leaders would achieve the same goals in vastly different ways.

Miller was brilliant, with a photographic memory and unmatched attention to detail. As I would later come to learn firsthand, he was an exceptional labor organizer and teacher with extraordinary communi-cation skills in both the written and spoken word. Warmth and humor, however, did not come naturally to Miller. Nonetheless, he soon out-negotiated the dimwitted and arrogant group that represented the baseball owners, including Bowie Kuhn, the lawyer-commissioner; John Gaherin and Ray Grebey, their labor guys; and owners like Calvin Griffith (Washington Senators and Minnesota Twins) and Charlie Finley (Kansas City / Oakland A's).

After the disappointing defeat of *Flood v. Kuhn* in the Supreme Court, Miller looked for new ways to attack baseball's reserve clause. In the early 1970s, he lobbied for a form of salary arbitration and got Major League Baseball to agree to an impartial grievance procedure and a neutral arbitrator to rule on contract disputes between the players and the clubs. (As a result, star pitcher Catfish Hunter was able to escape the Oakland A's and sign with the Yankees for big bucks when an arbitrator ruled that A's owner Charlie Finley had breached Hunter's contract by failing to make certain payments.) This wasn't free agency, but it helped players get something closer to their market value. Up to that point, the baseball commissioner, a lackey of the owners by definition, had held the power to settle contract disputes. You can imagine how those went.

By these steps, Miller had carefully laid the groundwork for dismantling baseball's century-old reserve system. In 1975, two players, Dodgers pitcher Andy Messersmith and Orioles pitcher Dave McNally, with union backing, agreed to play out their options and test whether baseball's interpretation of the option clause as infinitely renewable would hold up before a third-party arbitrator. This, Messersmith said, was "a fight for control over my destiny." Both he and McNally were pressured by their respective owners, who offered them lucrative new contracts in exchange for abandoning their campaigns. Both players chose the larger principle over their own immediate personal enrichment.

In December 1975, a three-person arbitration panel was convened, with Miller sitting on behalf of the union and labor negotiator John Gaherin sitting on behalf of the owners. The third-party neutral was Peter Seitz, a longtime labor arbitrator with a reputation for the utmost integrity and fairness. Seitz was in his early 70s and was a learned and jovial man with a full head of white hair to go along with a poetic sense of humor.

Dick Moss presented the players' case, and the owners' lawyer, Lou Hoynes, argued on behalf of the baseball owners. Hoynes was an excellent advocate, skilled in the art of obfuscation. Hoynes cited the 80-year history of the reserve system and claimed that it was the very system responsible for baseball's huge popularity. To change now, he warned, would likely destroy the sport, echoing the same "competitive balance" claptrap that the NBA had argued in the *Robertson* case. There were three days of hearings. Two months later, in February 1976 (the same month as the *Robertson* settlement), Seitz ruled decisively for the players. He declared that the so-called reserve clause was nothing more than a one-year option, which was not automatically renewable. Rather, looking at the "plain words," he ruled that the one-year option was just that, a one-year option. Naturally, the owners appealed and filed a countersuit in Kansas City, where they expected a sympathetic hearing. They were wrong. Federal district court judge John Oliver, a Kennedy appointee, upheld Seitz's ruling—a decision that was later affirmed by an appeals court.

The young lawyer the players hired to argue their case was a recent federal court clerk by the name of Donald Fehr. The baseball owners would later come to despise Fehr almost as much as they hated Marvin Miller. After the baseball owners lost their appeal, Miller negotiated a new collective bargaining agreement that, for the first time, included a new free agency system in baseball, the same one that survives in large part today. The baseball owners spent the next 20 years trying to undo Seitz's landmark decision without success, leading to a series of strikes and lockouts. Then, as we shall see, the owners and the players agreed to a luxury tax system in lieu of the salary cap revenue-sharing systems that had developed in the other major sports. I was to have a major role in that sorry development.

• • • •

Aware of what was happening in baseball and basketball, a dozen football players with union backing also sought to challenge the NFL's reserve compensation system. Though there were some technical differences, it had the same effect as the NBA and MLB reserve clauses. Football players were effectively prevented from moving to new teams at the end of their contracts. Over the years, as a handful of players had tried to negotiate with new teams, the NFL created its own version of an antitrust violation that came to be known as the "Rozelle Rule," named for NFL commissioner Pete Rozelle. If a team signed a player from another club, even though he was no longer under contract, Rozelle would determine the appropriate compensation. Remember what I just wrote about the baseball commissioner being a lackey for the owners? Well, that was Rozelle in spades. Each time a player tried to move to another team, Rozelle set the compensation so high that the new team invariably backed out of the deal. In one particularly egregious example in 1968, Rozelle ordered the New Orleans Saints to give up two first-round draft picks for agreeing to sign a journeyman 49ers receiver by the name of Dave Parks. After that, not a single player was able to exercise their right to sign with a new team. Free agency was a sham.

The NFLPA union first sought to challenge this system by threatening to strike the 1974 season. When that preseason effort collapsed, a group of players, backed by the NFLPA and led by Baltimore tight end and NFLPA president John Mackey, sued the NFL and each NFL team, attacking the Rozelle Rule as an illegal restraint of trade. The case was entitled *Mackey v. NFL*. One of the plaintiffs was Vikings Hall of Famer Alan Page, my Notre Dame classmate, who would later go on to become the chief judge of the Minnesota Supreme Court.

In February 1976, after a 55-day bench trial before federal court judge Earl Larson in Minneapolis, the court struck down the Rozelle Rule as a violation of US antitrust laws, a ruling that was upheld by an appeals court. One of the players' lawyers was Ed Glennon, a famous and colorful midwestern trial lawyer who, like his former partner, Ed

Garvey, had a knack for getting under the skin of the NFL, mercilessly cross-examining them. The NFL defense of the *Mackey* case was led by a Washington lawyer by the name of Paul Tagliabue, who would go on to become commissioner of the NFL and eventually, for me, both an adversary and a good friend.

Unfortunately for the NFL players, Ed Garvey was a traditional union labor lawyer whose focus was more on achieving league-wide benefits for NFLPA members than on meaningful free agency for football players. Garvey failed to recognize, as his successor Gene Upshaw surely did, that by obtaining real free agency, it would in fact benefit all the union members. Instead, in subsequent collective bargaining negotiations, Garvey proposed a 50/50 revenue split and a wage scale based on position, among other things. This and other concepts were rejected both by the league and by many players. The union unfortunately bargained away much of what they had gained in court in order to obtain certain league-wide benefits such as increased minimum salaries, pension increases, and severance pay. As a result, a whole new war against the NFL would have to be fought a decade and a half later in order to obtain meaningful free agency. Luckily for me, that was a war in which I got to play one of the generals.

Sadly, John Mackey ultimately succumbed to Alzheimer's disease at an early age. He was among the first former NFL players diagnosed with massive head injuries. Coincidentally, Mackey died just as the NFL players were involved in yet another struggle with the billionaire Lords of the NFL in the summer of 2011. Mackey would have been proud.

The same year the *Mackey* case was filed, the World Football League (WFL), another Gary Davidson brainchild, arrived on the scene to inject some short-lived competition for players into professional football. While the WFL was able to sign a number of NFL players, including a trio of Miami Dolphins stars (Larry Csonka, Paul Warfield, and Jim Kiick), it was doomed to fail from the start. The league had some colorful team names (the Fire, the Sun, the Bell, the Storm, the Thunder, etc.), but these franchises moved from city to city so quickly that one team, the Ambassadors, had three different homes before its first kickoff. That franchise didn't last a year, and the WFL folded in the middle of its second season. Competition for football players would be delayed for almost 20 years.

• • •

Hockey too had its first brush with the free market in the form of a rival league called the World Hockey Association (WHA), yet another Gary Davidson invention. Hockey has always had the most problematic business model of the four big professional sports—though it thrives in select markets, it has struggled to build a US national TV audience. The WHA had an interesting approach: they awarded franchises to fast-growing US cities with no hockey tradition (Houston, Miami), smaller Canadian markets where there was intense local interest (Quebec, Winnipeg, Edmonton), and traditional NHL strongholds (New York, Chicago). Right off the bat, they signed many NHL stars to lucrative deals, including Bobby Hull, Bernie Parent, and Derek Sanderson. The star Bruins goalie Gerry Cheevers successfully sued the NHL in federal court in Boston so he could sign with the WHA's Cleveland Crusaders. The court struck down NHL's so-called reserve clause insofar as it prevented players from jumping to a rival league. Another federal court in Philadelphia, at the urging of the WHA, also ruled that the NHL's reserve system was likely unenforceable under US competition laws.

The WHA ran into the same problems as every other start-up league—undisciplined spending and amateurish management. The unfortunately named Miami franchise, the Screaming Eagles, made a big splash by signing Parent but then couldn't nail down a home arena and had to move to Philadelphia as the Blazers before the inaugural season began. This proved typical.

As tough as the WHA was on the bank accounts of its owners, it worked wonders for those of the players. In the seven-year lifespan of the league, salaries for NHL players nearly tripled. But the gains might have been much greater if Alan Eagleson, the NHL union chief, had been a more honest advocate for his players. At one point in the mid-1970s, just as the *Robertson* case was proceeding to trial, Eagleson hired Weil, Gotshal & Manges to look into the possibility of filing a similar lawsuit but then decided not to pursue it. And when the unstable WHA ultimately sought a merger with the NHL, Eagleson did nothing to prevent it. Years later, it would be revealed that Eagleson's relationship with NHL owners was far too cozy, which would eventually lead to my involvement with the hockey players' union.

Ultimately, four teams from the WHA joined the NHL for the 1980 season (the Winnipeg Jets, the Hartford Whalers, the Edmonton Oilers, and the Quebec Nordiques). There would be many more hockey fights—almost literally—in the coming years as owners sought to balance their books on the backs of their players. Of all the sports, hockey has lost the most games to strikes and lockouts, greatly diminishing the league's standing among its peers.

•   •   •

The 1970s transformed professional sports. Free agency and competitive markets for players in various forms were taking hold. Television revenues began to explode along with player salaries. More than anything, however, players in all sports were now treated with some level of dignity and respect by most team owners. This only happened because the players learned to stick together through collective action, in court and on the picket line. Fleisher, Miller, and even Garvey were pioneers and unlikely heroes who, with the help of truly courageous players like Curt Flood, Oscar Robertson, John Mackey, and a handful of others, enriched future generations of professional athletes, few of whom would ever learn these names or understand the risks taken on their behalf.

CHAPTER 6

NBA and the "Phony Peace"

THE *ROBERTSON* SETTLEMENT, WHICH TOOK EFFECT in 1976 and was supposed to last for 10 years, boldly promised "peace in our time." But the ink had barely dried when skirmishes broke out in what turned into a new decade-long war between the NBA and its players. This conflict would draw in a former chief prosecutor of the Nuremberg trials, the former Yale University president and ambassador to the Court of St. James, and basketball Hall of Famers such as Red Auerbach, Bill Russell, and Dave DeBusschere, to name a few. Two future commissioners—my names for them were "King David" and "The Little Dickhead"—cut their teeth in the turmoil of that decade.

The new NBA antitrust settlement and labor agreements were hundreds of pages long—dense, complicated, and sometimes intentionally incomprehensible. I say that with authority, as I was closely involved in drafting them.

Our side—the players—wanted everything as vague and ambiguous as possible so that Fleisher and other clever agents could exploit loopholes and get around rules designed to suppress salaries. The owners and their herd of lawyers wanted each provision to be airtight and crystal clear. They were writing the IRS code; we were writing the Declaration of Independence.

But the differences between players and owners went much deeper than legal strategies. According to the preamble of the *Robertson* settlement agreement, the agreement's very purpose was "to increase players' freedom of movement and eliminate artificial restrictions on player salaries." In other words, free agency.

The owners demanded archaic rules to protect themselves. In the first five years of the *Robertson* settlement, teams that signed a free agent would have to "compensate" the former team for the loss of the player. For the second five years of the agreement, compensation rules would be eliminated and replaced by the right of first refusal, whereby the old team could match any offer for one of its players in order to retain his services—but now at a price presumably set by the free agent market. It sounded simple enough in theory, but in reality, these rules led to endless bickering and numerous arbitrations and lawsuits.

The owners kept trotting out their old shibboleth, "competitive balance." This notion had been around for years and is still preached to this day. If all players are allowed to sign with the highest bidder, wealthier big-market clubs will get all the best players and win all the championships, fans will lose all hope, and eventually the league will shrivel and die. This is pure bullshit. Nothing like this has ever happened, but it continues to be held out as the apocalyptic future that awaits us if players ever achieve unrestricted freedom of movement.

The reality is that during the glory days of the reserve system, the Yankees dominated baseball, the Celtics dominated basketball, and the Canadiens dominated hockey—*for decades.* During a 30-year stretch, the Celtics won 16 NBA championships. Add in the Lakers, and you have 63 percent of the championships in that period. Where's the "competitive balance" in that?

In fact, shortly after free agency reared its ugly head in the mid-1970s, the Yankee dynasty largely collapsed despite George Steinbrenner's frantic and costly efforts to resurrect it. In the 15 years following the dismantling of baseball's reserve system, 12 different teams won the World Series, including "small markets" such as Kansas City, Oakland, Minnesota, and Pittsburgh. In basketball too, free agency had an enormous impact on improving—not destroying—competitive balance. The Lakers and Celtics were cut down to size, winning barely 20 percent of NBA championships over the next 40 years—which, even accounting for the league's expansion, is a much lower percentage. One of the most successful teams over the last decade plays in the league's sixth-smallest market, San Antonio. The effect in the NHL has been even more dramatic. Since the early 1990s, 21 different teams have won the Stanley Cup—and not one of them was the Canadiens. The hapless Habs have gone a quarter century without winning the cup.

Ironically, in those stretches when minidynasties have emerged—Michael Jordan's Bulls, Wayne Gretzky's Oilers, Derek Jeter's Yankees, and Tom Brady's Patriots—the leagues have prospered like never before. That's the true nature of competition, and it's why people love sports. The rivalry between the Golden State Warriors and the Cleveland Cavaliers from 2015 to 2018 put the NBA in the stratosphere. As Al Davis, the iconic owner of the fearsome Oakland Raiders of the 1970s and 1980s, once told me, "Dynasties are good for the sport, whether it be the Yankees, Celtics or the Dallas Cowboys. Fans always need someone to hate."

The reason that owners keep fighting to impose limits on free agency is that they want protection from their own lapses in judgment, a way to ensure that they don't get caught up in senseless bidding wars and overpay for players who don't produce. This is a genuine problem, and it happens all the time. But that doesn't mean the players should be held responsible. Most athletes have short careers. Every year they stay tethered to a team is another crimp in their potential earnings.

If there's one thing I've learned over the course of my career, it's that team owners will always try to find ways to evade agreements. There is really no such thing as labor peace. The periods between all-out war—lawsuits, strikes, lockouts, and hostile negotiations—are filled with scheming and conniving. The basketball owners were no exception. Even before Judge Carter had a chance to formally approve the *Robertson* agreement, the owners were plotting a sneak attack to take back free agency.

It happened like this: On June 8, 1976, the NBA held its annual college draft, which went off smoothly enough. Point guard John Lucas from Maryland was the first player taken by Houston. Then came the surprise. A few days later, in a miraculous coincidence, all the players drafted in the top rounds were offered take-it-or-leave-it contracts with six- and seven-year durations. The idea was diabolically simple: by locking rookies to low-cost, long-term deals, owners robbed most of them of the benefits of free agency. The average career for an NBA player, after all, is less than five years.

Since Fleisher represented several first-round picks (Wally Walker, Adrian Dantley, and Mitch Kupchak, among others), we knew right away what was happening. The moment we uncovered this scheme, we told the owners that we would blow up the *Robertson* settlement if they persisted—but persist they did. The offers were not rescinded. We went before Judge Carter to explain that the NBA owners were once again acting in bad faith and trying to blow a hole in the settlement. The judge was not amused. He told the NBA and its lawyers, David Stern among them, that unless they ripped up those contract offers, he would not approve the settlement, and the case would go to trial within days. The NBA sheepishly backed down, and shortly thereafter, Judge Carter formally approved the settlement.

As part of the *Robertson* settlement and its accompanying new labor agreement, we had created an absurdly complex new legal structure with several new positions of power. There was a "Special Master," appointed and overseen by Judge Carter, to oversee free agency disputes. There was also a separate, aptly named "Impartial Arbitrator" to decide contract disputes between players, teams, and the league. There was even an "Impartial Basketball Expert" who was supposed to opine on technical basketball issues including relative skill levels—a role that was never precisely defined and almost never used.

The very first dispute under this new legal structure was a doozy, and it just happened to involve the president of the players' union, Paul Silas, who had just signed the *Robertson* agreement on behalf of the players.

Silas is smart and gregarious and one of the nicest men I've known in basketball. Our families, along with the Fleishers, would become very close. He was 6'8", with a fierce, muscled body he used to become one of the most effective rebounders in NBA history.

When this dispute arose, I had only known Paul for a short time, but I remember him telling me about growing up poor in Oakland, California, and what it was like being one of the few black athletes in the early 1960s in Omaha, Nebraska, where he attended Creighton University. He had a wonderful sense of humor and told stories of how he used Stickum on his hands to help his rebounding and how he had to hide it from the refs like baseball hitters hiding their pine tar from the umpires. He also told how he liked to take certain opponents mentally out of the game early by pounding the shit out of them in the first quarter. Elvin Hayes was one of his favorite victims.

This was to be my first NBA arbitration hearing. It was held at the Impartial Arbitrator Peter Seitz's wonderful high-ceilinged apartment in an old prewar building overlooking Central Park. Arrayed around Seitz's dining room table were Red Auerbach, president of the Boston Celtics; Fleisher, both as general counsel to the NBPA and Silas's agent; David Stern, as NBA counsel; and arbitrator Seitz. Only a few months earlier, Peter had delivered his *Messersmith* ruling in baseball.

There was no court reporter to take down the testimony; Seitz took handwritten notes.

White-haired and soft-spoken, he had both an elfin-like quality and a razor-sharp intelligence. He'd had a long career in labor law and commanded the utmost respect from our side for having just gutted baseball's reserve system.

Some years later, Peter would pen a poem to celebrate my admission to partnership at Weil, Gotshal & Manges. It read:

Lines to Celebrate the Apotheosis of James W. Quinn

By One Who Formerly Pulled an Oar As a
Helot in the Trireme of W. G. and M.

Felicitations, Mr. Quinn!

It seems that, finally, you're "in"!

You need no longer, James, repine
Since you are now "above the line"
Why is it that your noble firm
(With all the speed of pachyderm)
Took all these years to understand
Its partner force was undermanned;
And failed to note your versatile
Endowments and your legal skill?

The mills of Gods grind slowly, true;
But why, James, should they grind up *you?*
But now it's done! I'll not inveigh
I'll only sing "O frabjous day
When you sit with those mighty bosses
Sharing profits; also losses."

Peter (February 16, 1979)

Silas's dispute was quite simple: the Celtics desperately wanted to hang on to their leading rebounder, while Silas wanted to test the free market. When we got to the lobby of Seitz's apartment on the hearing day, Fleisher turned to me and said, "I want you to put Silas on the witness stand." I said fine, although I was a little taken aback, since I had never done a hearing like this before. I wasn't too worried, though. All I had to do was establish that Silas had not received a contract offer until after it was too late. We went up to Peter's apartment and commenced the hearing. Fleisher made a brief opening statement, as did Stern. Then I put Silas on the witness stand for a few short minutes, and our case closed.

I figured my work for the day was done.

Stern announced that he was going to call only one witness, Auerbach, who would later be in the Hall of Fame as a coach and executive. Auerbach proceeded to tell a convoluted, dog-ate-my-homework tale of misplaced folders, confusion about dates, unexpected illness, sick days, and so on—blah, blah, blah. He basically put the blame for the fuckup on his former secretary.

When he finished telling his story, I looked at Fleisher, expecting him to begin the cross-examination. Instead, Fleisher leaned over and said to me, "You cross him." I looked at Fleisher like he was crazy. Unprepared, I stumbled through a short session, trying to poke holes in what was little more than a cry for mercy. The Celtics merely wanted a do-over.

Arbitrator Seitz thanked both sides and informed us that he would make a ruling in due course. He then broke out a bottle of scotch and we all had a late afternoon libation. Although I thought he was leaning our way, neither side knew for sure how the arbitrator would rule.

Meanwhile, Fleisher had been talking to other teams about Silas. Carl Scheer, an old friend of Fleisher's who ran the Denver Nuggets, was particularly interested. In a matter of days after the hearing, Fleisher had arranged a trade with Auerbach: Silas went to the Denver Nuggets with a new contract and huge pay raise, and the Celtics got a second- or third-round draft pick. Fleisher had solved the issue with a bit of his vintage legerdemain. After the deal was done, I asked Fleisher why he made me cross-examine Auerbach. It was simple, he said. "I knew I was going to have to cut a deal with Red and I didn't want to piss him off."

Fleisher also knew he only had leverage until Seitz ruled, so he got the deal done right away. That was Fleisher: the deal came first, the law trailing somewhere behind. Some years later, Seitz showed me the decision that he had drafted. I had been right—he was going to rule in our favor.

It was around this time that Fleisher began talking to me about leaving Weil, Gotshal & Manges and joining him in the firm of Fleisher & Quinn. He offered me a big raise (something like $10,000, a lot of money back then) and the lure of a life representing NBA players in negotiations and the litigations and arbitrations that would surely follow. I was reluctant at first, but over several months, my interest grew. My wife, Katy, loved the idea. Working as an associate at a major firm like Weil had meant many long nights and lost weekends.

Before making a final decision, I went to talk to Ira Millstein, who had become my mentor at Weil. His advice was careful and concise: "If that's something that you really want to do, you should try it, but I know Larry, and you just might wind up being overpaid and bored." He added one last thing: "If you want to come back to the firm, just call me."

On March 1, 1977, Fleisher & Quinn was born. The new partnership got off to an auspicious start. I moved into a spacious office overlooking Central Park on Central Park West, in what was then the Gulf and Western Building. Fleisher's secretary/assistant, Curt Parker, worked with me as well. Several Weil clients continued sending me work, including Ross Perot and his colleagues Mort Myerson and Mitch Hart. Their disastrous foray into Wall Street in the early 1970s led to an explosion of litigation that had been going on for years.

I had a couple of memorable cases right off the bat. Angry season ticket–holders of the old New York Nets filed a lawsuit against the Nets owner, Roy Boe, and his star player, Julius "Dr. J" Erving, after Erving was traded to the Philadelphia 76ers. The plaintiffs alleged that they only bought tickets because of Erving's presence on the team and that trading him constituted fraud, which was ridiculous. I quickly got the case dismissed.

But the real payoff was that I got to know Erving's agent, Irwin Weiner, one of the great characters of the 1970s sports world. With curly, flaming-red hair piled high on top of his head, he was the shorter, Jewish version of boxing promoter Don King. He and Fleisher had gone to DeWitt Clinton High School together in the Bronx, and then he worked his way up through the garment business. Meeting Walt Frazier at a charity event in 1969, he somehow convinced Frazier to hire him as his agent. Frazier and Weiner partnered in a sports agency business that represented Ed Kranepool and a string of New York Mets as well as NBA stars George McGinnis, Marvin "Bad News" Barnes, and of course, Dr. J, among others. Weiner was as outgoing as Fleisher was shy, yet for years they were two of the most effective agents in sports.

When his sports agency business began to wane, Weiner turned to philanthropy, serving on several charitable boards and founding the Dr. I Foundation for medical research. Irwin was flamboyant in a good way. His secret, he once told some college students, was "to go by feel and experience, but it also doesn't hurt to have a good product."

During this period, I helped negotiate Willis Reed's first coaching contract with the New York Knicks. Reed was a loyal Fleisher client as a player and continued that relationship when he began his coaching career in 1977. Through Fleisher, I came to know Willis well over the years. A quiet man, he was enormously likeable and a true gentleman of the rural South. His former championship teammates (Bradley, DeBusschere, Frazier, and Earl "the Pearl" Monroe among them) not only respected him; they loved him.

His coaching career with the Knicks, and later the Nets, would be short and rocky, but he came into his own as an NBA executive with the Nets. Despite logging more than 30 years in the NBA, one moment we all remember: Game 7 of the 1970 NBA Finals, when he gamely limped onto the Garden's court to inspire the Knicks to their first NBA championship. Nearly three decades after that dramatic moment, Reed told me, "There isn't a day in my life that people don't remind me of that game."

In my dealings with the Knicks, I first met Steve Brenner, then assistant general counsel of Madison Square Garden, who would soon become a client and a lifelong friend. That friendship would lead to a series of hilarious encounters down the road.

During this period, Fleisher and I attended countless Knicks games, using his season tickets for seats situated right next to Marv Albert's radio booth. Those were lean years at the Garden—the team wavered between merely awful and truly atrocious. But at late-night dinners at Dave DeBusschere's East Side restaurant, George Martin's, with the likes of George Steinbrenner, DeBusschere, Willis Reed, and scores of NBA players and Fleisher clients, from superstars to bench-warmers, everyone was welcome.

But all was not well. Millstein had been right. I found myself with long stretches of time and very little to do. Fleisher took naps. I got bored. I was meeting a lot of interesting people—owners, ambassadors, real estate moguls, and the many diverse folks who flowed through Fleisher's eclectic life—yet I felt completely unchallenged. It all came to a head one Thursday morning around 11:30 a.m. when Fleisher popped his head into my office and said, "Let's go to the movies." I was appalled.

"Fleisher," I said heatedly, "you can't go to the movies in the middle of the day. It's just not done."

"Why not? We have nothing better to do," Fleisher responded. Gulf and Western owned Paramount Studios at the time and had a Paramount theater in the basement of the building. So we went to see a movie—*High Anxiety*, the hilarious Mel Brooks comedy. We entered the theater, the movie flashed on the screen, and a few minutes later I looked over to see that Fleisher had fallen asleep. I knew another career change was in order.

That same night, I told my wife that I actually missed the long nights and pressure-filled weekends of a high-powered law firm. She understood, and I called Millstein the next day. He was good for his word, as I knew he would be. I returned to Weil on March 1, 1978, exactly a year to the day since I had left. Within days, my plate was full again with the likes of the W. T. Grant bankruptcy and some new clients, including a struggling soccer league that was to take over my life for a while. I was looking to make partner, the pressure was on, and I was content once again. Meanwhile, my work in basketball continued at a faster pace than ever.

Despite the demise of Fleisher & Quinn, Larry and I remained very close. Just a few months after my return to Weil, my wife and I arranged to give Larry and his wife, Vicky, a surprise 25th wedding anniversary party. They arrived at our house in the pouring rain, thinking that we were all going out to dinner. They refused to come out of the car because of the torrential downpour. Finally, after half an hour, Dave DeBusschere ran out into the rain and yelled in frustration, "Fleisher, for Christ's sake, come into the goddamn house—half of the future Hall of Fame is inside!" It was true: Willis Reed, Bill Bradley, Oscar Robertson, John Havlicek, Paul Silas, and a half-dozen others were hiding around our house waiting to yell "Surprise!"

It was during this period of time that disputes among players, clubs, the union, and the league exploded. With the ABA expansion revenues and lots of money pouring in from television, the players rallied to get their fair share. I was back in my element.

One important showdown involved a journeyman player, Kenny Charles, who had been cut by the Atlanta Hawks early in the 1977–78 season. Superagent Bob Wolff represented Charles and claimed that the player had been illegally let go because the club determined he was making too much money. This was before guaranteed contracts.

Players got cut on the basis of skill all the time, of course, but under the terms of our labor agreement, a player couldn't be let go just because he made too much money. That was the team's fault, not his. Howie Ganz, the cigarette-dangling, wisecracking partner from Proskauer, was my adversary. Arbitrator Seitz ruled for the player, holding that Charles was cut for the wrong reasons, and therefore he was entitled to be paid in full under his player contract whether or not he played out the season. The NBA and the Hawks were not happy.

Another dirty, old-school tactic that teams tried to get away with was cutting a player while he was injured. We challenged that on behalf of a bench player for Seattle named Bruce Seals. This was the first and only time I got to cross-examine the great Bill Russell, then running the Seattle Supersonics. I had a sense from Russell's sphinx-like answers that he was conflicted about testifying against a player. Seitz once again ruled in our favor, establishing a clear prohibition of cutting injured players, a rule now taken for granted. This was trench warfare. We fought over every inch of ground.

Sometimes we got more, as we did in a dispute involving another little-known player, Rudy Hackett, who had played in the ABA with St. Louis and then signed a so-called "no cut" contract with the New Jersey Nets in their first season in the NBA, meaning he was guaranteed the full amount of the deal whether he played or not. A few weeks later, the Nets let him go, and he signed a contract with the Indiana Pacers for less money. The NBA and the Nets claimed that the Nets should be able to deduct from Hackett's guarantee the amount he was paid by the Pacers. We filed a claim on behalf of Hackett before Arbitrator Seitz. Once again, Seitz ruled in our favor and ended his decision with the following Shakespearian quote: "A rose is a rose and a guarantee is a guarantee."

That was the end of Seitz. The NBA fired him three days later. We weren't surprised. The parties agreed to replace Seitz with George Nicolau, a well-respected labor arbitrator. The new guy had his first big test in a case involving a young, volatile player named Bernard King. He had burst into the NBA in 1977, averaging more than 20 points a game for New Jersey in two seasons before being traded to Utah in the summer of 1979. Shortly after the season began, King was arrested in Salt Lake City for allegedly raping a woman described in the press as a "Mormon nun." Utah immediately suspended King without pay, even though King had already been released without bail and had yet to be formally charged. We filed for an expedited grievance arbitration before Nicolau, arguing that the suspension violated both King's contract and fundamental due process. In America, even a famous basketball player should be innocent until proven guilty.

The NBA's concept of due process was the opposite. The club and the league feigned outrage, whining that they could not allow King to be part of the team with such serious charges pending against him. Our response was simple: if you don't want to play him, then don't, but you do have to pay him.

The hearing was held a few days later, with representatives from both the team and the league testifying how this would have a heinous effect on their image. We called no witnesses, relying on the US Constitution. Nicolau ruled in our favor in less than a day. Within a week, all charges against King were dropped. As it turned out, the alleged victim was a prostitute, not a nun, and there had not even been any sexual contact, consensual or otherwise. However, the sad reality was that King had been an alcoholic for several years, and shortly thereafter, Fleisher, along with King's agent, Bill Pollack, got him into rehab. Fleisher then helped arrange for a trade to the Knicks, where King recovered his brilliance and became a Garden legend. He was the only active player to speak at Fleisher's memorial service. His closing words were, "Larry saved my life."

The NBA fired Nicolau less than a week later. He had only been on the job a few weeks. Once again, we weren't surprised. Owners hate to lose. Ironically, Nicolau later became an arbitrator in baseball, and a decade or so later he was fired by the baseball owners for ruling against them in another case. Thus both he and Seitz had the distinction of being fired by two separate sets of owners—quite an honor.

After Nicolau, a new Impartial Arbitrator was appointed, another well-known labor arbitrator by the name of Arthur Stark. By this time, the NBA salary cap had been put in place, and the battle shifted to new ground.

• • • •

On another front, after months of delay and stonewalling by the NBA, the league and the players finally agreed on a Special Master whose major responsibility was resolving free agency disputes. Under the *Robertson* agreement, a team that lost a free agent was entitled to reasonable compensation from his new team, as determined by the commissioner. It was in the players' interest to keep these awards as low as possible, so as not to freeze the free agent market. No team would sign a free agent if they risked losing too much in compensation. Furthermore, the agreement specified that any compensation awarded not be so high as to chill the market for free agents.

We got away with one in the selection of Professor Telford Taylor from Columbia Law School as Special Master. Taylor had been a chief prosecutor in the Nuremberg Trials at the end of World War II and was a leading constitutional scholar. Tall and regal, he had the bearing of an old country gentlemen and professed to know nothing whatsoever about basketball. He proved to be an extraordinarily quick learner.

What the NBA apparently didn't know—though we did—was that Taylor was an outspoken liberal who had been involved in ACLU matters for many years. He was liberal in other ways too. Then in his early 70s, he was married to a 23-year-old law student.

The NBA, of course, had a strong interest in pushing compensation to the max, and we were ready for them to overreach, which they promptly did. The first real test case involved center Marvin Webster (a.k.a. "the Human Eraser"), a Fleisher client who in 1978 had signed with the Knicks as a free agent from Seattle. Fleisher and Knicks general manager Eddie Donovan were close friends, so the Knicks were typically the first place Fleisher shopped for his free agents.

While the compensation awards technically were issued by the NBA commissioner Larry O'Brien, we all knew that David Stern, by then NBA general counsel and soon-to-be deputy commissioner, was the real author—the man behind the curtain, so to speak. Stern went for broke, awarding Seattle the Knicks' first-round draft pick as well as rising star Lonnie Shelton plus half-a-million bucks.

As class counsel appointed by Judge Carter, we challenged the award as being unreasonable, unfair, and intended to kill the very free agent market we had fought so hard to create. Professor Taylor soon became engrossed in the minutiae of NBA statistics: rebounds, assists, blocked shots, points scored, free-throw percentage—everything. These compensation hearings tended to become a hotbed of basketball arcana, with "basketball experts" testifying that the compensation was either too high, not high enough, or, in the parlance of the Three Bears, "just right." Our designated expert in many of these proceedings was Dave DeBusschere, a Hall of Fame player, former coach, and onetime ABA commissioner with a wealth of basketball knowledge. Who better to compare talent?

DeBusschere had by then also become a client and good friend. The son of a bar owner, DeBusschere had a blue-collar background and a white-collar smile. He was intelligent and funny, always joking around and playing tricks. My most vivid memory of DeBusschere dates from that year, 1978. Walking into one of our conference rooms to prepare his testimony for the Webster hearing, he blurted out, "We have a Polish Pope." DeBusschere and I were both Roman Catholic. The rest of our team was Jewish. OK, we said, what's the punchline? Naturally, we all thought DeBusschere was pulling our legs. "No," he said, "really—we have a Polish Pope."

We still didn't believe him, so he went downstairs to the newsstand and came back up with the *New York Daily News*, its headline reading, "Pope John Paul II from Poland Is the New Pope." We all laughed hysterically. DeBusschere, of course, went on to a successful career as a New York Knicks executive and then Wall Street. Tragically, he dropped dead of a heart attack in 2003 while walking down Wall Street with his son, Peter. He was only 63.

At the hearing before Telford Taylor, DeBusschere testified no one could justify the Webster compensation award—Webster was good, not great—and "there was no way he was worth Shelton plus a first-round pick and $500,000." Stern then tried to justify this award by unleashing all kinds of mumbo-jumbo about his supposed "methodology." Cross-examining him was a true match of wits. There was no point, no matter how small, that he would willingly concede. He was brilliant and clever, often sarcastic, sometimes hilarious, and always elusive. Whenever Stern testified, everyone in the room knew that the truth was hovering nearby. Stern gave new meaning to the concept of "truthiness."

As Special Master on free agency issues, Taylor ruled in our favor, voiding the award, and Judge Carter upheld Taylor's decision. In the end, Seattle received only Shelton. But Stern did not give up. When the San Diego Clippers signed Bill Walton as a free agent, the man behind the curtain mandated a king's ransom be sent back to Portland—the ransom being power forward Kermit Washington, center Kevin Kunnert, a first-round pick, their choice of high-scoring guard Randy Smith or another first-round pick, plus $350,000. We had to fight that one too, and we won again.

You can guess what the NBA did. After one more ruling in favor of the players, Taylor was sent packing, and we moved on to our second Special Master. You don't like a Nuremberg prosecutor, how about a former president of Yale and ambassador to Great Britain? The new man was Kingman Brewster, who, it turned out, had an ACLU background and a penchant for protecting the underdog. I still can't understand how the NBA did such a lousy job vetting these candidates.

Brewster hung on to his Special Master title long enough to get enmeshed in the next phase of the conflict: the fight over the salary cap.

Eventually, the NBA fired him too, though not before they fired Stark as Impartial Arbitrator.

One thing was clear—when Stern and his NBA owners didn't get their way, they didn't just sit around and pout. They fired someone.

CHAPTER 7

Soccer—the Sport of the '80s

ON A BRIGHT, SUNNY DAY IN JUNE 1978, A FEW MONTHS after my return to Weil, I was summoned once again to Millstein's conference room, where I met a man with a fierce look and a strange Welsh accent. He was introduced to me as Phil Woosnam, commissioner of something called the North American Soccer League (NASL).

Also in the room was my friend Steve Brenner, now general counsel of the NASL. They quickly explained their predicament: the NFL was trying to kill them. The NFL was about to enact a "cross-ownership ban" prohibiting their owners from holding a financial interest in other professional sports teams. This would effectively force the sale, if not the closure, of several NASL franchises.

The NASL was more like the ABA, the WHA, and the WFL than the established leagues I had been involved with. Their game may have been soccer, but what they really specialized in was shoveling money into a furnace. Since its founding in 1968, they had covered the continent in defunct franchises. Do you remember the Toronto Metros-Croatians, the Oakland Stompers, or the Caribous of Colorado? I didn't think so.

The NASL's origins dated back to the mid-'60s, when the 1966 World Cup, won in stirring fashion by England, drew surprisingly strong TV ratings in North America. A year later, two leagues sprang into existence, fielding a total of 22 teams. Expansion, contraction, and consolidation followed in short order. By 1969, the newly formed

NASL was down to 5 teams, then another round of breakneck expansion followed. By the summer of 1978, the league had 24 teams in the US and Canada.

During the NASL's 15-year lifespan, 65 teams played in 42 different cities, a failure rate that made the old ABA look like the Rock of Gibraltar. They had Atoms and Spurs, Lancers and Drillers, and Comets and Bays, although no Dashers or Blitzens. My personal favorites included the Boomers and the Earthquakes, with the Fury and Manic (pronounced "mah-neeg" by their French Canadian fans) coming in as close seconds.

Yet for one brief shining moment in the late 1970s—largely because of the popularity of the New York Cosmos and the signing of aging foreign superstars like Péle, Franz Beckenbauer, and Giorgio Chinaglia—the NASL looked like it might make it after all. The Cosmos, the pet project of record impresario Ahmet Ertegun, were attracting 50,000 fans to games at Giants Stadium, and several other teams were averaging crowds of 25,000. Corporate America was pumped up: Warner Communications owned the Cosmos, Louisiana Pacific Corporation owned the Portland Timbers, the Lipton Company owned the New England Teamen, and Molson Breweries acquired the Montreal Manic.

Fortified with such bullish indicators, the NASL owners began to believe their own bullshit. Unfortunately, the league's fundamental problems never went away. They had no regular television network contract, they were paying ridiculous sums for mostly washed-up foreign superstars, and outside of a few markets, attendance remained dismal. In truth, the NFL's cross-ownership ban was the least of their problems.

Nevertheless, showing appropriate outrage at the NFL's bullying tactics, we enthusiastically embraced the NASL's cause. I put together a legal team, which once again included Irwin Warren as well as a young lawyer by the name of Jeffrey Kessler and an even younger one by the name of Jeff Klein. A few days later, Millstein and I met with the NASL Board of Governors and made a presentation for a potential antitrust lawsuit against the NFL. The cross-ownership ban was in fact aimed primarily at two NFL/NASL owners: Lamar Hunt, the owner of the NFL's Kansas City Chiefs and NASL's Dallas Tornado; and Joe Robbie, the owner of the NFL's Miami Dolphins and NASL's Fort Lauderdale Strikers, which he cleverly put under the name of his wife, Elizabeth. Hunt and Robbie were the two leading owners in the NASL, and if they were forced out, we were told it could spell doom for the NASL.

Our team worked feverishly during that summer to prepare a lawsuit. Before filing, we met with the NFL and its lawyers to see if we could reach a compromise. The NFL was represented by the Washington law firm of Covington & Burling, but the firm had also been advising the NASL on several matters. We decided to ignore the conflict in the hope of reaching a settlement.

The meeting was held in late August at the NFL's offices on Park Avenue, in NFL commissioner Pete Rozelle's ornate, oak-paneled conference room. The room was filled with old pro football memorabilia: black-and-white pictures of Red Grange, the Canton Bulldogs, and one of the Baltimore Colts' mud-splattered Alan Ameche scoring the winning touchdown against the Giants in "The Game."

It was Millstein, Brenner, Commissioner Woosnam, and me from our side, and Rozelle and his Covington lawyers for the NFL. One of those lawyers was Paul Tagliabue, the future NFL commissioner. It was the first time I had met Paul, and I was immediately impressed with his intelligence, humor, and sense of fairness. Tagliabue, whose name means "cut the steer" in Italian, was also extremely tall. He had been the captain of the Georgetown basketball team in the pre–Patrick Ewing era. I would get to know Tagliabue well over the years and come to respect him as a lawyer, as a commissioner and, most importantly, as a person. Like Tagliabue, everyone at the meeting was quite pleasant. Views were exchanged frankly. We asked them to withdraw their cross-ownership rule and, in the nicest possible way, they told us to go fuck ourselves.

Game on.

A few days later, on the eve of filing our lawsuit, we were invited by Woosnam to attend the 1978 Soccer Bowl. The game was played on a glorious Sunday at Giants Stadium between the New York Cosmos and the Tampa Bay Rowdies. To our surprise, there was a massive crowd: 74,901 fans, still the largest ever to watch a professional soccer game between US teams in North America. They were noisy and enthusiastic, cheering and chanting and singing like they do in Europe and South America. Péle played, though it was Chinaglia who scored the winning goal in a 3–1 Cosmos victory. We were all blown away by the experience, which was to be the apogee of the NASL's tortured existence. But we didn't know that then. We just thought it was amazing, and for a few months, we all believed in the destiny of the NASL.

Ah, youth.

The very next day, October 1, 1978 (my 33rd birthday), we filed the lawsuit against the NFL and 26 of its then 28 teams, excluding Hunt's Chiefs and Robbie's Dolphins. The case was assigned to Judge Charles Haight, a lovely man whose legal background had largely been in admiralty law. He knew little about football and less about soccer. His preferences ran more toward sailing and skeet shooting.

Within days, Judge Haight held a hearing on our request for a preliminary injunction to ban the ban. Millstein stood up and, with marvelous, largely inaccurate flourishes, described our recent experience at the Soccer Bowl. He'd heard a cacophony of foreign languages, which convinced him, he assured Judge Haight, that soccer would definitely become "the Sport of the '80s," as the NASL's marketing phrase boldly proclaimed. But this would only happen, Millstein argued, if the illegal cross-ownership rule was enjoined before it killed soccer in the cradle.

Because of the ethical conflict, the NFL could not bring Covington & Burling, their regular counsel, to the proceedings. They turned instead to the old-line Wall Street firm of Sullivan & Cromwell. Bill Willis, their most senior lawyer, argued the ban was necessary to protect NFL trade secrets. Judge Haight demolished that line of argument. Not unlike what had happened a decade earlier when

Millstein successfully blocked the NBA-ABA merger, Ira's eloquence and hyperbole won the day. Haight granted our motion to enjoin the cross-ownership ban and ordered a full trial to determine its ultimate legality.

At that point, the senior men, Willis and Millstein, largely disappeared, and the young guns—Jim Carter, Sullivan & Cromwell's able partner, and me, not yet even a partner—were left to shoot it out. We launched into a year-long odyssey of discovery, with depositions and documents exchanged in the usual organized chaos of big lawsuits. Carter was very smart and truly tenacious but also a gentleman and worthy adversary.

Our side had one goal in mind: to show that the sole purpose of the cross-ownership ban was to stifle competition. The NFL countered with their "trade secrets" argument, citing also their institutional prerogative to ensure the undivided loyalty of NFL owners to the league. All of which sounded good until you thought about it. What were those trade secrets exactly? What did it mean to be loyal to a league? These weren't NFL employees; they were the actual owners of the NFL, who presumably should be free to invest in anything they wanted to. The NFL also concocted a brand-new concept: the "single entity" theory, by which they contended that the NFL, with its 28 separate teams, was but one entity. By this way of thinking, whatever actions they took jointly would always be legal and could never be anticompetitive. This despite the fact that the NFL had been routinely found to have violated US competition laws in a dozen cases around the country.

We felt good about our chances.

My first deposition was a multiday session with Pete Rozelle, the chain-smoking NFL commissioner. Rozelle had been a public relations man for the Los Angeles Rams before ascending to the commissioner job in the early 1960s, and he had cemented his reputation with two brilliant acts of diplomacy: getting the feuding NFL owners in 1961 to split network television revenues equally and engineering the NFL-AFL merger. Both moves helped the NFL leapfrog ahead of the other major sports and become the richest, most powerful league. Rozelle was both charming and elusive, some might even say slippery, but he was never good at winning lawsuits. He had been the star witness for the NFL owners in numerous lawsuits, all of which they had lost. Polished he was; believable he was not.

For two days, I pounded Rozelle with ammo collected from internal memos he and other NFL executives had written that showed the true purpose of the ban: to drive down competition from other leagues. Rozelle bobbed and weaved, squinting, denying, obfuscating, and always, always smoking. Like Colonel Klink, he heard nothing, saw nothing, said nothing. It was incredible.

Next, I flew to Houston to take the deposition of Bud Adams, the Oilers ornery owner. The son of an oil tycoon, Adams had been a founding member of the old AFL and was now thoroughly entrenched in the NFL owners' unique culture of privilege, power, and total conservatism. They liked the league exactly as it was and wouldn't consider changing a thing unless a gun was held to their collective heads, which, over the years, is what we tried to do on behalf of the players. Our gun of choice was antitrust law.

Adams remained reasonably calm through the morning session of his deposition. After lunch, though, he came loaded for bear—or rather, just plain loaded. Red-faced and belligerent, he ranted, mostly incomprehensibly, against the NASL and Lamar Hunt. Finally Jim Carter, the NFL's lawyer, took him outside to calm him down and sober him up. We resumed the deposition, with Adams proclaiming both ignorance and innocence but in a decidedly less belligerent manner.

The deposition of Wellington Mara, the New York Giants longtime owner, was a complete contrast. This was the first of several depositions I would take of Mara over the years in cases I brought against the NFL. Mara, a true Irish gentleman, was soft-spoken and polite, though thoroughly capable of the same studied obfuscation as his fellow NFL owners. He hewed carefully to the loyalty defense and swore that competition from the NASL had absolutely nothing to do with the cross-ownership ban.

I also took the deposition of Al Davis, the feisty owner of the Oakland Raiders, who dutifully spouted the NFL's line that they were all just one big happy "single entity" family. Within months, however, Davis was singing a different tune when the NFL refused to let him move the Raiders to Los Angeles. He filed his own antitrust lawsuit against the league and his fellow owners. In response, the NFL trotted out its "single entity" status, which Davis and his lawyer, former San Francisco mayor Joseph Alioto, attacked as legal nonsense. Suddenly, the NASL and the Oakland Raiders were on the same side: stranger bedfellows were hard to imagine.

Joe Alioto was as memorable as his iconoclastic client Al Davis. The former two-term mayor of San Francisco was the son of an Italian immigrant who ran a small fish-processing business on Fisherman's Wharf. Joe earned millions as one of the nation's most successful antitrust plaintiff's lawyers, suing big companies for their illegal, anticompetitive actions dating all the way back to his successful attack against the NFL in the Radovich case 25 years earlier.

Eventually, cracks appeared in the NFL's innocence narrative. During the course of discovery, we uncovered the minutes of several NFL Board of Governors meetings in which at least two owners, Leonard Tose (owner of the Philadelphia Eagles) and Max Winter (owner of the Minnesota Vikings), complained about Lamar Hunt coming to their cities to promote the local NASL teams, the Philadelphia Fury (partially owned by rock star Peter Frampton) and the Minnesota Kicks (owned by Jim Ruben, a local Minneapolis businessman).

At their depositions, Tose and Winter both claimed that Hunt's activities could hurt attendance at their games, a fairly preposterous notion given that the NASL played soccer in the summer, not the fall, and neither soccer team drew what could plausibly be called a crowd. Tose, a gambler and a drinker, was eventually pushed out of the NFL when his trucking company went bankrupt. Winter sold out a few years later in what became a messy litigation over NFL ownership rights. You have to give the NFL credit for its remarkable efficiency at weeding out misfits from its membership.

Now that the NASL had at least some evidence of the NFL's anti-competitive intent, the NFL lawyers zeroed in on the NASL's own mismanagement. In deposing Commissioner Woosnam, the NFL owners tried to expose the precarious economic state of the league. Woosnam was a tough SOB. He had captained the team for Wales in the World Cup in the late 1950s and was a staunch early believer in the future of soccer in America. In his deposition, he gave a spirited defense of the NASL and hit hard on the need for stable ownership and the importance of Hunt and Robbie to the league. He was right about that. Most of his other owners were complete clowns.

The question that hung over everything was why the NFL owners gave a damn about a league that already had a foot and a half in the grave. But NFL owners had become obsessed with exercising their power and stamping out this nuisance like an angry man chasing a fly all over the house. Tose would later testify that he was mad because "Lamar was promoting soccer instead of football." Art Modell, the owner of the original Cleveland Browns, told the press that there was "no way the NASL could win either in the market or in Court."

He turned out to be half right.

The depositions of Hunt and Robbie were key. Lamar was a likeable, soft-spoken Texan and one of the three legitimate sons of H. L. Hunt, the Texas oil billionaire. On the day before his deposition in Dallas, Lamar took one of my colleagues and me to lunch at the greasy spoon across the street from his office in downtown Dallas. As we walked in, all the regulars said, "Hi, Lamar, good to see ya again." The bill was $8.25, and he asked us to pay.

Nonetheless, Lamar was a very nice man and a good witness. He testified that the idea behind the cross-ownership ban was both anti-competitive and idiotic from a business point of view. "Some of the other NFL owners were out to get me because of my success and my willingness to take a chance on new ideas," Lamar said.

Joe Robbie also made an excellent witness for the NASL. Robbie, the son of a Lebanese immigrant, was smart as hell and one of the most belligerent people I have ever met. I was glad we had decided to waive a jury, because any jury would have hated him. He too was given to drink, although—thank God—he showed up for his deposition sober. He managed to come across as your slightly grumpy old grandfather—crotchety but wise and earnest and even occasionally funny. He testified convincingly that he and his wife, Elizabeth, should be able to own anything they wanted in sports or any other industry.

The NFL lawyers deposed many of our owners, but fortunately not all of them. They were a group who disagreed vehemently about everything—marketing, television strategy, player salaries, even the design of the NASL game ball. Some wanted to get rid of the offsides rule to allow more scoring. Others proposed time-outs so that viewers could safely use the bathroom without the risk of missing the only goal of the game.

The most volatile arguments were over, of all things, indoor soccer, a high-scoring version of the game played on a turf-covered hockey rink. The league's purists considered it sacrilege; others thought it might be the only way to get Americans interested in soccer. At virtually every meeting, there would be yelling and screaming between the pro- and anti-indoor soccer factions. Once there was an actual fistfight.

I heard some of the most outrageous things during these meetings. I remember the diatribe of one owner vividly. Bob Bell, a Beach Boy look-alike and real estate minimogul from San Diego who owned the San Diego Soccers, stood up in the middle of a strategy debate and posed an important question. "Are we businessmen," he asked, "or are we missionaries for the game of soccer?" He then passionately stated, "We need to be businessmen, because Jesus Christ may have been a missionary, but he never made any money."

I leaned over to Steve Brenner, the NASL's general counsel. "Did I just hear that?" I whispered incredulously.

He smiled and nodded. "Welcome to the NASL."

At that same meeting, another owner, Bob Hermann of the California Surf, offered this brilliant insight: "The problem with this league is there are too many away games and not enough home games." Someone else then suggested that the owners have a "gentlemen's agreement" that no team would pay their goalie more than a fixed amount. I quickly explained that people had gone to jail for just this kind of "gentlemen's agreement." The idea was abandoned.

There was also an impassioned discussion among several owners on the topic of how much you should tip a hooker. I never did find out.

But the NASL moment that trumped all others for me occurred mere weeks before the trial against the NFL was about to start. After a day of squabbling about indoor soccer and other important matters, there was an executive session that was interrupted by a knock on the door. Two owners, Peter Pocklington of the Edmonton Drillers and Nelson Skalbania of the Calgary Boomers, asked if they could present something to the executive committee for approval.

They came into the meeting room and sat down rather sheepishly. Pocklington was holding a small piece of paper that had some scribbling on it. He then announced that during the general session, he and Skalbania had decided to merge their teams into a single team based in Edmonton. As part of the swap, Pocklington, a wealthy oil guy, would give Skalbania one of his corporate jets, cash, and some real estate in Manitoba or Saskatchewan or somewhere up there. Skalbania would, in turn, give Pocklington several of his best players, the lease on a fleet of cars, and the marketing rights to all of Western Canada.

The executive committee took a vote and unanimously approved this once-in-a-lifetime transaction, which saved neither the league nor Skalbania and Pocklington, both of whom eventually went to prison (for matters unrelated to the NASL, to be fair).

Shortly after this incident, the NASL tried to prop up its image by convincing Dr. Henry Kissinger, a rabid soccer fan, to become honorary chairman of the NASL. During an NASL meeting at our offices in the General Motors Building, I got a call from a security officer in the lobby saying that there was a man insisting that he be allowed to come up to our office. When I asked who the man was, the officer admitted that he was having trouble understanding him. I came downstairs to find the diminutive Henry Kissinger waggling his finger in the face of the 6'5" security guard.

"This guy says he was a former secretary of state," said the guard, a fact I confirmed. Then, in a moment I will never forget, the guard roared, "I don't care who the fuck he is; he don't go upstairs without a pass!"

As tough a Welshman as he was, Commissioner Woosnam could not always control the NASL and its players. When he suspended the Cosmos' Carlos Alberto the day before the 1980 Soccer Bowl for spitting on a linesman, Alberto's teammate Giorgio Chinaglia phoned the league office and threatened that unless the suspension was lifted, they might "find Commissioner Woosnam floating in the East River." The suspension was lifted.

A month before the start of the NFL cross-ownership trial, Ira Millstein got a call from his friend Edward Bennett Williams, the most prominent trial lawyer in America at the time and the president of the Washington Redskins. Millstein and Williams had known each other since the late 1940s, when they both worked for the government in DC.

"I'm buying the Baltimore Orioles," Williams told Millstein. In other words, Williams was about to become a cross-owner, and he was concerned that the ban could be used to block his purchase. We flew down to DC the next day and met in Williams's opulent office, filled with memorabilia from his many famous trials. Williams had won acquittals for many a notorious defendant, including mobsters Frank Costello and Sam Giancana and politicians like Joe McCarthy and John Connally. It wasn't hard to see why: tall and trim, with a deep baritone voice and bright Irish eyes, Williams took over the room. He once famously said, "The dumbest owner in the NFL was smarter than the smartest owner in baseball." That's saying a lot!

Williams made us a remarkable offer: he would testify as a witness to the illegality of the cross-ownership ban if we dropped the Redskins as a defendant. This was a no-brainer. The greatest trial lawyer in America testifying for our side was a gift from the gods. The NFL's lawyers cried foul; we cried kickoff.

Then we got another phone call. I fielded this one.

"Hey, Jim, it's Al."

"Al as in Al Davis?" I responded.

"Yes."

"Al, why are you calling me?" I asked, flustered. "Does Joe [lawyer Joe Alioto] know you are calling me?"

"Of course, no problem," he replied dismissively.

I pointed out that there very likely *was* a problem, because as he was a defendant in my case, he shouldn't be talking to me directly. He responded with typical Al Davis insouciance.

"Don't worry, Jim, it's OK. I waive everything."

He asked me whether I was going to call him as a witness.

"No, I don't plan to," I told him. "I've already deposed you under oath, and you didn't say anything particularly helpful to our case."

But as Davis reminded me, things had changed. Now the Raiders had sued the NFL to force the league to let his team move to Los Angeles.

"We're really on the same side now," said Davis, who then delivered a bombshell. "I'm willing to testify to whatever you want. If I help your case, it would help my case."

Al Davis was a very practical, if not entirely honorable, man. Suspecting that he could well be taping this call, I thanked him for his offer and immediately declined. He had offered to perjure himself, and I wanted no part of it. Man, I thought to myself, does this shit really happen?

Davis did not testify in the trial for either side, but he and the Raiders, relying largely on our earlier injunction victory, did win their case against the NFL. The Oakland Raiders became the Los Angeles Raiders.

Our trial began on March 1, 1980, in the old federal courthouse in downtown Manhattan. Both sides agreed to defer discussion of damages and to try the legality of the NFL's cross-ownership rule directly to Judge Haight without a jury. We thought we had the edge because the judge had already granted us the preliminary injunction. We thought wrong.

As the trial moved along, the New York City transit workers went on strike, strangling the city for two weeks and forcing us to move the trial to the City Bar Association offices on 45th Street in midtown Manhattan, which was easier for everyone to get to. The judge and I walked down 5th Avenue together almost every day.

This was also Passover season, which would result in a particularly amusing clash of cultures as we prepared Lamar Hunt for his testimony. The day before Lamar was to testify, we were having lunch in one of Weil's conference rooms. Steve Brenner (NASL general counsel), Irwin Warren, and I were munching on sandwiches alongside a plate of unleavened bread from a box of matzoh traditionally eaten at Passover time. Lamar looked at the plate and at the box and in his soft-spoken southern drawl asked, "Pardon my ignorance, but what exactly is a matzos anyway?" Irwin patiently explained a little bit of Jewish history, and we all smiled and continued our preparation, thinking that Lamar probably hadn't attended many Seders in his life.

The next day, Lamar testified at length about his experiences in multiple sports and why such experience can be critical in finding suitable franchise owners. He was smart, direct, credible, and enormously likeable, and Judge Haight thanked him effusively for his testimony. We thought we were flying high.

Next came Joe Robbie. That evening we arranged to meet Joe and his lawyer (whose name I've long since forgotten), a law partner of Washington insider and former secretary of defense Clark Clifford, at the uptown Carlyle Hotel on East 76th Street. The trial was continuing at the City Bar Association's building, so at the end of the day, we packed up our bags from court with the key documents to review with Robbie and walked 30 blocks north to meet them at their hotel. Because we were running a little late, we assumed we would be meeting Robbie and his lawyer in their hotel suite. Not so. When we got to the lobby, we were pointed in the direction of the hotel bar.

Sure enough, Robbie and his lawyer were sitting somewhat bleary-eyed at the bar. It looked like they had been there all afternoon. We got a table and started—futilely—to prepare Robbie for his next-day testimony. Both Robbie and his lawyer were shit-faced and neither showed any interest in getting prepared. We tried six ways from Sunday to get the preparation going, but it was no use. They just kept ordering more drinks. After a while, we gave up and began drinking with them. By the time we staggered out of the bar several hours later, I was convinced that Robbie would be a disaster on the witness stand the next day. All was lost.

I was wrong again. The next morning, we met for five minutes in the lobby of the City Bar Association, and then I put him on the witness stand cold and hoped for the best. He performed brilliantly. He turned out to be the best witness in the entire case. So much for preparation.

We thought the next witness we called would be the killer. Here I was, a newly minted partner (I had made partner at Weil the previous February), and I was putting on the stand as a witness the greatest trial lawyer in America. What could be better? On direct examination, Williams was smooth, amusing, and convincing in his argument that the cross-ownership ban was illegal and should be scrapped. He wasn't really testifying so much as persuasively arguing our case, which was fine with me.

Everything was going our way until the NFL got its chance to cross-examine Williams, which had been the least of my worries. First, lawyer Jim Carter got Williams to admit that he was in the process of buying the Baltimore Orioles and that the ban could impact this purchase. In the law, we call that bias. Score one for the NFL.

Then it got worse. We had said all along that the market for sports ownership was limited and, in addition to having lots of money, required significant experience—specifically, knowledge and skill that had been acquired over the years by running other sports franchises.

Unfortunately, when Carter asked Williams how highly he valued experience, Williams pooh-poohed the idea. "You don't need any special skills to operate a sports franchise," Williams said. "Any bright, reasonable person could assimilate those skills in two days."

I winced. With that line, Williams torpedoed a fundamental piece of our case. We closed with our economic expert, Lou Guth, and the extensive data he had assembled about cross-ownership in sports. It was solid stuff, but not exactly riveting. We rested with fingers crossed.

By the time the NFL's case began, we were back downtown at the federal courthouse. The NFL's case was much shorter. Their lead witness was Rozelle. I tortured him for nearly two days on cross-examination, knowing that he desperately needed a cigarette break. I tried a little Pavlov's dog trickery on him; if he gave a little good testimony, he could have a cigarette. Eventually, he got the idea and conceded that some of his owners may have had concerns about competition from soccer.

The NFL then blundered big time by putting Leonard Tose on the witness stand. On cross-examination, he had a meltdown trying to explain why the NFL needed the ban. The easily riled Tose couldn't help himself, attacking Lamar for competing against him in Philadelphia. The real anticompetitive reason for the ban was now out in the open.

Carter finished the NFL's case with their own economic expert, who argued, persuasively, that the only reason the NASL had trouble finding owners was that the league itself was poorly managed, lost tons of money every year, and had no future. Hard to argue with any of that. After the NFL rested their case, Judge Haight indicated that he would issue his ruling as soon as possible. That turned out to be six long months.

In the meantime, the NASL continued to disintegrate. The Houston, Memphis, and Philadelphia franchises all folded shortly after the trial ended. In 1979 alone, the league had lost an average of nearly $1 million per team. By the time the judge's decision came in November of 1980, the NASL had fewer than 20 clubs, of which a half dozen were on life support.

Judge Haight's decision only hastened the decline. Relying almost totally on Williams's devastating testimony, he ruled that our sports ownership market did not exist. Even if it did, he said it didn't matter because the NFL was really a "single entity" and therefore couldn't be sued for the ban. It was a complete disaster.

But just as the NASL was tottering on oblivion, Millstein reengaged and appeared at a league meeting for the first time in two years. In one of his Douglas MacArthur moments, he guaranteed the beleaguered owners a victory. Then he disappeared again and dumped the job on me and Kessler, our young antitrust guru.

Although he had gutted our case, Judge Haight also threw us a lifeline. He agreed to keep the injunction against the ban in place until the outcome of the appeal, which meant Hunt and Robbie could keep their NASL franchises at least for now.

It took nearly a year for our appeal to be heard by a three-judge panel of the US Court of Appeals in New York. Millstein, arguing on behalf of the NASL, was brilliant—other than the fact that he repeatedly referred to our client as the "NHL" and in some instances the "National Hockey League." At one point, I had to yell out, "We represent soccer, not hockey!" Fortunately, the judges didn't seem to mind. We left the courthouse feeling pretty good about our chances.

Unfortunately, in the year between the lower court decision and the appeals court ruling, another dozen franchises had dropped out of the NASL, including, ironically, Hunt's own Dallas Tornado. The blood was in the water.

Our appeal optimism was well founded. On January 27, 1982, the Court of Appeals reversed Judge Haight's decision in its entirety. They found that the NASL had indeed been the target of the NFL's anticompetitive cross-ownership ban, and they sent the case back to Judge Haight to determine the NASL's damages.

But it was too little too late. While we fought the NFL over the amount of our damages and legal fees, the NASL went out of business—though not without a couple of priceless last hurrahs. When the NASL's general counsel was dispatched to Vancouver to collect on a letter of credit from the owner of the defunct Whitecaps, the lawyer threatened the owner with bad publicity, unaware that he was already under indictment for child molestation, among other crimes. Stiffing the NASL could only improve his reputation. And in a last-ditch attempt to save the Seattle Sounders, the league offered the team to a pair of brothers in the construction business. When asked what their net worth was, they said zero. The franchise was granted anyway. It folded within weeks.

So many teams folded so quickly that we had trouble locating recipients of the NFL settlement money and got stuck with nearly $400,000, which we donated to charity. I directed a large chunk of it to help find a cure for diabetes, since my son, Chris, is a juvenile diabetic.

Soccer never did become "the Sport of the '80s," though the current professional league, Major League Soccer, has achieved the stability and professionalism that the NASL never did. It doesn't seem nearly as much fun, though. I've seen the inner workings of every top sports league in America, and nothing can touch the sheer lunacy of the old NASL. There is nothing like watching grown men go to pieces over indoor soccer, trust me.

I had several takeaways from this half-decade-long debacle: expect the unexpected, and keep fighting if you know you are right. I also learned that the NFL owners as a group were the most arrogant and powerful people in all of sports. That was a lesson I would learn over and over again in the coming decades.

CHAPTER 8

Cable TV: Baseball's "Pot of Gold"

IT WAS IN THE LATE 1970S THAT THE SPORTS WORLD
became what we know it as today: a cultural juggernaut. We have
cable television to thank. Though cable had been around for years,
the technology had mostly been employed to serve remote areas that
couldn't get a proper signal. But in the 1970s, cable moved into major
metropolitan areas with a vengeance, bringing a heretofore unimagi-
nable volume of TV options. Cities that had been served by just three
or four broadcast stations (New York had a whopping seven) soon had
15, 30, 40 channels. Some of the first slots were allocated to so-called
superstations, like WGN from Chicago and WTBS from Atlanta,
which happened to show lots of baseball games (the Cubs and Braves,
respectively) to a national audience.

There were also many brand-new cable channels that focused
on sports, like the USA Network, the Sports Channel (later MSG),
the Prime Ticket Network, Sports Southwest, and a half-dozen other
regional sports networks. The most significant one was a satellite
farm in isolated Bristol, Connecticut, called ESPN, which couldn't
afford the rights for big-time sports but somehow built a following with
obscurities like beach volleyball, Australian-rules football, and weight-
lifting. Men, the lesson was, would watch anything remotely related
to sports. As their reach grew, cable networks went after pro hockey,
basketball, and baseball for weeknight games, which then forced the
three broadcast networks CBS, NBC, and ABC to pay much higher
rights fees to the leagues for the lucrative weekend packages as well as

for the playoffs and championships. The networks went from paying a few million to a few hundred million and eventually to billions for the rights to major league sports. It was becoming a very big pie.

The players, understandably, wanted their piece. A new tool at their disposal was the "right of publicity," a legal concept spawned from a 1950s US Supreme Court case involving baseball cards. It recognized that an individual had a right to control how his or her name, image, and likeness were used, especially for commercial purposes. In the Supreme Court case, the majority had ruled that baseball card companies like Topps and Fleer had to pay each player to publish their card. Shouldn't television be subject to the same legal principle?

That's the question Irwin Warren and I asked in an article we wrote for the *Indiana Law Review*. Our goal was to inject this issue into labor negotiations as another bargaining chip for the players in their effort to get a fair share of the new cable TV revenue.

Sure enough, Larry Fleisher, ever the innovator, seized on the right of publicity. He anticipated the NBA's position—that games had been televised for years without the players mentioning anything about their right of publicity. So Fleisher focused on the emergence of cable television, attempting to differentiate the new revenue streams from the old.

In June 1979, the NBPA filed a test case. With Paul Silas, the union president, serving as lead plaintiff, we sued the NBA and the Manhattan Cable Company, the local New York cable provider. We argued that its showing of NBA games violated Silas's and other players' rights of publicity.

It took us until 1983 to settle the case by folding it into a landmark collective bargaining agreement, which, for the first time, included a salary cap and a designated player share of all revenues, including cable television revenues.

Marvin Miller and the baseball players' union were also focused on this television issue but for different reasons. I had known Miller from the *Robertson* case; we occasionally held meetings with officials from all four players' unions. I had also recently become friendly

with Don Fehr, who became the MLBPA's new general counsel after
Dick Moss resigned in 1977 to become a baseball player agent.

In the fall of 1981, Miller and Fehr called me. They wanted to
discuss launching a lawsuit similar to the one we had going in basketball. Baseball had just suffered through a miserable season as owners
insisted on trying to impose punitive compensation for the loss of free
agents, the same crap Stern and the basketball owners had tried a few
years before. The baseball players called a midseason strike, canceling
more than 700 games. Robbed of their antitrust rights by the infamous
Flood decision, the players had been backed into a corner. The stoppage of play ran from June 12 to July 31. The owners' resolve slowly
evaporated, and they meekly capitulated, gaining nothing and losing
millions of dollars and thousands of fans. There was so much bad
blood that at the press conference to announce their collapse, Miller
refused to shake the hand of Ray Grebey, the owners' negotiator.

The dispute over the baseball players' rightful share of TV revenue
had a long and complicated history. From the very first TV deal, a
group of veteran players had successfully earmarked a sliver of the
World Series television proceeds for a modest pension plan. But no
consensus had ever been reached as to what rights were owned by
whom or how those revenues should be divided. This became a major
bone of contention when Miller came to the union in 1966, but the
owners simply refused to negotiate, claiming that it was not a proper
subject of collective bargaining. The issue came to a head in the wake
of the bitter 1981 strike.

Before long, the MLBPA hired us to organize a lawsuit, and over
the next few months, we had extensive discussions with Miller, Dick
Moss, and Don Fehr as they filled us in on the unique history of television in baseball. We were all ready to go, but there seemed to be some
reluctance, particularly on the part of Miller (who was about to retire),
to pull the trigger.

Before filing suit, Miller wanted to send a letter to the Lords of
Baseball setting forth our position. Fehr and I thought we should sue
first and bargain later, but Miller thought that the labor laws required

otherwise. His was not an easy mind to change; he sent the letter, and it backfired immediately. The baseball owners jumped the gun and sued the MLBPA in federal court in Chicago. It came to be known as the *Baltimore Orioles* case, simply because they were the first team name on the pleadings. We fired back with our own lawsuit in New York federal court on behalf of three players, all of whom were prominent members of the MLBPA leadership: Steve Rogers, a five-time All-Star pitcher for the Montreal Expos; Bob Boone, a four-time All-Star as a Phillie who then played for the California Angels; and Steve Renko, a solid starting pitcher also with the Angels.

Now we had dueling cases and a pair of less-than-ideal judges. In Chicago, we had Charles Kocoras, newly appointed and no genius. He was like a numbskull fan who instinctively sides with owners because he thinks players make too much money. In the New York case, we drew Judge Irving Ben Cooper, who had been the baseball union's nemesis in the *Flood* case 10 years earlier. Cooper had particular contempt for Miller, so we chose what we thought was the lesser of two evils and picked Chicago.

The owners hired Lou Hoynes, by then a senior partner at Willkie Farr & Gallagher, to lead their team. Willkie was baseball's traditional law firm, and Bowie Kuhn had been a Willkie partner before becoming MLB commissioner in 1969. Hoynes had argued the *Flood* case at the Supreme Court. Hoynes was assisted by a young partner named Bob Kheel, who was the son of Ted Kheel, a nationally known labor lawyer. My team consisted of Irwin Warren and Jeff Klein, the young lawyer who had gotten his feet wet in the NASL case. Because publicity rights under the law are a form of intellectual property, I also drafted my partner Bruce Rich, an intellectual property expert, to weigh in on those issues.

The baseball owners had two principal arguments. First, they said whatever publicity rights the players might have were trumped by copyright law, and they owned the copyrights to all baseball games, so that was that. Second, by failing to sue over the past 35 years, the players had long ago waived any rights to television revenues. Our response was that live performances could not be copyrighted and that we had always reserved our rights on television going back to 1947. It was the litigator's version of "Play ball!"

The owners' first big move was to test our financial resources by forcing us to do tons of depositions—the same trick the NBA had tried in the *Robertson* case. Also, the more players they got to interview, the more likely one would say what they wanted him to say, which is that players were well aware they were being televised and had never raised an issue about it. The truth was the players had maintained for decades—both orally and in writing—that they were not waiving their right to a fair share of television revenues.

Bob Kheel took many of the depositions. Most of the players had been heavily involved in union business as officers or team player representatives. They were among the smartest and most accomplished players in the league, and many of them went on to distinguished postplaying careers as managers, coaches, and broadcasters. In addition to our plaintiffs (Rogers, Boone, and Renko), we also included Don Baylor (manager and coach), Tommy John (of elbow surgery fame and a broadcaster), Jerry Reuss (coach and broadcaster), Mark Belanger (MLBPA executive until his untimely death in 1989), Phil Garner (manager of several clubs), Pete Rose (manager and player still not in the Hall of Fame), Tom Seaver (broadcaster and Hall of Fame player), Dave Winfield (broadcaster and Hall of Fame player), and Reggie Jackson (a.k.a. Hall of Fame player "Mr. October").

Apart from a few memorable moments, the player depositions were uneventful. Pete Rose, despite his faults in the eyes of the Lords of Baseball, turned out to be a Hall of Fame witness, respectful of the process and staunchly supportive of the players' right to a share of television revenue. Reggie Jackson was the opposite; he pulled a Wilt Chamberlain and gave Jeff Klein a very tough time when he went down to Miami Beach to prep him. Jackson, a world-class pain in the ass, insisted that Klein put on a bathing suit and join him in the pool at his hotel. For all that, Reggie was a lousy witness, arrogant, forgetful, and dismissive of the entire process.

These players knew they were sticking their necks out. More than any other sport, baseball owners had a history of punishing the players who dared to speak out, Curt Flood being a prime example. Flood was essentially banished from baseball after his unsuccessful free agency battle.

The owners also took depositions from a bunch of agents, including superagents Jerry Kapstein and Ron Shapiro, for no particular reason other than to harass our side.

Dick Moss, the MLBPA's former general counsel who left the union to become one of the leading baseball agents, gave a lengthy deposition. As an agent, he represented such superstars as Nolan Ryan and Fernando Valenzuela. A little rounder and a little balder than when I first met him nearly a decade earlier, Moss still had the same wisecracking intelligence that had made him an effective second-in-command in building the MLBPA. He testified effectively and at length as to the long and tortured history of television revenue negotiations and its funding of the players' pension plan.

It was during this period that I really got to know Marvin Miller on a personal level as Klein and I spent days huddled together in his midtown Manhattan apartment preparing him for his deposition. By then, Miller was retired and less voluble, but he hadn't lost one iota of his commitment to the cause. He had a biting sense of humor and a gift for storytelling and was able to recall conversations word for word from 15 years earlier. He did not suffer fools lightly, as he made clear when he regaled us with tales of his often fruitless dealings with baseball commissioner Bowie Kuhn and his labor henchmen, John Gaherin and Ray Grebey. A true believer in both the union movement and his players, he also recognized the irony of a Brooklyn-born, one-armed Jewish atheist having achieved fame, if not fortune, as the head of what was by then considered the most powerful union in sports. If you want to know why baseball is alone among the four major leagues in never having a salary cap, the answer begins with Marvin Miller.

During discovery, we unearthed a treasure trove of documents that went back decades into the 1940s; they proved that everything

Marvin remembered was, in fact, true. We even had transcripts from owners' meetings where the Lords of Baseball had actually agreed to set aside a portion of television revenue to fund the players' pension plan. Marvin believed that the baseball owners now were simply reneging on that earlier promise.

Marvin had a long memory not only for facts but also for slights and insults. He was a hater. He particularly despised Calvin Griffith (Twins) and Charles Finley (A's), whom he described colorfully as either Neanderthals or clowns or both. As for Kuhn, it was a mixture of professional contempt and personal dislike. Miller considered Kuhn to be a bit of buffoon and a bit of a liar.

Miller had a grudging respect for John Gaherin, a professional management labor negotiator with a gruff Irish demeanor. Miller believed Gaherin was just doing his job as the mouthpiece for the Lords of Baseball. Years later Miller said of Gaherin, "Of all the management people I dealt with in baseball, he was clearly the most knowledgeable and skilled. He had the most integrity plus a wonderful sense of humor."

However, Miller did have contempt for Ray Grebey, Gaherin's replacement, with whom he'd had a stormy relationship from the start. Grebey, who had been chief labor negotiator at General Electric, was hired by the baseball owners to replace Gaherin in 1978 with the stated purpose of "getting tough" on the players. It had been his idea to gut free agency by insisting on an unreasonable compensation for free agents, a strategy that led to the 1981 strike. Miller blamed Grebey for mishandling the issue from the start. Ironically, as years went by, their feud cooled, and Grebey eventually wrote a letter to the Hall of Fame urging the induction of Miller, saying that despite their differences, he deserved admission: "the history of the game must prevail." The Lords of Baseball said, "No, thanks."

Lou Hoynes took Miller's deposition for several days, and I defended. There was no love lost between Miller and Hoynes, who had also unsuccessfully represented the owners in the *Messersmith* free agency arbitration. The deposition was contentious, with Hoynes and

Miller going at it over every aspect of the 35-year television dispute. I acted as umpire. True to form, Marvin was a phenomenal witness, remembering detail on detail of every negotiation and pointing to the earlier transcripts and documents that proved that players had never waived rights to television revenues. We believed we were on very solid ground. Though retired, Miller spent countless hours preparing the case, including helping us structure the depositions we would take of the Lords of Baseball and their representatives.

While all this was going on, the players' union itself underwent a crisis of leadership. When Marvin announced his retirement shortly after the end of the 1981 strike, he gave no recommendation for his successor. To some, his silence reflected poorly on Don Fehr, who had replaced Dick Moss as MLBPA general counsel in 1977 and had only been in that job for less than four years. That wasn't the case; it was just that Marvin believed that the players should select their next executive director and did not wish to influence them in any way. Fehr had by then developed good relationships with many of the player leaders, and several players expressed surprise that Marvin had not formally recommended or even suggested Fehr for the role.

So in the fall of 1982, the players hired Ken Moffett, a former head of the Federal Mediation Board. He lasted less than a year.

I had been convinced all along that Fehr was the right person for the job, and I told Marvin as much. I knew Fehr to be brilliant, if a bit spacey, and he was also devoted to the players. Fehr analyzed problems from many sides, sometimes too many sides. He often seemed to talk in code. He had a unique way of thinking outside the box, occasionally way outside the box. After a year of turmoil, Fehr was appointed acting executive director in the fall of 1983. In 1985, he was elected as the full-time executive director.

Despite the union's internal strife, the television lawsuit lumbered on. I took the deposition of Bowie Kuhn, who was the polar opposite of Miller. Tall and heavyset, with a booming voice, Kuhn gave the impression that he was "to the manor born," though he had actually grown up in a middle-class suburb of DC. He was a big man physically—6′5″ and 240 pounds—but not intellectually, a perfect fig-urehead for the Lords of Baseball. As a partner at Willkie Farr, he had spent a decade or more representing MLB owners as his only clients. When he ascended to the throne in 1969, he was just in time to lead the fight against Curt Flood. In a letter to Kuhn, Flood declared that he was "not a piece of property." Kuhn was unmoved. Beating Flood in court was probably the high point of his career.

Players, in his view, had to be policed. Kuhn prided himself on being the "moral conscience" of baseball, cracking down hard on players for trivial drug offenses (his indefinite suspension of pitcher Ferguson Jenkins for drug possession in 1980 was promptly over-turned by an independent arbitrator, as were many of the other pen-alties he handed down as commissioner). He was always purporting to do things "in the best interest of baseball," though federal judges repeatedly reversed his decisions because, as they pointed out, even the commissioner of baseball is bound by basic legal principles like due process.

Throughout the 1970s, Kuhn battled hard against free agency, sincerely (and moronically) believing it had to be stopped. During his deposition, I spent several hours trying to get him to admit the obvi-ous: that he was merely the employee of the owners, paid to do their bidding. Kuhn kept insisting that he was the commissioner of all of baseball, including the players, as if his job were some divine appoint-ment. It was just plain silly.

I also took the depositions of baseball's lead labor negotiators, Gaherin and Grebey. True to form, Gaherin was honest, engaging, intelligent, and a good storyteller in his own right. He readily admit-ted that the players had always sought to reserve their rights with regard to television. Grebey, on the other hand, was both unpleasant and not particularly wedded to the truth. He would admit nothing. It was easy to see why Miller detested him.

As we went along, I began to have some doubts. Judge Koco-ras had made it clear from the outset that he wasn't in our dugout. Baseball salaries were exploding, which made it difficult to garner much sympathy for the notion that players were entitled to even more money. I was convinced that legally we were right, but sometimes that doesn't matter.

We took the depositions of the president of the American League, Lee MacPhail, and the National League, Chub Feeney. I recall taking the deposition of at least one owner, Nelson Doubleday, the owner at the time of the New York Mets. Doubleday was a distant relative of Abner and the scion of the Doubleday publishing empire. He proved every cliché you ever heard about silver spoons—dull and detached, though polite.

As the case progressed, Klein and I were drawn into a sideshow involving Dave Winfield and George "the Boss" Steinbrenner. In December 1980, Winfield signed a deal with the Yankees that was the moonshot of free agency—$23 million for 10 years. Even now, it still seems like a lot of money, but back then, it was insane—the league-wide average for the previous season had been $143,000.

Winfield's deal was complicated, and there was an extra chunk of it—approximately $3 million—that was supposed to fund his charitable foundation, which benefited underprivileged kids. Support for the Winfield Foundation was actually in a separate contract signed by the Boss, not by the Yankees. It was a little added sweetener to bring Winfield to New York.

When Winfield's deal was announced, Steinbrenner was smiling along with everyone else. After Winfield went 1 for 22 in a six-game World Series loss to the Dodgers in 1981, however, the Boss was no longer smiling. He began to call Winfield "Mr. May," a satiric comparison to the "Mr. October" nickname earned by Reggie Jackson for his clutch postseason play in the late 1970s.

In the spring of 1983, Dave and his agent, Al Frohman, met with Klein and me to tell us that Steinbrenner had reneged on funding the Winfield Foundation. They hired us to force Steinbrenner to live up to the deal, and we threatened to sue. In response, Steinbrenner hired the meanest attack-dog lawyer in the history of the bar, the infamous Roy Cohn.

Among his many career lowlights was suborning perjury to help convict Julius and Ethel Rosenberg of espionage, chasing down alleged communists for Senator Joe McCarthy, and mentoring a young Donald Trump. Cohn, twice indicted for stock fraud and bribery, represented himself in both trials and won acquittals. He was indicted a third time for perjury and witness tampering but again somehow avoided conviction, although he was later disbarred.

In the summer of 1983, Steinbrenner summoned Winfield to Cohn's palatial townhouse in midtown Manhattan on the pretext of resolving the foundation dispute. Klein and I came along. Cohn, who took the meeting in a bathrobe, was in bad shape, his pockmarked face drawn and most of his hair gone. We didn't know it at the time, but Cohn was dying of AIDS.

Cohn was still plenty sharp. He kept calling me "John," an old ploy of his to rattle adversaries, so I called him "Ray," which caused him to stop. After an hour or so of banter, I went into a separate room with Steinbrenner, and we worked out what I thought was a deal. The Boss was charming and earnest, and he assured me that it was all "just a big misunderstanding." We came back into the room, announced a settlement, and shook hands.

The next day, after I sent over a draft letter to confirm our agreement, Cohn called to say George was refusing to acknowledge the handshake agreement and that there was no deal. Cohn actually sounded embarrassed, an emotion he was not widely known to possess. I immediately remembered Billy Martin's famous double-barreled insult of Reggie Jackson and Steinbrenner—"one's a born liar and the other's convicted"—referencing Steinbrenner's guilty plea to felony perjury in connection with Watergate. But the thrice-indicted Roy Cohn was, in my personal experience, more honorable than the Boss.

Over the next few years, we hounded Steinbrenner to live up to his obligations to the foundation. After Cohn died, we dealt with a series of vicious, unethical lawyers. Steinbrenner did everything he could to dodge being deposed, but federal judge Robert Ward finally forced him to go under oath, and the case was settled in 1987 with full payments made to the Foundation. (Meanwhile, Klein had replaced Al Frohman as Winfield's agent. Their families became close, and Winfield became godfather to Jeff's son. Klein guided Winfield through several more negotiations until Dave retired in 1993.)

Two years later, it was revealed that during this period, Steinbrenner had hired a petty gambler with Mafia ties named Howard Spira to dig up dirt on Winfield and his Foundation. There was no dirt to dig up—the Foundation had for years made good on its mission of helping underprivileged kids in New York, Minneapolis, and San Diego—and the whole tawdry episode backfired on Steinbrenner when Spira tried to blackmail him, which ultimately led to Steinbrenner receiving a "lifetime" ban from baseball in 1990. The ban lasted barely two years.

Meanwhile, there had been a major setback in the TV revenues case. In May 1985, Judge Kocoras ruled—unsurprisingly—that the owners' copyright superseded the players' right to publicity. My intellectual property expert partner, Bruce Rich, was appalled by this unheard-of application of copyright law, so we appealed the Federal Court of Appeals in Chicago, convinced the law was on our side. We were apparently wrong. A panel of three judges upheld Judge Kocoras's ruling, a decision that is still criticized today by copyright law scholars. I was bitterly disappointed; the decision was just flat-out wacky. I felt particularly bad for Don and Marvin and the players who had funded this multiyear fight with nothing to show for it. In hindsight, it's hard to feel sorry for the baseball player of today, when the average salary is over $4 million and superstars are now routinely signed to long-term $200 million deals. Who knew?

Maybe we were 25 years too soon. In more recent times, a series of lawsuits by college athletes have asserted with some success the same right of publicity claims relating to television. In a twist of fate, I ended up defending several of the television networks (including my longtime client CBS) in these lawsuits, relying on the old *Baltimore Orioles* case.

I simply followed Justice Joseph Story's famous admonition that "the law is a jealous mistress that requires constant courtship." In this case, I was courting the TV networks.

• • •

In 1984, the baseball owners dumped Commissioner Kuhn, who they blamed for free agency, and replaced him with Peter Ueberroth, who had just orchestrated the wildly successful Olympics in Los Angeles. He swept into office with a powerful message to the owners.

Echoing Ed Williams, he called them "damned dumb" for throwing millions at free agents. He stuck to this theme, and soon enough, the owners absorbed his message. They made an agreement—clearly anticompetitive and clearly collusion—to limit contracts to three years for position players and two for pitchers.

The result: of the 35 players who were free agents after the 1985 season, only 4 changed teams, and only because their old clubs didn't want them back. Proven stars such as Kirk Gibson, Tommy John, and Phil Niekro received no offers. After the 1986 season, again only 4 free agents switched teams, and three-fourths of the free agents were forced to sign one-year contracts. I watched from the sidelines appalled as this obvious conspiracy to cripple free agency in baseball continued.

It turned out to be a very costly gambit by the owners. Over the next few years, Fehr, his new general counsel Gene Orza, and Don's younger brother Steve brought a series of collusion cases before arbitrators and won almost $300 million in damages. Fehr proved every bit as combative as Miller had been, and so did Orza, his pugnacious and wisecracking number two.

But the baseball owners were undaunted; they stepped up their campaign to splinter the union in the early 1990s. When the owners attempted to unilaterally impose a salary cap in 1994, the players went on the longest strike in baseball history, wiping out a third of the season and the World Series. I was pissed because the Yankees were leading the league when the strike began, headed for the postseason for the first time in 13 years.

At one point, Fehr asked Ira Millstein, long gone from the world of sports, to try to help settle the dispute. Although Millstein was an old friend and political ally of Richard Ravitch, who was representing the baseball owners, the attempt failed. Even the intervention of President Clinton went nowhere. It wasn't until a federal judge named Sonia Sotomayor, now an associate Supreme Court Justice, ordered the owners to withdraw their efforts to impose a salary cap that the strike ended. Fehr and Orza came to be despised by the new Lords of Baseball almost as much as the earlier Lords had hated Marvin Miller and Dick Moss. Marvin Miller has been shamefully punished by being kept out of the Hall of Fame for almost 40 years. Fehr is not likely to fare any better.

In 1998, at the baseball players' urging, Congress passed a law permitting baseball players to utilize the antitrust laws in the same way as other professional athletes. That law would be known as the Curt Flood Act. Since then, relative peace in baseball has prevailed.

The most important thing I learned from my involvement in baseball was to communicate openly with the players, involving them in every key decision. Players are smart—they "get it."

I had one last run-in with the Lords of Baseball. In the spring of 2002, I was retained by the 14 minority owners of the Montreal Expos in a last-ditch effort to keep the franchise from leaving Montreal. The Expos, who joined the National League as an expansion club in 1969, had been something of a cursed franchise. After many years of futility, false hopes, and underachievement, they had the best team in baseball in 1994, the year of no World Series. After that, Montreal abandoned ship.

Then along came a shifty New York art dealer named Jeffrey Loria, who obtained a majority interest in the Expos and then put the squeeze on the minority investors to either pump money into the club or lose their shares. Confusing signals were coming out of Major

League Baseball—did they want to fold the team, move it somewhere else, or what? Those questions were answered when baseball commissioner Bud Selig engineered a complex three-way deal in which Loria sold the Expos to the MLB and simultaneously bought the Florida Marlins from John Henry, who in turn bought the Boston Red Sox.

The Expos minority owners were royally screwed, and on July 16, 2002, we filed suit in federal court in Miami, Loria's new home, charging him—as well as commissioner Bud Selig, his deputy Robert DuPuy, and Major League Baseball—with fraud and violations of the Federal Racketeering Influenced and Corrupt Organization Act, known as RICO. I learned later that DuPuy's sister was a tax partner of mine in Weil's Washington, DC, office. Small world. The case was a bit of a stretch, but it sure as hell got their attention. The Lords of Baseball were outraged.

A few months later, in October, my friend and client Steve Brenner, then president of USA Network, invited me to go with him to that night's playoff game at Yankee Stadium—Yankees versus Angels. When we got to the game, the seats turned out to be three rows back from home plate.

"Whose seats are these?" I asked Brenner.

"This is the commissioner's box," Brenner replied.

"Holy shit," I said. "If Selig knew I was his guest, he would not be pleased." Brenner told me not to worry, that no one would ever know. Wrong. The next day, Brenner was told, "Don't ever bring Quinn to another game as the commissioner's guest." Like Pete Rose and Steinbrenner before me, I had been banned.

In the end, we couldn't do anything for the guys in Montreal. At the end of the 2004 season, the MLB transferred the franchise to Washington, and they became the Nationals. Our RICO claim, which had previously been sent to an arbitration panel in New York City, was dismissed.

In a last bit of irony, in 2010, Bob DuPuy hired me and Jeff Klein to represent him against Major League Baseball in a potential dispute relating to a falling-out he'd had with Bud Selig. We successfully negotiated a lucrative retirement package for the former alleged rack-eteer with my old nemesis from Proskauer, Howie Ganz, who by then was one of MLB's chief outside lawyers. Obviously, DuPuy harbored no hard feelings. Now we're golfing buddies.

The extraordinary success of the baseball union was the direct result of its leaders—Miller and Moss, then Fehr and Orza. They were the Koufaxes and Drysdales of the labor movement in sports. But the success was also due to the unique solidarity of the players. Curt Flood set an example that was emulated by Messersmith, Rogers, Winfield, and many others, making the MLBPA the most formidable sports union in the entire country.

Through the years, Fehr and I remained close. We would consult on whatever issues we were working on across all four major sports. In 2011, he signed on as executive director of the National Hockey League Players' Association (NHLPA), and together we went back to the barricades.

CHAPTER 9

The Salary Cap Is Born

BY THE LATE 1970S, THANKS TO THE *ROBERTSON* settlement, a lot of NBA players were rich beyond their wildest dreams, and deservedly so. The average player salary would soon reach $250,000. For the players, it was the best of times—and, for most NBA owners, the worst of times.

Their business had problems everywhere you looked. Network TV ratings were sagging—blamed in part on the string of small market franchises (e.g., Portland, Washington, and Seattle) winning NBA championships—and new cable revenue was not rising fast enough to keep up with the escalating salaries. The four franchises that had come over from the ABA were in particularly tough shape; the onerous conditions set by their fellow owners had forced them into heavy debt. Attendance in many cities was down—in Chicago and Philadelphia it was way down—and storied franchises like the Knicks, Lakers, and Celtics had suffered through several years of ignominy.

But the biggest problem was thought to be cultural—namely, a festering perception that the NBA had become "too black." Since the league's color line had been broken in 1950 by Earl Lloyd, the percentage of African American players had steadily grown to more than 70 percent by 1980. For some time, people around the league had worried about sustaining the interest of a mainstream white audience, especially since there were also rumors of rampant cocaine use by some of the NBA's emerging young black stars. The drug stuff was certainly a problem, but not any more than it was a problem for society as a whole. In terms of race, the NBA would distinguish itself as a force for positive change over time. But in those high-anxiety years of the late 1970s and early 1980s, there were serious fears—among mainly owners but also coaches, TV executives, and even some journalists—about the viability of a black-dominated league.

This obviously affected our labor negotiations. Black players were well represented in union leadership, and we tended to look at the race issue as just another convenient way for the owners to blame the players instead of themselves for the league's struggles. Although the *Robertson* antitrust settlement ran through the end of the 1985–86 season, a separate three-year collective bargaining agreement also agreed to in 1976, covering player benefits and related issues, had expired after the 1978–79 season and had to be renewed. So negotiations began in 1979 with the NBA owners crying poverty once again and blaming free agency and demanding givebacks and financial concessions. Naturally, one of the first things we did was ask to see their audited financial records. Naturally, they refused. We concluded that their claims were probably bullshit. As it turned out, we were wrong.

It was already a busy time for me—I was up to my ears in the NASL's long-shot crusade against NFL, and the baseball television revenues case was about to pop up on my radar screen. But because of my history with Fleisher and Robertson, the basketball work had always consumed me. We filed the Silas cable television lawsuit in June 1979, just as the old labor agreement expired.

The NBPA and the league were still optimistic enough about a new labor deal that we tacitly agreed to keep negotiations out of the media. Not that the media much cared. Before the 24-hour sports news cycle, you couldn't make much news unless there was about to be a strike or a lockout or a lawsuit.

Our team consisted of Larry Fleisher, Paul Silas, and me. Silas, coming off a championship season with Seattle, was nearing the end of his playing career. This would be his last negotiation; he retired the following year and was hired almost immediately to coach the San Diego Clippers, a team newly purchased by one Donald Sterling (more about him shortly).

The NBA was led by Stern and his new general counsel, Russ Granik, along with Angelo Drossos, chairman of the NBA Board of Governors and owner of the San Antonio Spurs. Drossos was another unforgettable character of the precorporate era. He was short and feisty, with steel-gray hair and a Texas-sized ego. When the ABA's Dallas Chaparrals were gasping for breath, he and a group of San Antonio businessmen swooped in and bought them for nothing. Renamed the Spurs, they became the ABA's model franchise—and eventually the NBA's model franchise too. Drossos had a good sense of humor, and he thought he could sell anything. His role in the negotiations was to sell doom and gloom. Small-market franchises like his would be screwed, he told us over and over again, if the NBA free agency bazaar was not reined in.

Other owners, usually also from small markets, would occasionally show up to describe their woes, but Angelo was the NBA's whiner-in-chief. Let me tell you, there are few things that are more enjoyable than watching a bunch of aging white millionaires whine. Well, it's funny, then it gets annoying.

Drossos kept telling us that "We have to be partners." Our response: How can we be "partners" if you won't show us your financials? After Drossos said the word *partners* for what must have been the hundredth time, Silas, the tall, silent one, lost his cool. He rose from his seat at the conference table and walked slowly around the table, looking down at the diminutive Drossos, and bellowed, "Angelo, I don't want to be your fucking partner!"

We never heard that word out of Angelo's mouth again.

The negotiations dragged on into the 1980 season before we finally reached an agreement on a few modest points: an increase in minimum salaries, a reduction in the number of draft rounds, and some improvements in pension and other benefits. The owners got us to defer the issue of cable revenues. I don't know if anybody was happy, but a three-year deal was signed, which was probably a mistake on both sides. Often, the best you can do in the moment is kick the can down the road, and that's what we had done. By not dealing with the facts and illusions of the NBA's financial predicament, we all set ourselves up for a confrontation in the summer of 1982 that would throw the league's very existence into doubt.

It was during this period that Fleisher and the players went into overdrive to transform NBA stars from regional heroes to international celebrities and ambassadors for the sport. He and the players of that era have never received proper credit for being way ahead of the league in recognizing international opportunities. After our secret trip to Brazil in 1975, Fleisher began arranging similar goodwill missions around the world for the players, plus their wives, girlfriends, and assorted hangers-on (which included Katy and me). These midsummer player jaunts involved exhibition games and basketball clinics, activities that, to be frank, were in direct violation of the players' NBA contracts. The legal language was clear: players could not engage in organized games in the off-season. We had a simple workaround: we didn't tell the league where or when we were going. At one point, the NBA heard about an upcoming trip and actually got a court injunction to stop it. Unfortunately for them, we had already left the country. Since there was no one in Fleisher's office to receive it, the injunction was ignored.

The next trip after Brazil was to the Ivory Coast, not the most obvious choice. But there were some, shall we say, synergies at work. Fleisher and a group of former players, including Bradley, DeBusschere, Havlicek, Silas, and several others, had purchased an interest in the Hotel Ivoire, an upscale business hotel in Abidjan, the capital of the Ivory Coast. The Ivory Coast, a former French colony, was one of the poorest nations in the world, but Fleisher convinced the government to underwrite the expenses for two dozen players and their entourage. The guys played in an All-Star game and gave clinics, and we all toured Abidjan and nearby regions.

One day we visited a fishing village not far from Abidjan. We bargained at the local bazaars, watched native dancers wearing Nike sneakers, and drank in the local culture, both literally and figuratively. I can still smell the sweet yet acrid odors of the many items sold at an ancient bazaar in downtown Abidjan. We were all struck by how these people lived such primitive daily lives in the shadow of the city's ultramodern skyline.

The following summer, we went to Greece, where we took in the Acropolis, visited the island of Mykonos, tearfully sang the "Star-Spangled Banner" on the Fourth of July, and rode motorbikes on the island of Corfu. There is nothing quite as ridiculous looking as a 6'8" basketball player on a tiny motorbike—except maybe a 6'8" basketball player on a donkey. On the island of Hydra, Havlicek, Silas, and I rode donkeys through bleached white villages, drank too much ouzo, and ate plenty of a local fish called barbudi. We also played a series of games against the Greek national team. When Oscar Robertson, now in his new role as our coach, walked onto the court in the Athens arena, 18,000 Greek fans stood up in unison and began to chant "O, O, O." They knew Oscar well because he had been the star of the 1960 US Olympic basketball team, which had won the gold medal in Rome. When they started that chant, chills went up and down my spine. It was incredible to see how far the love and respect for NBA players had traveled.

The following summer, we toured Italy and Yugoslavia, which was then still under Communist rule. The highlights of that trip included a 3:00 a.m. train ride from Bologna to Rome, something that Fleisher had forgotten to tell the players about until after a postgame feast. There are certain guys who still bitch about that train ride to this day. We toured Rome on a hot, sunny afternoon, ending up at Trevi Fountain, where a lot more than three coins were tossed into the water. The next day, we arrived at a beautiful resort north of Dubrovnik on the Adriatic Sea in what is now Croatia. We held a tennis tournament, and Marvin "the Eraser" Webster was my doubles partner. His strokes were awful, but he was murder at the net. We lost in the finals to Havlicek and Buffalo Braves star Randy Smith, a truly amazing athlete who had never held a tennis racket before the tournament. Later, on a giant-screen television set up in the lobby of our hotel, we all gathered to watch the five-set Wimbledon final between Bjorn Borg and John McEnroe, which kept our American basketball players entranced for nearly five hours. The nude beaches in Croatia weren't bad either.

By far, the highlight of our globetrotting summer trips was "the NBA China tour." In the summer of 1982, Fleisher, working through his son Marc (who was then in the music business and had contacts in the Far East), arranged a series of games in Communist China, secretly sponsored by their government. Ronald Reagan was president, and relations between the US and China were at an all-time low. The afterglow of the Nixon-era détente had long since faded. We could not keep this trip a secret.

One of Fleisher's old friends was married to Rita Satz, a producer for NBC's *Today Show*. She arranged for an NBC camera crew to record this latest version of "Travels with Larry." It was an extraordinary experience, a true effort at "Hoops Diplomacy." Aside from a Red Auerbach–led State Department tour to Communist Eastern Europe with a team of NBA players in 1964 and an exchange of Ping-Pong teams in the 1970s, there had never been an organized visit of American athletes to what was a completely closed Communist society. Though our guides and translators were perfectly nice to us, we were sure they were all government agents.

My first impressions remain vivid in my mind. The country was dirt-poor. The tallest buildings in Beijing and Shanghai were no more than four stories high, with gray, Communist-style facades. The infrastructure—roads and bridges—was crumbling, and the people were all dressed in black and white. No one looked very happy. This was before the "China Miracle"; the only miracle at that point was that we were there at all.

Our player group was as good a team as you can imagine: Kareem Abdul-Jabbar, Dennis Johnson, Bernard King, Alex English, Gus Williams, Maurice Lucas, Bob Lanier, Buck Williams, Artis Gilmore, Jim Paxson, Steve Mix, Freddie Brown, and a dozen more. Our first stop was Peking, now Beijing. I'll never forget Fleisher sitting the group down in the lobby of our hotel, which was closer to a Motel 6 than a Four Seasons, and lecturing everyone on Chinese culture and their particular quirks and habits. He reviewed some dos and don'ts and then explained that Chinese drug laws were extremely strict; possession of illegal drugs, including marijuana, was punishable by life imprisonment or even death. Incredible to think he waited until we were in the country to enlighten the players about that one! Panic spread around the room. Within moments of checking in to our rooms, which had walls as thin as paper, you could hear toilets flushing all over the hotel.

Every few days, a short segment on our trip would appear on the *Today Show*, narrated by Rita Satz. We toured the Great Wall, the Forbidden Palace, the Great Hall of the People, and Red Square. I remember visiting Mao's tomb in the center of Red Square after a night of hard drinking. As we walked around Mao's fully exposed body, Houston Rockets center Billy Paultz, a.k.a. "the Whopper," looked down from his 6'11" perch at Mao and stage-whispered, "He looks like I feel." We thought the guards were going to shoot Billy as laughter erupted all around.

The streets were a sea of bicycles—they outnumbered cars at least 50 to 1—and huge multiunit buses jammed to the roof with people and belching acrid black smoke. We were followed everywhere, particularly by children in awe of the overgrown giants in their midst. The players had packed plenty of candy and handed it out instead of autographs.

Then there were the games. The Chinese teams had good players, but they were neither fast enough nor physically adept enough to keep up with our superstars. One team featured Mr. Mu at center, who, at 7'8" and 470 pounds, looked quite formidable but couldn't jump more than a half inch off the ground. Jabbar had little trouble sky-hooking over Mr. Mu.

Our last game was against the Chinese Red Army team that had won the silver medal in the 1980 Olympics in Moscow, which had been boycotted by the US. For the first time, we had real competition, and we were actually down with a couple of minutes to play. Coach Robertson, eyes bulging, called our team over and started yelling, "We cannot lose to these damn Commies!" The players, always afraid of the Big O, got it together and scored 15 straight points to beat the Commies one more time.

The success of the China trip—and others like it—was a testament to Fleisher and his belief in the game and the appeal of the players. At a time when the NBA couldn't make its way in Buffalo, Kansas City, or New Orleans, he charted a course for the future dominance of the league. Fortunately, the league was paying attention. After the China trip, the NBA and Stern organized an NBA Friendship Tour underwritten by the league. Today, the NBA generates hundreds of millions of dollars a year overseas in TV rights, apparel sales, and more. I don't recall Stern ever saying thank you to us.

Back in the US, however, the league was in free fall. *Sports Illustrated* ran a cover story with the headline blaring, "Can the NBA Save Itself?"[8] It was a legitimate question. Cocaine scandals swirled around Phoenix Suns star Walter Davis, the Knicks' Michael Ray Richardson, Bulls rookie Quinton Dailey, Rockets star John Lucas, Utah Jazz player John Drew, and the Los Angeles Lakers' Marques Johnson, to name a few. Meanwhile, when the NBA owners weren't desperately throwing millions at free agents, they were calling each other names. Drossos accused the 76ers' Harold Katz of "not playing with a full deck"[9] after he signed Moses Malone to a $13.2 million contract, by far the largest in the history of the NBA at the time. Celtics executive Red Auerbach decried "a new breed of owner[s]" who "make moves to get their name in the paper and trade players that their wife doesn't like."[10]

Auerbach was not wrong about that. A big problem for the NBA was that they had admitted some truly dumb, pernicious guys into their ownership ranks, none dumber or more pernicious than the aforementioned Donald Sterling. A Los Angeles slumlord who passed himself off as a real estate mogul, Sterling bought the San Diego Clippers in 1981 and immediately ruffled feathers. In his first season, rumors swarmed that he was telling his team to lose games so they could snag the number one draft pick, slated to be 7′4″ center Ralph Sampson from Virginia. Sterling had hired Paul Silas as coach, and Silas introduced me to him at a 1982 All-Star Game party in New York. I remember he was wearing what appeared to be a bearskin coat. When Silas told Sterling I was the union's lawyer, he hugged me and kissed me on the cheek. Right then, I knew there was a problem.

A few weeks later, Sterling, claiming he had no money, delayed his contribution to the league for pension and other player benefits. He also stopped making deferred salary payments to a number of retired players, including his own coach. Kansas City also claimed they couldn't make the payments. The players threatened to strike, and under intense pressure from the league, Sterling and Kansas City coughed up the dough.

Within a year of Sterling buying the Clippers, everybody had come to loathe him, and I do mean everybody: players, league executives, and the good people of San Diego. Among his many dubious moves was hiring an ex-model he had dated named Patricia Simmons to be assistant general manager. According to one San Diego reporter, she had "no known basketball background but a decidedly stunning foreground."[11] Things got so bad that Stern asked sports lawyer Alan Rothenberg to run the team on a day-to-day basis until Sterling could figure out how to pay his bills on time.

Worse than Sterling was the owner of the Cleveland Cavaliers, Ted Stepien, another real estate guy with a low basketball IQ. In his first couple of years, Stepien dumped all his draft picks and brought in middling free agents like James Edwards, Scott Wedman, and Bobby Wilkerson on huge contracts. All turned out to be busts. When the Cavaliers ended with the worst record in the NBA, the Lakers used a pick acquired from the Cavaliers to select James Worthy, who played 12 highlight-filled seasons in a Lakers uniform, won three NBA championships, and was elected to the Hall of Fame. After the Cavaliers traded away all their picks for the foreseeable future, Auerbach remarked that the team's "next pick right now is probably a freshman in high school."[12]

Stepien's contribution to the NBA was "the Teddy Bears," a nearly nude group of cheerleaders who entertained the sparse crowds at Cleveland Arena. Around the league, the team became known as the Cleveland Cadavers. A 1982 *New York Times* article christened Cleveland "the worst club and the most poorly run franchise in the history of professional basketball."[13]

One thing that wasn't funny about Stepien was his view on race. In 1982, his team had six white players and six black players, which he called "racially balanced." He also claimed that he "was really big on desegregation." This from a man who said, "There were five percent black fans and seventy-five percent black players, and black fans don't buy tickets or products that we sell."[14] Stern privately told Fleisher that he (Stern) had to get this moron out of the NBA as quickly as possible. The damage of the Stepien era was significant—during his four-year reign, the team had a 66–180 record under five different coaches and lost over $15 million. But in a deal orchestrated by Stern, he sold the team for over $20 million, nearly doubling his money in four years. Amazing what you can do when you are part of a monopoly.

With owners like Sterling and Stepien, it's no wonder the league was in trouble. A number of teams were reportedly on the brink of collapse, including Cleveland, Denver, Indiana, Kansas City, San Diego, and Utah. Several teams were on the market with no buyers in sight, effectively dropping their value to zero. There were rumors that Denver and Utah were talking about merging and that Cleveland and Indiana might not make payroll. "Forget about the players," one member of the NBA Board of Governors proclaimed, "it will be the owners who will go on strike."[15]

At one point, *Newsweek* referred to the NBA as "the sorriest mess in all sports." Ralph Sampson, slated to be the NBA's number one draft pick, was quoted as saying, "I just hope that the NBA is still around when I get there."

Whatever economic problems existed in the NBA, they were self-inflicted, brought on by the owners themselves. Nobody forced Katz to pay Moses $13.2 million. Not a single gun was put to a single owner's head in signing a player contact. They wanted to be saved from their own insanity. Bob Lanier, the new president of the NBPA, said it plainly: "The owners have got to keep tabs on themselves; if they stop paying these humongous salaries, there won't be a problem."[16]

Lanier, of course, spoke the truth. I got to know "Bob-a-Dob" well over the next couple of years. He was a giant of a man—6'11", 260 pounds, and with size 18 sneakers, he had to have had the largest feet in America. He also had a tough-guy veneer to go along with a big heart and an even bigger smile. He was a good listener and an even better talker. The greatest player in the history of St. Bonaventure, he was a perennial All-Star. He became one of the few members of the Hall of Fame who never won an NBA championship, but not for his lack of trying. He was a blue-collar kid from Buffalo; his father owned a small trucking outfit, and Lanier started hauling boxes at age nine. Lanier was destined to play a key leadership role as the NBPA president in this difficult time and would make critical decisions that would change the NBA and professional sports forever. After he retired, he became the NBA's Ambassador for Community Relations, ran their Stay in School program, and served as assistant to two NBA commissioners—Stern and later Adam Silver.

First free agency was ruining the NBA, then it was drugs. What would be next, sex and rock 'n' roll? One thing was sure: the NBA owners refused to blame themselves. But their spending was out of control, and there was no doubt the problems had been exacerbated by some of the clowns the league had admitted as new owners.

To rebuild the league, owners promised a new "get-tough approach." Some of their ideas allegedly included cutting roster sizes from 12 to 10, requiring players to fly coach despite their size, and drastically reducing pension and health benefits. But the big play was the so-called salary cap. Stern and other NBA officials began laying the groundwork for the imposition of hard limits on how much each club could spend on players. At first we thought they had to be kidding; when it became clear that they were serious, we mobilized for action.

Fleisher's initial response to talk of a salary cap was blunt: "It will never happen."[17] Irwin Warren and I quickly drafted a new lawsuit blocking any effort by the NBA owners to unilaterally impose a cap, filing our lawsuit before the first collective bargaining meeting was even scheduled. NBPA president Bob Lanier was our lead plaintiff. We brought the case on an expedited basis, and by early July 1982, we were before the new Special Master, Kingman Brewster. Stern argued for the NBA. I argued for the players. The NBA feigned innocence and maintained—absurdly—that such a cap would have absolutely no effect on the free agent market. Brewster said he would rule promptly, and we refused to meet with the owners until he did so. The "NBA China Tour" was about to start. Before we flew off, Fleisher told the press, "We have no intention of saving them from themselves, which is what they want. They say they are a sick and dying industry. That's ridiculous. What they are really saying is that there are a few teams in trouble, but that they want us to make concessions that would help the whole league."[18] Lanier was even blunter in response to their threat that some teams might go under. "It might actually improve the league," he said. "We may have to lose players in the process, but it might make it a more quality League."[19]

Bold statements, indeed; we were going to call their bluff. But we soon learned that it wasn't a bluff.

The Special Master issued his *Lanier* decision on September 7, 1982, ruling that any attempt to unilaterally impose a salary cap would violate the *Robertson* settlement agreement. The upshot was that the league would have to deal with us directly at the bargaining table, and within a week, we had our first formal negotiating session with the NBA owners.

When our side arrived promptly at 10 o'clock that morning, at a splendidly decorated art deco conference room in the Waldorf Astoria, we found a dozen or so NBA owners and their minions already seated along one side of a huge oak table. They seemed agitated and glum all at the same time. They were led by Deputy Commissioner Stern and General Counsel Russ Granik. Commissioner O'Brien was also present, though it was immediately clear that Stern was running the show (and would soon replace him as commissioner).

As we exchanged phony pleasantries, my eyes were drawn to a neat stack of leather-bound folders, carefully guarded by one of Stern's assistants. It reminded me of the leather-bound White House transcripts behind Nixon when he released them on network television during Watergate.

"Larry, we may have a problem," I whispered to Fleisher. "If those really are their books, they may not have been bullshitting us about their financial problems."

Fleisher nodded. I knew he got it.

Moments later, Stern pointed at the folders and announced with annoying flair, "Go ahead, take a look and decide for yourself if we're not telling the truth." We had no choice but to accept the challenge. We told him with some hesitation, "Send them over, we'll study them."

The meeting quickly got heated as Stern and Fleisher exchanged barbs over who was to blame for the league's troubles. It went back and forth for another half an hour or so until the meeting broke up with nothing resolved, no firm proposals, no handshakes, and no further meetings set. Not a good day for the collective bargaining process or the future of the NBA.

Though it was barely eleven o'clock in the morning, our side adjourned to the bar of the Four Seasons two blocks up Park Avenue. We talked next steps for a few minutes. Everyone was nervous; we had no idea what might come next. I soon excused myself to go back to the office to work on some motions in the baseball case.

Fleisher called me there later that afternoon. "You have to come over to the [NBPA] office right away, it's really important," he said.

"What's going on?" I asked.

"We're all here," Fleisher slurred.

"Who is all?"

"Me and Bob [Lanier], Mo [Lucas], Stern, and Howard Cosell," he said.

"What the hell are you people doing?" I asked.

"Drinking."

I told him I'd be right over.

I literally ran across Central Park to the NBPA's office on Columbus Circle and made it in less than 10 minutes. As I went up the elevator, all I could think was, What in God's name are these people doing and why was Howard Cosell there? I only hoped they weren't negotiating while under the influence.

I walked into the office where I had once worked, passed Curt Parker (who himself had a healthy glass of vodka on his desk), and positioned myself in the doorway to Fleisher's office. Sure enough, sitting around the table were Lanier, Lucas, Fleisher, Stern, and Cosell, with one empty bottle of vodka next to another that was still half full.

At that point, I had never met Cosell, and it was an introduction I'll never forget. As I walked in, he looked up and said in his famous Brooklyn-accented staccato delivery, "A n d—you—m u st—be—TH E—M IGH T Y—Q UIN N!"

It was obvious they were all drunk. I knew better than to ask why. Sometimes it is a lawyer's job to simply commiserate. I sat down and poured my own large vodka. We shot the shit for the next several hours, talking politics, religion, sex, organized crime, organized sports—anything other than basketball or the NBA. It was a delightful time and not a damn thing was accomplished. Everyone in the room that day knew that the NBA was in trouble, and we silently acknowledged that something had to be done about it.

Later, I would get to know Cosell very well. Katy and I had many long dinners with him and his wife, Emma, often with the Fleishers, where he would drink heavily and entertain us with the most outrageous statements. I even became a regular on his weekly radio program, *Cosell Speaking of Everything*. He had an opinion on everything, and he could be gracious and kind and spectacularly mean. But he was never dull.

One of my fondest memories of Cosell was a small dinner he hosted the night he was inducted into the Television and Radio Hall of Fame in midtown Manhattan. After the induction, where he gave a witty and incisive acceptance speech, he invited my wife, Katy, and me to join him in a small dining room for a special catered dinner. The only other guests were David Stern and his wife, Dianne, and Jackie Robinson's widow, Rachel. Over more glasses of wine than I could count, we spent hours telling stories—about sports, politics, history, our lives growing up. We seemed to truly enjoy each other's company. Even King David was at his benign and jovial best, and I realized that, at least once in a while, Stern was capable of being human and even a little humble. Of course, I attributed that to his wife, Dianne, who was charming and funny and seemed easily able to control her husband's worst instincts.

After the disastrous Waldorf Astoria meeting, Fleisher hired the accounting firm then known as BDO Seidman to vet the league's financial documents. Fleisher had a good grasp of numbers, but he wanted to be absolutely sure we were being told the truth. Seidman's forensic team spent several weeks scrubbing each team's financials, looking for bookkeeping shenanigans. They didn't find any. They interviewed several team representatives, as well as the NBA's CFO, to be sure they weren't putting something over on us.

The bottom line was that at least half a dozen teams in the NBA were on the brink of bankruptcy, and many more were financially unstable. Their books showed that many teams had borrowed heavily to meet escalating payroll and other expenses, while revenue had remained flat. Fleisher was flabbergasted. In early November, he confided to me that he thought the league "might be beyond help."

Only a handful of teams—the Knicks, Lakers, Supersonics, 76ers, and Mavericks—were making money but not very much. For the first time, we realized that there was a real possibility of teams going out of business and, with them, players losing jobs. The impact on the league and its credibility would be disastrous. We knew from the experience of the ABA, the NASL, the WFL, and the WHA that once teams start to fold or hastily relocate, a league can slip into a downward spiral from which it cannot recover. Tens of millions of dollars in guaranteed player salaries were tied up in the league. The players understood well what was at stake. It was gut-wrenching, but we were convinced that unless players made certain concessions, the NBA might collapse.

We held a series of meetings in hotels around New York City. The talks were informal, both sides feeling each other out about possible solutions. Stern, Granik, and Alan Cohen participated for the NBA, and Fleisher and I (and occasionally a player or two) showed up for our side. Since the season was in full swing, it wasn't always easy to get players to attend. The discussions kept circling back to the NBA's salary cap idea, and we kept pushing back. Fleisher and I discussed it endlessly. After having fought so hard for free agency, there was no way we would agree to salary limits of any kind without some substantial benefit coming back our way. The cable TV issue was still out there, and Stern made vague references to revenue guarantees. Ironically, the NBA's weakness put them in the strongest bargaining position they'd had in years.

As Russ Granik recalled years later, "We knew that Fleisher knew as much about the business as we did. There weren't a lot of secrets. And Larry was able to see that this really was a problem. So he was at least amenable to having conversations that would preserve jobs. He knew that to put the league in financial trouble was not in the best interest of his clients. We still had one of the toughest negotiations I've ever been involved in. But we got to the point that we were talking about a salary cap."[20]

Christmas came and went with no solution. Neither side was yet threatening a work stoppage; we were just trying to figure out what the hell to do. I remember thinking one morning in the shower that if a salary cap could be tied to overall revenue increases from the gate and all forms of television, with job guarantees and guaranteed minimum salaries both by player and by team, maybe, just maybe, we could sell it to the players. It turned out Fleisher was thinking along those same lines. Hesitantly, we began to discuss these ideas with the league.

Alan Cohen, a co-owner of the Nets, now took on a critical role; it was clear that Stern was relying on Cohen's advice because he was a respected businessman. Cohen had started out as a corporate lawyer at Paul, Weiss, then began a remarkable ascent that saw him become CEO of Madison Square Garden. Most recently, he was trying to buy the Boston Celtics. He was known as "Bottom Line Cohen"—he was a strong negotiator but fair and evenhanded.

Late one cold winter afternoon, with negotiations bogging down again, Stern informed us that the Bird-Magic show was playing at Boston Garden and the NBA corporate jet was warmed up and ready to go across the river in New Jersey. We all piled into a big black limousine to the airport and flew to Boston to watch Bird beat the Lakers at the buzzer with a jumper from the corner. Such were labor negotiations in the NBA in the 1980s. It wasn't all pain and suffering. There was some beautiful basketball too.

In early March 1983, we held the first formal bargaining session since the Waldorf meeting six months earlier, and it also ended in disaster. The NBA owners insisted on a cap without any firm guarantees, and the meeting devolved into a screaming match. Fleisher's face reddened. "If nothing is settled by April second," he told the owner committee, "the players won't finish the season."

Now our war spilled over into the press. Shortly after the meeting, Ira Berkow, sports columnist for the *New York Times*, summed up the hostilities:

Dr. Strangelove, it may be remembered, had this unusual problem with his right arm. It had a tendency to jerk up, and he controlled it only by wrestling it down with his left hand.

The National Basketball Association's owners also have a compulsion, though a substantially different one. They cannot contain themselves from giving away huge chunks of money, and are now pleading with the players to help them stop.

The average N.B.A. player draws $246,000 a year and $20,000 in benefits. Moses Malone, for one, gets $2 million a year,

Julius Erving $1 million. A player named Dave Corzine, of the Chicago Bulls, makes a half-million dollars a year. Someone else, named Steve Hawes, a third-string center somewhere, trundles home with $250,000 a year.

As high as the salaries are, the players are not to be blamed. A market was created by the owners—no one else—and each player, blushing, accepted with both arms. It's an honest living, so to speak.

Of course, both sides have a stake in a robust N.B.A., but a salary cap seems a strange thing for a union to accept—establishing, in effect, a maximum wage. But Fleisher believes that revenue-sharing from future cable and television would make it at least as profitable for the players as the current arrangement.[21]

The next day, Stern called Fleisher and begged him to resume meeting in secret without formal committees. Fleisher agreed. By late March, we were still trying to nail down the final points of a landmark agreement. The playoffs hung in the balance. As the stakes mounted and time grew short, Bob Lanier flew in to participate in person.

After a secret, all-day meeting at the New York Hilton, we knew we were close. Stern and Cohen had finally conceded to our guaranteed team minimum proposal as well as our proposed revenue share number. The three of us—Fleisher, Lanier, and I—still loathed the idea of a salary cap, but the alternative seemed worse. As we left the Hilton Hotel and walked up Sixth Avenue toward Fleisher's office, we continued debating. At the time, Moses Malone was the highest-paid player in the NBA at just under $2 million a year. As we walked, Bob Lanier looked down at Fleisher and me and said, "I guess fucking Moses will just have to get along on two million dollars a year." That's when I knew we would make a deal.

Within days, both sides agreed that, starting with the 1984–85 season, the total salaries for each team would be capped at $3.6 million. The cap, based on a projected revenue number, came with a guarantee that the players would get 53 percent of defined gross revenues, which was intended to include all revenue from basketball operations (mainly TV, radio, gate, etc.). The formula also called for the players to receive up to 57 percent of gross revenues, depending on annual projected growth over the course of what was to be a four-year agreement. There were five teams—the Knicks, Lakers, 76ers, Nets, and Supersonics—that were already over the projected cap number, and they were allowed to remain there as long as the cap grew and their individual team salaries remained comparable. Those five, incidentally, were among the few profitable teams in the league.

Throughout the negotiations, Stern had insisted that the cap be "hard," with no exceptions other than the five aforementioned teams. Ironically, it was the owners who lobbied for loopholes, the most important being the "Larry Bird exception." This was the brainchild of none other than Alan Cohen, about to be the new owner of the Celtics. Knowing that Bird's contract renewal was coming up soon, he wanted to be certain he could re-sign him at any number, regardless of the cap. Bird was a superstar, and Cohen was adamant that the Celtics had to be able to pay whatever it took to retain him. Hence the first exception: a team could sign its own free agent without restriction.

Several more exceptions crept in at the insistence of other teams. The players couldn't have scripted it any better. We were now relying on the competitive impulses of the teams to keep salaries rising. After all, general managers are paid to build winning teams; a salary cap made their jobs appreciably harder. What happens, some asked, if a player gets injured or teams trade a player? "We need to be able to replace an injured or traded player," they said. We said, "Yes, you do!" Exceptions were carved out for injured players and for traded players. This is how Stern's hard cap became a soft cap.

It was all brand-new territory. No other league had tried this before. Fleisher and I told the NBA lawyers to work up a first draft as the strike deadline loomed. According to Russ Granik, he dragooned his deputy, Gary Bettman, and his Proskauer lawyer, Jeff Mishkin, into a conference room at the league office. "The three of us sat there with yellow legal pads to make up a salary cap," Granik later recalled.

"We'd gotten a handshake with Fleisher. Now we had to go try and write it up. Honest to goodness, that was it. We sat there, the three of us, for two or three nights with a couple of secretaries. And we wrote sports's first salary cap."[22] They gave us a draft the following morning; we marked it up with our changes, and that was that. The salary cap era began the very next day.

"This is a landmark labor agreement in professional sports," said the outgoing Commissioner O'Brien, whose involvement was purely ceremonial. "It maintains the principles of individual bargaining and free agency, which the players have fought for over the years."[23]

Lakers owner Jerry Buss was more direct. "If we had not been able to get a limitation in the salary," he said, "the league wouldn't have been here in two or three years."[24]

Our side was spinning too. "The players are delighted with the settlement,"[25] said Fleisher, which was mostly true. There had been remarkably little pushback about the cap from our union members, probably because many were making big salaries for the first time in their lives and had no desire to mess that up. NBPA vice president Jim Paxson expressed confidence that the cap "wouldn't limit free agency, and the better players are still going to get their money." He turned out to be right.

Lanier, as usual, said it well: "The key to the agreement is that we were able to maintain player movement. I'm getting along in years, and I may not reap the benefits of this agreement, but we have worked on behalf of the younger brothers and those who are still to come. Guys like Oscar Robertson and Paul Silas sacrificed for me. We won because the guys stuck together."[26]

Alan Cohen trotted out Angelo Drossos's favorite word and called the agreement "a partnership between the league and players."[27] Within a matter of weeks, the NBPA and the league also announced the first ever league-wide drug agreement. Lanier had been adamant that it was up to the players to take the initiative to rid the NBA of the scourge of drugs. Only a tiny minority of players were actually involved with hard drugs. The use of marijuana was more widespread, though no more so than in the rest of America. We agreed to set up a program to deal with drug problems, particularly those involving cocaine, with an agreement that emphasized treatment and rehabilitation rather than testing. The program eventually evolved into testing in basketball and in all the major team sports. The early programs focused primarily on recreational drugs, not on so-called performance-enhancing drugs (PEDs), which have become the focus of drug programs in more recent times. The use of growth hormones, testosterones, and so on was virtually unheard of back then. People just wanted to get high.

The entire 1983 salary cap revenue-sharing agreement consisted of six pages. Today that same provision is 150 pages and still growing. As the years passed, a half-dozen new exceptions were added, including things like the "Early Bird" exception and the "Mid-Level" exception. There's even a "Non-Bird" exception. The cap is rapidly approaching $100 million per team and increasing. While the players' share of revenue has since been sliced to 50 percent, the pie itself has grown enormously, which is what we had hoped would happen when we insisted on the revenue guarantee.

Today we take for granted the idea of salary caps and drug agreements in sports, but back then, they were truly revolutionary. Or maybe the better word is reactionary. Think about it: in what other industry could a group of competing executives agree not to hire each other's employees or, worse, agree on limiting the amount they would pay their own employees? People could go to jail for price-fixing. Back in the 1980s, the oil industry tried it and was promptly sued by the US Department of Justice and faced huge fines. A few years later, several Silicon Valley tech companies, including Apple, Intel, and Microsoft, made an agreement not to hire—or at least to limit how much to pay—each other's programmers. They too were sued by the government for price-fixing, and they, too, quickly settled.

In other words, it's just not allowed. Except in sports. Why? It all goes back to the antitrust labor exemption, which allows a union to agree as part of collective bargaining to set limits on salaries in exchange for other benefits. Outside the labor framework, you could be led off in handcuffs. Likewise, a person's drug use or drinking habits are not usually regulated by industry agreement. After all, these guys aren't air traffic controllers; their work does not in any way impinge on public safety. They are basketball players. Nonetheless, to save the league from the lousy business practices of its owners, we agreed to these restrictions.

These agreements immediately boosted the NBA. Teams now had "cost certainty," which increased their value enormously almost right away. Even incompetent buffoons like Ted Stepien were able to sell their teams for a profit. Stern emerged from behind the curtain and formally became commissioner in 1984. Alan Cohen became the chairman of the NBA Board of Governors the following year. The Bird-Magic show came to full fruition, and the excitement and success it generated as well as the enormous new television revenues pushed the NBA into an upward spiral that continues today.

• • • •

The "partnership" supposedly born from the new salary cap revenue-sharing agreement, though, was strained almost from the beginning. Because the cap had been negotiated and drafted in less than two weeks, there were holes in it a mile wide.

Enterprising GMs and agents (particularly Fleisher, who had a hand in structuring it) rendered the cap as soft as a marshmallow. Fleisher, a brilliant architect of mayhem, was in his element; he relished the opportunity to drive holes in the cap every chance he got. In the opposite corner were Stern and his new "capologist," Gary Bettman, who were driven nuts by Fleisher's tactics. Bettman, a combination of Inspectors Javert and Clouseau, tried relentlessly to make every dollar count against the cap.

Our very first cap throwdown involved the aging superstar (and Fleisher client) David Thompson. This initial dispute was all about timing. Under the Larry Bird exception, the team could always sign its own free agent for any amount without regard for the cap. But because payrolls could be in flux during the off-season, teams could game the system.

Which is what the Sonics tried to do. In the fall of 1983, Thompson, still a good player but on the downward slope of his career, had played out his contract with Seattle and was a free agent. His club wanted to re-sign him. One of the five teams with a payroll that already exceeded the cap, Seattle was allowed to spend up to $4.6 million. Fleisher, working with his old friends, Seattle coach Lenny Wilkens and GM Zollie Volchok, waited to sign a deal for Thompson until they had signed all their other players first. Those 11 players had salaries totaling approximately $4.5 million. Then Thompson signed for $400,000, putting them several hundred thousand dollars "over the cap," which was technically permitted by the Bird exception.

Capologist Bettman, claiming that Fleisher and the Sonics had violated the spirit of the agreement, refused to approve the contract. So we filed a grievance before Impartial Arbitrator Arthur Stark.

At the hearing, I pointed out that there was nothing in the salary cap agreement about when you had to sign your own free agent, and the fact that such a signing might put a team over the cap was the point of the Larry Bird exception. Stark ruled for us.

The NBA was apoplectic and insisted that we had misled them. We asked how we could have done that. The league, after all, had more lawyers working on the agreement than we did. "Any actual or potential inequities must be remedied by the parties themselves," Stark had written. In other words, he told the parties to work out their differences in collective bargaining. Some years later, we did. But for now, the first gaping hole in the salary cap was opened.

That was the beginning of a pattern. Over the next year or so, we blew several more holes in the salary cap. Each time, Bettman protested, we all got together before Stark, and he ruled in our favor. Our battles with Bettman culminated in a crafty deal Fleisher worked out for his client, guard Jim Paxson, with the Knicks. Paxson, who was also an NBPA vice president, signed a complex six-year deal with New

York worth more than $10 million. Since the Knicks had little cap room, most of the money was in the form of prorated signing bonuses and back-loaded salary.

In the NBA's view, this contract put the Knicks nearly $1 million over the cap, and Bettman nixed it. We went back before Stark, who did what he'd always done and ruled in our favor. That was his last rodeo. The NBA fired him. By then, the league office was under serious fire from NBA owners who did not understand why this damn cap thing was not working out. Personally, I thought Fleisher was pushing it, and I told him so. We were due for blowback—and we got exactly that on the next case.

The player in question this time was Albert King, Bernard's younger brother and an up-and-coming star for the Nets. Fleisher, working once again with the Knicks, concocted another monument of financial engineering that eclipsed the trickery of the Paxson deal. In a preliminary ruling, the Impartial Basketball Expert Billy Cunningham judged the King contract to be technically invalid. But Fleisher would not give up. He fixed the technical problem and resubmitted the contract for approval.

This time the NBA woke up. The league brought a proceeding before Special Master Brewster, arguing that the Albert King contract violated the circumvention provision of the amended *Robertson* settlement agreement, which said that a contract could not "serve the purpose of defeating or circumventing" the salary cap. We had always been afraid that they would make that argument. Now they had.

The dispute led to one of the more bizarre events in the history of NBA jurisprudence. As it happened, Brewster, a partner at the Winthrop, Stimson, Putnam & Roberts law firm in New York, had recently moved to London to run Winthrop's UK office. We had all agreed to keep Brewster as the Special Master, thinking that he could always fly to New York for a hearing. Unfortunately, Brewster was tied up in another case and also under doctor's orders not to fly. With the regular season set to begin in less than a week, the proceeding had to be done quickly. Everyone would have to fly to London.

The media, of course, had a field day with this absurd spectacle. Sam Goldaper nailed the story for the *New York Times*:

N.B.A. people will be going to London not to see the Queen but to make a choice on a King named Albert. How much will it cost to find out whether the Knicks circumvented the salary cap with their offer sheet to Albert King? Regardless of the ruling by Kingman Brewster, who will decide the outcome after tomorrow's hearings in London, airlines and British hotels and restaurants will benefit. The six participants in the hearings will spend a total of $16,945 in air fare for a hearing that might last only a few hours. Larry Fleisher, the general counsel for the National Basketball Players Association, flew to London yesterday on British Airways. Total roundtrip cost—$3,979. Jim Quinn, whose law firm represents the players, will arrive in London today by way of San Francisco where he was attending to other business. He is going on British Airways and returning on the Concorde. The total air fare—$3,984 with benefit on the exchange rate.

Dave DeBusschere, the executive vice president of the Knicks, and Ken Munoz, Madison Square Garden's assistant general counsel, will leave today on the Concorde and return tomorrow night on the same airliner. Since the Concorde has a special two-for-one deal, the total cost will be $4,491. Gary Bettman, the general counsel of the N.B.A., and Jeff Mishkin, whose law firm represents the league, will take advantage of the same deal when they fly to London today on the same flight.[28]

We held a one-day hearing in Brewster's plush offices overlooking Hyde Park. The setting may have been old English, but the subject was nouveau NBA all the way. We called DeBusschere as our main witness and, as usual, he performed magnificently. We also called Albert's agent, Bill Pollak, who testified as if the dog had eaten his homework. His guilty demeanor wasn't helpful.

The NBA called a couple of witnesses, including Bettman, to show how the contract had been jerry-rigged to get around the salary cap. Mishkin argued vigorously about the outrageousness of not only the contract but also the behavior of the union and the Knicks in making a mockery of their beloved salary cap. We feigned outrage and made arguments similar to those that had been successful in the Paxson case.

Much to our surprise and glee, we won again. Brewster ruled that "the salary cap agreement was written to cover any signing bonuses without restrictions of any kind." We breathed a huge sigh of relief. The Nets had no choice but to match the Knicks' offer, and Pollak called it "a wonderful victory for Albert's career."[29]

DeBusschere added, "My feelings all along were that we were acting in compliance with the guidelines of the salary cap."[30] Of course, this was all bluster. We knew we had ducked a fast one.

The NBA had another card to play, appealing to our old friend Judge Carter. Within days, Mishkin and I were back before the good judge arguing our respective positions. At one point during the hearing, Carter looked down with me with a rueful smile and said, "Mr. Quinn, you're not serious, are you?"

Uh oh.

Carter's ruling came out a few days later. He not only reversed Brewster's decision, but he lectured us in words that still sting 35 years later: "The events and circumstances of this case present a stark case of intentional circumvention. If the Court were to let it stand, the Special Master's determination would eviscerate the salary cap limitation." He went on to say that our actions were "an egregious disregard of the agreement, which would leave the league in shambles."

The NBA was giddy. Bettman kept a copy of the decision, along with the *New York Times* report, on his wall in his office at the NBA and, even later, when he became commissioner of the NHL. So be it. We didn't deserve the win in the first place?

Having been one of the architects of the salary cap, first in the NBA and later in the NFL, I have decidedly mixed feelings about it now. The NBA salary cap was necessary in the moment we did it—somebody could make a good argument that it was the tipping point in the league's renaissance. But it quickly outlived its usefulness. By the Michael Jordan era of the 1990s, there was no good reason to restrict the earnings of players. There was an obscene amount of money sloshing around the league. But having been forced to abandon the reserve system a decade earlier, the NBA owners—and eventually owners in football and hockey—would cling to salary caps like a drug. These fabulously rich men could not imagine being unprotected by this form of socialism. But was it really so important? Of the four major sports, baseball was the lone holdout against a salary cap, thanks to Marvin Miller and Don Fehr. And did that league go down the tubes? Hardly. If I had my way, I would abolish the damn thing forever. The owners of sports teams as much as anyone ought to know that competition is the essence of capitalism. Isn't that what made them rich enough to buy sports franchises in the first place.

CHAPTER 10

Trump's "Three-Dollar" League

NEW FOOTBALL LEAGUES USED TO COME ALONG every decade or so. In the 1940s and early 1950s, it was the All-American Conference, whose Otto Graham–led Browns might have been better than any team in the NFL. In the 1960s, it was the AFL, which established footholds in growing cities like Houston and Denver and boasted colorful personalities like Joe Namath and Fred "the Hammer" Williamson. In the 1970s, it was the hapless WFL, with their big dreams and extraordinarily naïve grasp of basic economics. The 1980s had one too—the United States Football League (USFL)—and that one could have, and should have, been the one with the greatest staying power.

The USFL was the brainchild of David Dixon, a New Orleans businessman and art dealer who, back in the 1960s, had played a key role in building the Louisiana Superdome and luring an NFL football franchise to New Orleans. Dixon, always a font of new ideas, had also worked closely with Lamar Hunt in the formation of World Championship Tennis. Dixon's idea for a rival new football league was based on sound principles. It would start slowly with just 12 teams, all in major TV markets; obtain a network contract immediately, even if it didn't pay much; include only wealthy owners; and maintain a strict budget on expenses, particularly player salaries. To all that, Dixon added a major innovation: the league would play in the spring because, as Dixon said, "it would be suicidal to try to compete head-to-head with the NFL in the fall."[31]

It took Dixon a decade and a half to put his baby together, but by the early 1980s, it was looking good. His initial ownership group had some seriously rich guys, including Al Taubman, shopping center mogul (Michigan Panthers); Bill Daniels, cable TV billionaire (Denver Gold); J. Walter Duncan, Oklahoma oil tycoon (New Jersey Generals); Edward DeBartolo Sr., real estate magnate whose son ran the NFL's 49ers (Pittsburgh Maulers); and John Bassett, Canadian oil man and sportsman (Tampa Bay Bandits). Actor Burt Reynolds also signed on as a minority owner with Tampa Bay.

The original 12 teams did, in fact, cover most of the major markets, including Washington (Federals), San Francisco Bay Area (Invaders), Boston (Breakers), Chicago (Blitz), Philadelphia (Stars), and Los Angeles (Express), plus the small-market Birmingham Stallions and Arizona Wranglers. The first season was set to start in the spring of 1983. The USFL hired Chet Simmons, an ESPN founder, as its commissioner, who negotiated two TV contracts, one with ABC for Sunday afternoon and one with ESPN for a spring version of Monday Night Football. Dixon expected his new league to incur operating losses for the first few years, but he believed they could be kept at a sustainable level as the league focused on putting out a quality product and set itself up for more lucrative TV deals down the road. All in all, it made a lot of sense.

From the beginning, the USFL attracted a host of future Hall of Fame talent: coaches George Allen and Steve Spurrier signed on, and Hall of Fame players like Reggie White and Jim Kelly started their careers in the USFL. In fact, the famous Buffalo Bills trio of coach Marv Levy, quarterback Jim Kelly, and general manager Bill Polian, all of whom are now in the NFL Hall of Fame, started their professional football careers in the USFL. Even ESPN's Lee Corso coached in the USFL. Other great NFL players on USFL rosters included Gary Zimmerman, Marcus Dupree, Bobby Hebert, Anthony Carter, and Kelvin Bryant.

The first season went reasonably smoothly. Average attendance was more than 25,000 per game. The losses, though higher than expected, seemed manageable, at about $3 million per team. The Michigan Panthers beat the Oakland Invaders to win the inaugural USFL Championship, playing to a sold-out crowd in Denver's old Mile High Stadium.

I went to my first and only USFL game that inaugural season, on a sunny day in early May. The New Jersey Generals hosted the Philadelphia Stars at Giants Stadium in the Meadowlands. A friend of mine had bought season tickets to the Generals because they were cheap, and we dragged along our then 12-year-old sons. The stands were reasonably full, the beer and the hot dogs tasted fine, and frankly they played pretty good football. The baseball season had barely begun, the hockey and basketball playoffs were winding down, and it was a nice way to spend a sunny Sunday afternoon with my son. I remember thinking to myself, This could work.

Then things began to get crazy. In the fall of 1983, Duncan, the Oklahoma oilman, sold the New Jersey Generals to 36-year-old Donald Trump, who immediately made a big splash by signing Heisman Trophy winner Herschel Walker to a huge $5 million contract.

At the time, Trump, in his usual understated way, described Walker as "the greatest college player in history." Competition heated up for players around the league. In addition to Walker, millions more were spent on Heisman Trophy winners such as Boston College's Doug Flutie and Nebraska's Mike Rozier. The Los Angeles Express signed All-American BYU quarterback Steve Young to an unheard of $40 million multiyear contract.

Early on, Dixon had urged USFL owners to abide by an informal salary cap. But just as in the NBA, the owners hated being hemmed in even by rules of their own devising. To get around the cap, owners began signing players to so-called personal service contracts, which supposedly bound the player only to the owner, not the team, a sham if ever there was one. Like, what was Herschel Walker going to be doing for Donald Trump that was worth $5 million other than playing football?

Salaries soon began to skyrocket upward, which was bad for Dixon's slow-growth model. Worse was that Trump began lobbying his fellow USFL owners to move their season to the fall and compete head-to-head with the NFL. Trump had earlier tried to buy the Baltimore Colts but was turned down by the NFL. He now harbored a not-so-secret fantasy of shotgunning his USFL franchise, now populated with stars, into the NFL.

In need of additional cash, the owners added six new franchises to begin playing in the spring of 1984—twice as many as Dixon had envisioned. Seeing the writing on the wall, Dixon bowed out prior to the start of the 1984 season. "This isn't the league I founded," Dixon told the press. He sold his franchise rights to a group headed by Steve Ross, which became the Houston Gamblers. Ross, another real estate tycoon, would years later become the owner of the NFL's Miami Dolphins. By this point, the USFL had teams called the Outlaws, the Wranglers, the Gunslingers, the Bandits, the Renegades, and the Stallions. Sound like the Wild West? It was.

As the 1984 spring season got under way, the league remained popular, attendance and TV ratings held steady, and television revenues kept trickling in. But the crazy bidding war with the NFL for players was taking its toll. Teams started to move—the Boston Breakers became the New Orleans Breakers and then the Portland Breakers. Despite winning the 1984 USFL Championship, the Philadelphia Stars moved to Baltimore the following year, where they again won the league championship.

In the fall of 1984, things came to a head. Just as he would hijack the country three decades later, Trump hijacked the USFL by convincing his fellow owners to move the playing season to the fall for 1986. Trump was every bit the shameless huckster then as he is now. He became the face of the USFL, dominating the media's coverage of the league. Within months of buying the Generals, he had made it clear that spring football was for losers. "If God had wanted football in the spring," he famously opined, "he wouldn't have created baseball."[32] The only USFL owner willing to stand up to Trump was Tampa Bay Bandits owner John Bassett, who had unfortunately been

TRUMP'S "THREE-DOLLAR" LEAGUE   137

diagnosed with terminal brain cancer. The other owners soon caved to Trump's insane plan.

To top it off, Trump also persuaded his fellow owners to sue the NFL for a billion-plus dollars, claiming that the NFL conspired to run the USFL out of business. Trump's farfetched hope was that the lawsuit might force a merger of the two leagues, and the USFL hired none other than Roy Cohn, a Trump confidante, to quarterback the case. When Cohn's illness rendered him too sick to proceed, Trump picked another of his own lawyers to replace him, one Harvey Myerson. Myerson, described by some as a "pit bull" in the courtroom, acquired the nickname "Heavy Hitter Harvey," although he had never won a major jury case in his life. Short, with a wavy, black toupee, he chewed on foot-long cigars and enjoyed buying mansions and expensive cars. He didn't have a clue about the antitrust laws, which was, of course, what the lawsuit against the NFL was supposed to be about.

On the media front, Trump banged the war drums and assured the world with his now familiar slogan, "We're gonna win." The USFL's case focused on the claim that the NFL had tied up all three television networks with exclusive contracts, effectively freezing out the USFL. I was interviewed by the *Wall Street Journal* shortly after the lawsuit was filed:

> But winning the legal battle won't be easy. "In today's world of antitrust, just being big and powerful isn't enough," says James Quinn, a partner in Weil, Gotshal & Manges and a professor of sports law at Fordham University. "The fact that the NFL successfully entered into agreements with all three networks adds at least a patina of truth to the (antitrust) allegations, but the USFL has to show more, some kind of tacit agreement to keep the league off the air."
>
> USFL sources have been hinting at the existence of a secret NFL committee to combat the USFL, which Mr. Quinn concedes would be "pretty sexy stuff."[33]

There were other allegations about miniconspiracies relating to the Oakland and New York markets, but the key was TV. The case meandered through the courts over the course of the next year and a half, finally going to trial in federal court in late spring 1986 before a jury of six native New Yorkers. The judge assigned to the case was Peter K. Leisure, who had been appointed by President Reagan in 1984, the same year the case was filed. He was a big, brawny, good-natured man, a former assistant US attorney who had also spent time at the prominent New York law firm Donovan, Leisure, Newton & Irvine, where his father, George Leisure, had been a founding partner.

In January 1985, the USFL commissioner Chet Simmons resigned in protest of Trump's plan to move to the fall, and he was replaced by Harry Usher, who had been Peter Ueberroth's deputy in running the successful 1984 Olympics in Los Angeles. Usher, a lawyer with a business background, was smart, quick-witted, and eminently likeable. He clearly had no idea what he was getting himself into.

Prospects for the league were dimming every day. On July 14, 1985, before more than 50,000 fans at Giants Stadium in the Meadowlands, the USFL closed out its third season, with the Baltimore Stars edging out the Oakland Invaders 28–24. The league thereupon announced it was suspending play until the fall of 1986, awaiting the outcome of the Trump-led lawsuit.

Chaos ensued. The Breakers moved for the third time, and the Arizona Wranglers swapped franchises with the Chicago Blitz and then merged with the Oklahoma Outlaws to become the Arizona Outlaws. Days later, the Maulers, the Blitz, and the Los Angeles Express announced they were folding. Over the course of the next few months, several more USFL teams threw in the towel. Commissioner Usher reluctantly announced that if and when the league resumed play in the fall of 1986, it would field only eight teams. In that third season, attendance had held steady and TV ratings were actually up because of the star-studded rosters. In fact, had the USFL continued to play in the spring, it likely would have been a financial success. Instead, the decision to move to the fall meant forfeiting nearly $50 million in television contracts with ABC and ESPN.

To defend the USFL's lawsuit at trial, the NFL hired Frank Rothman, considered the top entertainment trial lawyer in America. Rothman, tall with a large hook nose, had a deep, stentorian voice and was known and admired for his eloquence in the courtroom. Rothman was well into his 60s but still at the top of his game. So the stage was set: two showman litigators, Myerson and Rothman, about to do battle. Although we were not yet involved, my Weil sports team was keeping a close eye on it.

When the trial finally started in late April 1986, it opened with a bang. Myerson promised the jury of five women and one man that he would show them conclusive proof that the NFL's rich and arrogant owners, fearing competition, had done horrible things to his client, the USFL. He told the jury that only they could save the USFL from extinction by awarding it a billion dollars or more in damages. Rothman countered, with shades of the NFL's old NASL defense, that the USFL's problems were a product of its own gross incompetence.

Myerson relied heavily on what he repeatedly called "the smoking gun," a report written for the NFL by a Harvard economist entitled "How to Conquer the USFL." It laid out a strategy for raising salary bids for players, shutting down potential franchise locations, and most importantly, making sure there were no open television networks. By this point, TV was the lifeblood of pro sports. There was also a memo written by NFL general counsel Jay Moyer that stated in reference to USFL competition, "Don't allow an open network." Over the next few weeks, Myerson called a virtual Who's Who of the sports world as witnesses, including Trump, NFL owner Al Davis, and even Howard Cosell.

Trump testified that he had met Rozelle at the Pierre Hotel a few months after he had joined the USFL and that Rozelle had offered him an NFL franchise if he backed out of the USFL. Rozelle vigorously denied Trump's claim, saying that the meeting was just a friendly lunch that Trump himself had set up. Al Davis, still a renegade, accused his fellow NFL owners of trying to run the Oakland Invaders out of business. Cosell testified that Chet Forte, head of ABC Sports, had told him that the NFL was pressuring ABC not to deal with USFL. Forte, in a sworn deposition, said it never happened. Cosell by this time was long gone from ABC's Monday Night Football and maybe not the most reliable witness on anything to do with his former employer. Years later, Cosell told me that he thought the case was a farce and that Myerson in particular was "a buffoon."

Rothman subjected each of them to withering cross-examination, poking huge holes in their testimony. Myerson tried to do the same to Rozelle, but slippery Pete got the best of him.

Rothman repeatedly waved around a memo written by Invaders owner Tad Taube, in which Taube quoted the famous Pogo line: "We have met the enemy and he is us." When the USFL later appealed, claiming that Judge Leisure should have kept this type of damning evidence out of the trial, the appeals court wrote, "Courts do not exclude evidence of a victim's suicide in a murder trial."

As the case came to a close, Rothman told the jury that the USFL owners were "mercenaries" and said that Trump was motivated by "abusive blind greed and was also a liar."[34] He said Cosell and Davis had their own vendettas against the NFL and Rozelle in particular. Myerson countered—quite correctly—that the NFL owners possessed "an arrogance of power," and they acted as if they were "above the law."[35] All true.

At the conclusion of a 10-week trial, the jury deliberated for five full days before reaching its verdict on July 29, 1986. It was a disaster for the USFL. This is how it was reported by the *Los Angeles Times* that same day:

The National Football League was found guilty Tuesday of violating an antitrust law but survived the United States Football League's $1.69-billion suit here when a bothered and bewildered jury of five women and one man awarded damages of just $1 to the failing football league.

Damages in antitrust cases are tripled, so the award given to the USFL will actually amount to $3.

The verdict, coming after about two years of pretrial litigation and 2 1/2 months of trial testimony, shook Courtroom 318 in Manhattan's U.S. District Court. But it will shake the USFL far more, perhaps to the ground. Although the decision certainly discredits the NFL, it probably dooms the USFL which, in its fourth year, had planned to switch to fall play in direct competition with the NFL but without the established league's television revenue sources.

What the jury decided, after 31 hours of deliberation over five days, was that not only does the NFL enjoy monopoly power, but it also unfairly conspired to gain its competitive edge and did in fact violate antitrust law—"to exclude competition within major league football."

As far as the USFL goes, the NFL said the new league's failure was simply bad management and, finally, a merger mania mandating that it play opposite the established league in the fall. As NFL Commissioner Pete Rozelle said, "They shot themselves in the foot."

"We're lost now," said Rudy Shiffer, vice president of the Memphis Showboats. "We're dead."

The jury understood that the NFL was a monopoly but rejected the notion that the NFL had done anything to actively hurt the USFL. According to Rothman, "What the jurors said is that the NFL monopolizes football, not TV."[36] The USFL was reduced to a punch line. Johnny Carson compared the league to one of his ex-wives: "Like the USFL, I expected a bit more."

As to Trump's allegation that Rozelle had tried to bribe him at the Pierre Hotel, the jury chose to believe Rozelle over Trump, probably one of the few contests for personal honesty that Rozelle could ever win.

Ironically, although Rothman claimed that the USFL's case was "smoke and mirrors,"[37] the case would have been quite winnable if only Myerson and Trump hadn't made so many blunders. Myerson, who had never tried an antitrust case, was the wrong lawyer. He focused on the wrong section of the Sherman Act, emphasizing monopoly instead of conspiracy, which is much easier to win. They filed the case in the wrong place; it should have been brought in Memphis or Birmingham, small markets where the USFL had teams. With these moves, the USFL's "smoking gun" evidence might have had a chance.

The surviving USFL owners wouldn't survive for much longer. Without a TV contract, and hemorrhaging nearly $200 million in three years, the USFL scrapped the 1986 season and awaited the outcome of an appeal. Things got so bad that, acting on a federal court order, a Florida sheriff confiscated the Tampa Bay Bandits' team equipment and souvenirs because of a lien placed on the team by a former player who was owed $150,000.

Up until this point, my team at Weil was still on the sidelines. But within days of the verdict, Trump called Ira Millstein for help. The next day, Millstein and I met with Trump, Usher, and the USFL's TV guru, Eddie Einhorn, at our offices to discuss Hail Mary options.

Trump did most of the talking, and I won't lie to you—he was impressive, sharp, energetic, and funny. Not that it wasn't also obvious how self-absorbed he was, motivated solely by what was best for the Donald. He called his fellow USFL owners "morons." Einhorn, a short, chubby guy from Patterson, New Jersey, with the face of a cherub, was equally smart but much more open-minded. He was a legitimate TV expert and wanted to do what was best for the league. Network television was critical to the USFL's survival; everyone was in agreement about that. Millstein and I mostly just listened, trying to absorb the full arc of the USFL's four-year odyssey in an hour-long meeting.

After the meeting, I called in my old standbys, Jeff Kessler and Jeff Klein. I also added a brand-new face, Bruce Meyer, to my quickly assembled USFL team. The group knew from the start that this was going to be an uphill battle. We spent hours batting around ideas, trying to figure out a rescue plan for the USFL.

Trump informed his friend Myerson that the league was bringing in additional counsel, and Myerson was not a happy camper. A few days later, Millstein and I presented our plan to the remaining team owners. The room was tense: Myerson sat there silently, glaring at us the whole time. Our idea was to convince Judge Leisure to order that the USFL be given a time slot on Sunday afternoon in the fall with at least one of the networks. Everyone liked the idea, even Myerson, but we had to move quickly. We were like doctors with a patient who had no pulse but might still be alive.

First, we met with Myerson and his team to get a quick rundown, where Myerson tried to bully and belittle us. His colleagues, thankfully, were more professional. Then we met with USFL brass and team owners past and present. We even got Al Gore involved because, as a US senator from Tennessee, he had an interest in the survival of the Memphis Showboats. We worked literally around the clock over the next several weeks to prepare for a hearing before Judge Leisure in early September 1986.

As part of our strategy, we insisted on deposing Rozelle and several key NFL owners, including Wellington Mara and Art Modell, who was head of the NFL's TV committee. It was déjà vu all over again from the NASL days. Rozelle was, as usual, evasive, always smiling, and always smoking. Mara repeated his polite know-nothing act, and Modell reprised his ornery demeanor and poor memory.

Judge Leisure held an all-day hearing right after Labor Day. We had convinced ourselves that our open network television strategy was nothing short of brilliant. Millstein and I whipped out fancy charts and affidavits from owners and politicians showing how giving the USFL a network slot in the fall would make the business of pro football genuinely competitive. Kessler, our resident antitrust genius, had formulated wonderful arguments, and Millstein, as usual, waxed eloquent. I spent an hour or so on the more technical stuff. It was all to no avail. Judge Leisure wasn't buying it. He denied our request for an injunction within a matter of days.

So it was off to the appeals courts. But rigor mortis was setting in on our patient. Over the next year, we worked closely with Myerson's team on appealing the three-dollar verdict as well as reversing Judge Leisure's refusal to order the television network relief the USFL needed to survive. Hundreds of pages of briefs were filed before the US Court of Appeals in New York, and the appeal was finally argued in June 1987. Myerson insisted on taking the lead. It did not go well.

On March 10, 1988, the USFL's death knell sounded. In a unanimous decision, the three appellate judges upheld the three-dollar verdict, rejecting each and every one of the USFL's arguments. The court found that it was moving to the fall—Trump's grand gesture—that caused the league's demise, not the NFL monopolizing the airwaves. The court chided the USFL for its "decision to seek entry into the NFL on the cheap." As for our request for an open network, the court rejected what it called "sweeping injunctive relief," refusing to order "a judicial restructuring of major league professional football." The final whistle had blown on the USFL.

Naturally, we lawyers stayed busy for a while longer as we haggled over the legal fees owed to the USFL because of the single finding of illegal monopoly. The USFL was eventually awarded $5.5 million, virtually all of which went to Myerson's firm, which had fallen into bankruptcy. As for Weil, we got stiffed on half of our fees. That can happen, we learned, when you do business with Donald Trump.

Because I am a lawyer and not a businessman, I said yes a few years later when Trump asked me to represent him in a $100 million tax abatement dispute with the City of New York relating to his United Nations Plaza project. We won a total victory. A few weeks later, Trump called to niggle about our legal fees. I thought he would be embarrassed, but he wasn't in the least. At one point, he offered us a third of one of his racehorses as payment. I told the Donald in no uncertain terms, "We at Weil don't take hay or coal or horses—we only take cash." I then insisted that he pay every penny, which he eventually did. The next time he called, I told him I was too busy to work with him again. I'd learned my lesson.

Shortly after the collapse of Myerson's old firm (Finley, Kumble, Wagner, Underberg, Manley, Myerson & Casey), Myerson announced the founding of a new "powerhouse" law firm, and he asked former MLB commissioner Bowie Kuhn, of all people, to join him. At an ABA lunch, Bowie took me aside and asked me about Myerson. "He is an asshole," I told Kuhn. "Stay away." Kuhn ignored my advice. The law firm of Myerson & Kuhn lasted less than a year when Harvey was indicted and later convicted for fraud and tax evasion. Bowie never did listen very well.

Trump, naturally, was unrepentant. When asked about the demise of the USFL, he said the USFL was nothing without him and referred to the league as "small potatoes." Some years later, ESPN produced a *30 for 30* documentary on the USFL with the title *Small Potatoes*. Much later, as Trump campaigned for the presidency, the media honed in on the Donald's spectacularly unsuccessful foray into professional sports. ESPN wrote a story entitled "Trump Widely Blamed for the Demise of the USFL," and the *New York Times* followed with an article by Joe Nocera entitled "Donald Trump's Less Than Artful Failure in Pro Football." Trump's involvement with the USFL was hardly "amazing"; the only thing "huge" about it was just how colossal a failure it truly was. And as of this writing, he is running the country. That's anything but small potatoes.

CHAPTER 11

Let's Blow Up the Union

IN THE SPRING OF 1987, THE NBA WAS IN THE MIDST of a spectacular renaissance: the Bird-Magic show was at its apex, and new exciting stars like Michael Jordan and Patrick Ewing were coming up right behind them. In just three years, the NBA's gross revenues had doubled, and franchise values had gone through the roof. The Boston Celtics had sold shares to the public, which put the value of the franchise at $125 million—a nearly 800 percent increase in value in less than three years. Attendance and TV ratings were soaring. In the fall of 1986, Commissioner Stern told the *Los Angeles Times* that they were "looking at what will be the best season in the history of the league with most teams in the black."[38] Soon after, he told the *Washington Post* that they had "found the collective holy grail of sports."[39]

Stern and his acolytes were hailed as marketing geniuses, but we knew what was really behind the league's astonishing return from the near dead—the players! And yet, because of the salary cap, their overall percentage of the revenue pie was shrinking, and fewer players were enjoying the fruits of free agency. Salary increases had been brought to a virtual standstill. Fleisher and the players, especially Junior Bridgeman, Bob Lanier's successor as NBPA president, were livid. Free agent offers were virtually nonexistent: some teams were abusing their first refusal right by publicly threatening to match any free agent offer (which was in direct violation of the *Robertson* settlement agreement), and other teams were using the cap as an excuse not to sign free agent players. We suspected that the NBA owners and the league office were up to their old tricks by encouraging these shenanigans.

At Fleisher's request, Bruce Meyer and I prepared a document we called "Players Position on Free Agency Issues," which we delivered to the NBA in the spring of 1987. Both the *Robertson* settlement agreement and our collective bargaining agreement were due to expire in June 1987. As we wrote to the NBA owners, "We believe that the drop in our share of revenues and the lack of meaningful salary increases are a direct result of the economic restraints on player movement which continue to exist in the NBA and which significantly impair each player's ability to obtain a competitive market value for his professional basketball services. The players believe that it is no longer in their self-interest to accept any of the existing restrictions on their economic freedom."

This was the opening barrage in the next phase of the NBA owner versus player wars. We told them that the players wanted to eliminate the salary cap, the right of first refusal, and the college draft. We threw in the attack on the college draft because we knew just how much the owners cherished this particular form of restriction. The draft had been around forever, and the league used it not only as a way to eliminate bidding for rookies but also because it had become a successful marketing tool, generating huge fan interest in the off-season. While the draft did have some effect on reducing player salaries overall, the reality was that most veteran players didn't feel strongly about eliminating it because it no longer impacted them directly. Our real focus was the restrictions on free agency.

The owners' response to our position paper was swift and direct: it'll never happen.

Beginning late in the spring and all through that summer, we held a series of frustrating collective bargaining meetings with the NBA. As in the past, David Stern and Russ Granik led the negotiations for the league; they also added their newly minted general counsel, Gary Bettman, to their team. Fleisher and I again took the lead for the players. By this time, we too had added a new member to our team, a bona fide labor lawyer by the name of George Cohen. Fleisher had finally recognized that we actually were a labor union, that neither he nor I knew jack shit about labor law, and that it was time to add some real labor expertise to the team. Cohen had done work for the baseball players' union, and Marvin Miller and Don Fehr recommended him to us.

George was a thin-faced, wisecracking, Brooklyn-born lawyer schooled at Cornell Law School, which specialized in labor management law. He had spent most of his career representing unions and was no pushover at the bargaining table. He was the recognized dean of the union-side labor bar. Plus, he knew everything about sports. His father, Leonard Cohen, had been a sports writer for decades at the *New York Post*. George had literally grown up going to games at the old Madison Square Garden on 8th Avenue between 49th and 50th Streets. The NBPA had originally hired Cohen to help draft new agent regulations in basketball as he had done earlier in football and baseball. (Many years later, he was appointed by President Obama to head up the Federal Mediation and Conciliation Service, and I would spend long days with him in his role as a mediator.)

By this time, Charlie Grantham, the NBPA's executive vice president, had begun to take a more active role in union activities. In the late 1970s, Fleisher had hired Grantham, who had been director of admissions at Wharton School of Business, on a part-time basis. Later, he joined the union full time as director of administration and marketing. Grantham, who had played college basketball at Cheyney State University, was streetwise and very ambitious; he hoped to replace Fleisher as head of the union someday soon. I liked Charlie, but I never trusted him. He spent too much time ingratiating himself with players and not enough time focusing on the complex issues we faced with the NBA.

As the summer wore on, discussions got heated. At one meeting in the commissioner's office, Stern made one snide comment too many, and he and I nearly came to blows. He of all people accused me of lying, which really pissed me off; Granik and Fleisher had to separate us. Later that evening, when Fleisher told my wife that I had almost gotten into a fistfight with the man we referred to as "King David," she laughed and said, "For God's sake, it's only basketball!"

By mid-September, with the season fast approaching, it was clear we were getting nowhere. The league simply refused to make any concessions on the cap or any of the related free agency issues. The owners saw no reason to concede anything at this point. Even though the old agreement had expired, they believed they could keep us at the table and legally retain all the free agency restrictions. Antitrust was moot in their view because they were protected by the labor laws. We warned them that if they continued to impose restrictions on free agency, we would sue. It was hard to imagine resolving this any other way than in court.

The great unanswered question in professional team sports at that time was, How long could a league keep free agency restrictions in place given that the players no longer agreed to them in bargaining? We said this protection ended when the prior agreement expired or, at the latest, when there was an impasse in negotiations. After that, as far as we were concerned, we could sue them under the antitrust laws for an injunction and damages, just as we had in *Robertson*. There were some prior cases that seemed to support our position, particularly earlier rulings in the *Robertson* case in basketball and the *Mackey* case in football. The question, however, had never been definitively decided. We were prepared for another legal fight, but first we needed some players to agree to sue on behalf of all NBA players.

As in the past, union president Junior Bridgeman, then a free agent, stepped forward. Bridgeman had been drafted in 1975 by the Lakers and was part of the package that went to Milwaukee in exchange for Abdul-Jabbar. He spent his entire career as a small forward and a highly regarded sixth man with the Bucks and was the first Milwaukee player to have his number retired.

We needed both free agents and rookies because they were the most directly impacted by the free agency restrictions, salary cap, right of first refusal, and rookie college draft. It wasn't always easy because many players feared retaliation by the owners if they stepped up. We did manage to round up nine players to act as plaintiffs, with Bridgeman as the lead. Junior, who would later become very wealthy as a major Coca-Cola bottler and the owner of hundreds of fast-food franchises all over the Midwest, had a keen mind for business. He and I had first bonded when we found ourselves, along with our wives, crammed in a tiny compartment on the awful train ride to Rome during "Travels with Larry."

Of the eight other plaintiffs who stepped forward, there were four rookies, including the number one draft pick in the 1987 NBA college draft, David Robinson, known as "the Admiral" for his Naval Academy roots. He was joined by Armon Gilliam, the number-two draft pick from UNLV; Reggie Williams, the number-four pick from Georgetown; and Ken Barlow, who had been drafted out of Notre Dame the year before. We also recruited three other veterans: Rory Sparrow, Darrell Walker, and Phil Hubbard, all of whom were solid players whose contracts were about to expire and whose careers could be impacted by the free agency restrictions.

On October 1, 1987—my 42nd birthday—we filed yet another antitrust lawsuit against the NBA owners: *Bridgeman v. NBA.*

We decided to file the case in federal court in New Jersey because we wanted to avoid New York. Ralph Winter, the former Yale law professor and author of the leading article on the owners' labor defense, entitled "Superstars in Peonage," was now an appellate judge on the Federal Appeals Court in New York. Judge Winter plainly favored the labor laws over the antitrust laws. Since this issue was critical to our case, we could not take the chance of Judge Winter ruling against us.

Our case was assigned to Judge Dickinson Debevoise, a Jimmy Carter appointee who had been on the bench for 10 years. A war hero who had fought in both the Second World War and the Korean War, he had spent the bulk of his legal career doing commercial litigation in New Jersey. He was tall, friendly, and utterly clueless about both the game of basketball and the labor and antitrust issues that were the key to the case. He was neither a friend nor a foe of unions; he just plain didn't get it.

Both sides recognized that the real issue revolved around when the owners' labor protection ended. We argued that the owners' labor defense had ended either in June, when our agreement had ended, or at the latest in September, when we had reached an impasse. We believed we were now free to attack the NBA's free agency restrictions under the antitrust laws.

The NBA owners, on the other hand, argued that as long as a collective bargaining relationship existed, they were protected from antitrust claims. This meant that we would be stuck with the rules in place, which we thought were both illegal and unfair unless we just stopped being a union. That made no sense. Each side filed cross motions, and within a few weeks, we had a hearing before Judge Debevoise. I argued for the players. My adversaries Jeff Mishkin and Mike Cardozo argued for the NBA. On December 29, 1987, Judge Debevoise issued his ruling. We didn't like it one bit.

In an effort to reach some kind of compromise, Judge Debevoise unwittingly created a standard that played right into the NBA's greedy hands. According to the court, "The labor [defense] survives as long as the employer continues to impose a restriction unchanged, and reasonably believes that the practice or close variant of it will be incorporated in the next collective bargaining agreement."

That phrase, "reasonably believes," was like a punch in the neck. Imagine trying to argue in court what constitutes another person's reasonable belief. How could you possibly do it? It was like some existential riddle.

The ruling left both sides peering over their foxholes, not sure what to do next. We recognized immediately that continuing the lawsuit would be expensive, lengthy, and fraught with uncertainties. The union, as usual, had no money for a prolonged fight. Player unions back then relied primarily on membership dues and whatever minimal revenues came in from group licensing agreements, which were barely enough to pay union expenses (even with Fleisher taking no salary). There was no money left to fund another lengthy antitrust lawsuit that could ring up millions in legal fees and expenses.

As in the past, the NBA owners had the financial upper hand. Worse, even if we proved that the restrictions were illegal, an appeals court could ultimately rule that the NBA owners were protected by their labor defense. Fleisher wanted us to find a way out.

It was the third week in January 1988. A group of us were sitting around a conference room at Weil feeling flummoxed. Our labor guru, George Cohen, was there, along with Junior Bridgeman, who had decided to retire as a player and so was now a full-time participant. There was no agenda; we were looking for a new strategy, a way to bring this mess to a quick conclusion. We were also looking for leverage. We discussed litigation timing and whether to seek an immediate appeal or call a strike and, if so, when. No one liked any of those options. The hours dragged by, stale sandwiches and empty soda cans littering the room.

I finally looked up with an idea: "What if we weren't a labor union anymore? If there's no labor union, how could there be a labor defense?" George Cohen's jaw dropped. He was appalled. He had spent his entire life fighting for labor unions, and I was suggesting that we blow ours up. He kept saying over and over, "You can't do that; it just isn't done." His way of fighting management was to strike, to picket, to boycott—not to disband.

Others chimed in. Kessler said he thought it might work under the antitrust laws, but Cohen remained skeptical. "Look, under my theory, the Players Association wouldn't disappear," I said. "We would become a professional trade association, like the American Bar Association, the American Medical Association, the Society of Professional Engineers." Fleisher's face lit up with a smile. He liked the idea, but Cohen kept shaking his head. Junior listened carefully, then finally nodded and said he was willing to go along with it.

By remaining a trade association, we could keep the organization intact as we continued the antitrust court fight and fund it through trading card and other licensing revenue. The threat of unlimited free agency was Armageddon for the owners. Even worse for them, without a union to deal with the players collectively, it would be chaos for the NBA clubs, who would be forced to deal with each player on an individual basis for everything from medical insurance to meal money. This could also potentially expose them to millions of dollars in antitrust treble damages for having conspired to hold down player salaries and benefits after the expiration of the old collective bargaining agreement.

We went from being powerless and afraid to fully armed and dangerous. Nothing like this had ever been done before. We didn't even know what the hell to call it. Cohen told us about a process before the NLRB called "certification," when a group sought union status. We decided to call what we were doing "decertification."

Actually, as we later learned, what we were suggesting was properly called a "disclaimer," where a majority of the union members would vote to "disclaim" union status. We asked George if we could legally do this. He told us that there was no precedent for this kind of thing, but presumably if the majority of the players voted to decertify (in reality, to disclaim), that should be enough to satisfy the labor laws and gut the owners' labor defense. We had a plan. The only alternative was to strike the playoffs, something that also had never been done before in basketball. We were reluctant to do it for fear of the impact it would have on the NBA's rising popularity.

The NBA All-Star Game in Chicago was set for early February. We called for a meeting of the player reps before the game. On Friday, February 5, the player reps, plus most of the All-Stars, gathered for a meeting in a downtown Chicago hotel.

There were more than 40 players in the huge ballroom, including Magic Johnson, Larry Bird, Kareem Abdul-Jabbar, Michael Jordan, Moses Malone, and Karl Malone. The situation was tense; everyone was nervous. Fleisher, Cohen, and I described the situation to the players and laid out the alternatives, including a possible strike of the playoffs. We ultimately recommended that the player reps authorize a decertification vote of all the players. The players asked a lot of questions: What would this mean? Would players still get benefits? What about player arbitrations? How would players be protected?

We explained that the nonunion Players Association would be essentially a professional organization that would continue to assist players in developing pension plans and medical and other benefits but that each player may have to negotiate his own per diem expenses and other benefits. A few players raised questions about timing and possible lost benefits. We responded that these were legitimate concerns, but we believed that by making this move, it would likely lead to a quick overall settlement. Everyone in the room was anxious; it grew very quiet. Minutes ticked by.

Finally Junior spoke. He said that he was convinced that this was the right move. Stripped of the labor defense, the league would run the risk of virtually all their rules and restrictions being declared illegal. Plus, there was the possibility of hundreds of millions of dollars in treble damages.

His words carried weight. The player reps voted unanimously, 23–0, to authorize a vote of all players to decertify the union. Junior then said he was retiring and stepping down as president. The player reps unanimously chose Alex English, a union vice president, as the new president of what was about to become a professional organization.

At the meeting, Fleisher also dropped one more bombshell. He told the player reps that at the end of this fight, he would step down as general counsel and head of the Players Association. He told the players, "It may take one year, five years, two years or a week. I'll be here only for as long as it takes." I sat there stunned. He had never breathed a hint of this to me before the meeting. Nearing 60, and with almost a quarter century in this post, I sensed Larry believed it was time to move on.

We immediately set out to collect the votes we would need to put the decertification plan into action. George Cohen drafted a one-sentence form:

DECERTIFICATION

I do hereby vote to decertify the National Basketball Players Association as I no longer wish to be represented by a collective bargaining agent.

Date: _____, 1988 _____
Player's Signature

With those 24 words, the relationship between professional athletes and team owners would never be the same again.

We handed out the forms at the All-Star Game meeting and asked the player reps to get signatures from their teammates as quickly as possible.

The forms began trickling into Larry's office from each team. And I do mean trickle. We were a little worried by the slow pace. I called Fleisher every morning to check the mail. But soon it became a tidal wave. By the beginning of March, we had gathered the forms from all 23 teams and it was a landslide in favor of decertification. Of the 276 players who were eligible to vote, we had 268 signed forms voting to decertify the union—about 99.5 percent. To this day, I don't know what happened to the missing 8, but I do know that not a single player voted against decertification.

Once we had gathered all the forms together, we organized them by team, made copies, and put the originals in a big brown envelope. At Fleisher's request, I called Jeff Mishkin over at Proskauer to tell him of the overwhelming vote for decertification and that I had the forms in my office if he wanted to inspect them. He did. He immediately walked over to our offices and took a look. He was convinced. I then told him that before we delivered these forms to the NBA and NLRB, it might be productive to meet one more time, off the record and in secret.

Now we had the league's full attention. They knew that if we delivered the forms to them and the NLRB on a formal basis, everything would change. Free agency restrictions, including the salary cap, would almost certainly not survive an antitrust challenge, and owners could potentially be on the hook for hundreds of millions of dollars in damages. Within hours, Fleisher got a call from Stern taking us up on our offer to reconvene discussions. The media, for the moment, would be left out of it. A day or so later, we met, with the understanding that all discussions would be confidential and without prejudice to either side's position in the still-pending *Bridgeman* case.

The NBA brought a new figure to the table: Abe Pollin, chairman of the NBA Board of Governors and a member of their labor committee. Pollin was the longest-standing owner in the NBA, starting with a half share of the Baltimore Bullets back in 1964. He later purchased the other half and moved the Bullets to Washington, where eventually they became the Wizards. Pollin was highly respected by both the owners and the players; he and Fleisher, from similar backgrounds, got along especially well.

The mood was somber but calm. This was no time for tantrums or lost tempers. Both sides recognized that we were edging into unknown territory. Stern begrudgingly acknowledged that the specter of decertification was a powerful incentive for both sides to reach an agreement quickly. We had also never taken the idea of striking the playoffs off the table. We felt good about our position.

We immediately got down to hard bargaining. The players were prepared to live with a salary cap and a college draft but not owners' rights of first refusal. We insisted that the first refusal restriction be eliminated totally or seriously modified so that most veteran players would not be subject to any restrictions when their contracts expired. Free should mean free.

In exchange for us accepting the continuation of the cap, Stern offered to more than triple its size over the next several years, to $12 million. He also offered to knock a round off the draft, taking it from three to two rounds, which was mostly a symbolic gesture. Not many players drafted beyond the second round stick on a roster. But there were other concessions too, such as large increases in benefits, including a new pension for players who had retired before the union obtained its first pension plan back in 1965.

We met over the next couple of weeks and hammered out most of the terms of a new agreement. The right of first refusal remained a sticking point. They wanted it to apply for the first six years of a player's career; we countered with three years. And back and forth we went for several weeks until Fleisher and Pollin—in what amounted to face-saving for both sides—went behind closed doors alone. They talked for over an hour. When they came out, they told the rest of us they had agreed on four years.

To keep pressure on the owners, we set a deadline: the new agreement had to be wrapped up before the playoffs started, which was only days away. Easter Sunday turned into a full workday, which caused a bit of a crisis in my household. Our team agreed to meet at Fleisher's Chappaqua, New York, home to finalize the papers over lox and bagels early on Easter Sunday morning. The group included Fleisher, Cohen, Kessler, and Bruce Meyer. I was the only goy in attendance.

As the day wore on, I received periodic calls from my wife about our family Easter dinner. I kept telling her to push Easter Sunday dinner back, hour by hour. As dusk approached, the calls got more frantic, and it looked like the Easter ham would go uneaten. Finally, I left my colleagues to finish the details and rushed home for some cold ham and my wife's famous (but now burnt) macaroni and cheese. I have been reminded many times about the year the NBA stole Easter.

But cold ham was a small price to pay for a new seven-year deal known as the *Bridgeman* settlement agreement. At the owners' insistence, we also signed a new labor agreement, which provided the owners with an antitrust exemption for the same seven-year period, through June 1994.

In hindsight, it was a very successful negotiation—we never had to strike or actually decertify the union. There would be peace. We agreed to keep Judge Debevoise on as the new basketball judge to replace Judge Carter, and we appointed a new Special Master, a New

York lawyer named Ted Clark who was then the president of the New York City Bar Association. The players had not gotten all that we wanted, but a costly, drawn-out war had been averted.

As promised, Fleisher announced to the players and the media that he would be stepping down after the playoffs in June. Unbeknownst to me, he had been interviewing candidates since early January. He believed strongly that the next NBPA union head should be black and had talked to several former players and prominent African American politicians and lawyers.

Meanwhile, behind the scenes, Grantham had been lobbying the player reps to choose him as Fleisher's successor. Fleisher took a dim view of this. "Charlie is smart enough for the job but he's out for himself," he told me and a few others. But considering how strongly he felt, Fleisher didn't do nearly enough. When the player reps met the following summer without Fleisher for the first time, Grantham was elected the new executive director. He was the wrong choice. Years down the road, Grantham's leadership, or rather lack thereof, resulted in chaos at the NBPA and a major crisis for the league.

But that would come much later. Fleisher, my friend and mentor, had gone out on top. He gave his life to the union, and despite his many shortcuts, quirky deals, and funky work habits, he had built it into a major force to be reckoned with. His final battle, in which we threatened to blow up our own union, may have been his greatest of all, and it became the centerpiece of the labor struggles in major team sports for the next 25 years. The next battleground after basketball was football, and I would be right in the thick of that one too. But not before a crushing personal loss.

CHAPTER 12

Larry Died

I PICKED UP THE PHONE IN MY SUITE AT THE WEST-
wood Marquis in Los Angeles. It was May 4, 1989, a beautiful sunny
morning in California. My new secretary, Diane Brandi, was on the
line. It was her first day on the job, and I could hear panic in her voice.
"Your wife's calling," she told me, and she transferred the call. Katy
didn't mince words. "Larry died," she said.

Since leaving the NBPA, Larry had become head of basketball
operations for IMG, the large Cleveland-based sports agency. We had
remained as close as ever, talking almost daily about the sports agency
business he was building with his sons, Marc and Eric, and everything
else imaginable. But this day, I was out of town. Larry had just finished
playing squash with an old college friend at the New York Athletic
Club when he had a massive heart attack in the men's locker room. It
killed him immediately. He was 58 years old.

I was devastated. I had never lost a friend like that—and I have
never had another friend like Larry. I knew I couldn't get back to New
York right away, so I called then senator Bill Bradley about funeral
arrangements. I was in California to argue an appeal for one of my
nonsports clients, Westinghouse. The appellate argument was set for
10 o'clock the next morning (Friday), somewhere in Burbank.

Back east, Katy, Bill, and Larry's son Marc struggled to put
together burial arrangements for Saturday and a memorial service
the following Monday. Still in shock, I somehow argued the appeal. I
was told it went well.

The next day was the graduation of my eldest daughter, Kellianne, from Denison University in Ohio. Marc Fleisher had graduated from the same school just a few years earlier. I knew immediately that Larry's death was going to make it impossible for Katy and me to be there to see her graduate. I called to explain. She understood. I remember her exact words: "It's OK, Dad. Grandma and Grandpa will be here. I know how much Mr. Fleisher meant to you." I had tears in my eyes, both for Kellianne and for Larry. When I got home that evening, well after midnight, Katy outlined the arrangements.

There was to be no funeral; Larry would be buried at noon the next day at the Gate of Heaven cemetery in Valhalla, New York. A reception would follow immediately after the burial service at our house in nearby Armonk. That Saturday turned out to be a spectacular day, sunny and warm, with the flowers of spring blooming to life. There must have been nearly 60 cars in the funeral procession to the burial site, which was high on a bluff overlooking the rolling hills of Westchester. At least 100 people gathered around the gravesite—NBA All-Stars present and past, college friends, law school classmates, and his family—all the people who loved Fleisher. At the grave, Lee Sarokin, a federal judge from New Jersey and Fleisher's law school roommate, gave the eulogy. Sarokin had been Bradley's first campaign manager, and Senator Bradley later recommended him for a spot on the federal bench. An accomplished trial lawyer, Sarokin spoke eloquently about Larry's life, his accomplishments, and most importantly, what he had meant to so many people. He spoke for no more than 15 minutes, but by the time he was finished, people who barely knew each other were hugging and sobbing uncontrollably. Larry's was a life well lived.

After the burial service, everyone was invited back to our house for a luncheon celebrating his life. It was as if the Basketball Hall of Fame had temporarily moved from Springfield to Armonk. There were Oscar Robertson and John Havlicek; Bob Lanier, Willis Reed, Dave DeBusschere, Bill Bradley, Earl Monroe, Maurice Lucas, and a dozen more All-Stars and friends. Diane and David Stern were there.

Stern, at his warmest, expressed enormous affection and respect for Larry.

In Larry's *New York Times* obituary, Stern described him as "a remarkable man and a personal friend . . . who always worked for the good of the sport of basketball."

Larry's wife, Vicky, still in shock, was comforted by many of the wives who had also known Larry well: Beth Havlicek, Gerri DeBusschere, Yvonne Robertson, and Katy among them. Katy also played hostess, making sure everyone was comfortable. Friends from Larry's 30 years in sports and business filled the room. My daughter Kerrin, seven years old at the time, still remembers Bob Lanier banging his head on the chandelier in our dining room. She says she looked up at Lanier and asked, "Did that hurt?" Lanier looked down and said, "All the time," with a big smile on his face.

The hours passed quickly. The group spent the time eating and drinking and telling "Fleisher stories," with laughter filling the room over and over again—the time we got lost in Monaco, the time Larry sneaked the uniforms onto the plane on the way to Brazil, his drug lecture in Beijing, and on and on. As the afternoon drew to a close, people lingered. Nobody really wanted to leave because they didn't want to leave Larry.

On Monday, there was a memorial service in a hall we had rented in midtown Manhattan. Hundreds more came to celebrate his life, nearly 500 in all. Robertson, Bradley, Havlicek, Don Fehr, and David Stern all spoke. Bradley called Fleisher "the older brother he never had." Oscar spoke haltingly and openly sobbed. "Sorry," he said, "I will cherish his memory." Bernard King sat in the front row. He had tears in his eyes, recalling what Larry had done for him.

I spoke last. With tears in my own eyes, I talked about Fleisher's critical role in changing the face of professional sports in this country forever. I said that it was about much more than money; it was about respect, decency, fairness, and integrity. I also talked about our travels with Larry—both literally and figuratively—and his impact on me and almost everyone in this huge room. At a luncheon afterward at his favorite restaurant, Mama Leone's, there were tributes, more funny stories, more tears, and more laughter.

The very last time I had seen Fleisher alive was in a restaurant parking lot in Westchester after one of our family dinners, just two days before he died. He was proudly showing us the new BMW he had bought for his wife, Vicky. He never got to drive it.

Meeting Fleisher back in 1973 changed my life. Through Larry, I met and later came to represent Marvin Miller and Don Fehr in baseball; Ed Garvey and Gene Upshaw in football; and Alan Eagleson, Bob Goodenow, and Don Fehr again in hockey—the once and future leaders of sports unions from the 1970s to today. Each of them would be involved in the struggles between players and owners that played out over the past several decades. During the years I knew Larry, I grew from a young acolyte learning the business of law and the business of sports to a mature first-chair lawyer able to attract clients from both the sports world and the corporate world. Plus, I found a home in the courtroom that I came to love. Much of this I owed to Fleisher—his insights, his intelligence, and his introductions. Through Larry I came to believe that whoever I represented in the courtroom—pro athlete or giant company—I would treat them as the underdog and fight for them as hard as I could with integrity and a sense of humor. Just like Larry.

The days passed. I went back to work. I thought of Larry almost every day, but we all moved on, as people do. Less than two years later, with the help of both David Stern and Russ Granik, who sat on the Hall of Fame's board, Larry Fleisher was inducted into the Naismith Memorial Basketball Hall of Fame, the first and only labor union leader to be inducted into a sports Hall of Fame. To their great credit, Russ and David made this happen because it was the right thing to do.

I was there at the ceremony along with Larry's wife, Vicky, and his son Marc, who spoke for his father at the induction dinner. Bradley, DeBusschere, Robertson, and several other Hall of Famers filled out our table. There was more laughter and a few more tears as we toasted Larry one last time.

As the months went by, I resigned myself to thinking my life in sports was coming to an end. On the day Larry died, I was 43 years old, the same age as Fleisher had been when I first met him a decade and a half earlier. I had been involved in sports virtually my entire professional career—representing basketball players and baseball players and even a couple of defunct professional sports leagues. I had loved being a "sports lawyer"—hanging out with players past and present, fighting for players' rights, and bonding with Fleisher. It had been both challenging and lots of fun. But maybe it was time to grow up. The law of sports was narrow, not particularly lucrative, and rarely ended up in the kind of full-blown trials that natural-born courtroom lawyers like me dream about. A larger world was opening for me. I was now running Weil's 400-person litigation department. By 1989, I was just coming into my own as a nationally recognized trial lawyer, representing corporate icons like Westinghouse, General Electric, General Motors, and soon ExxonMobil, CBS, Disney, Procter & Gamble, and Johnson & Johnson, among others. High-stakes jury trials really got me excited. The money and prestige weren't bad either. I had also just become the youngest member of Weil's management committee. It was a natural evolution.

My decision was made easier by the fact that I had no interest in working closely with Charlie Grantham. He was no Larry. So I began slowly to drift away from day-to-day involvement with the NBPA, leaving that to Jeff Kessler and Bruce Meyer, in order to build a litigation powerhouse at Weil.

I could not have predicted that within a matter of months I would be embroiled in the biggest sports case of my life in football—and that a few months later I would get dragged into hockey. To quote Yogi, "I came to a fork in the road and I took it."

CHAPTER 13

"We Can Always Get More Cattle"

I KNEW DICK BERTHELSEN (A.K.A. "RICHARD," AS HE sometimes insisted on being called), the general counsel of the NFLPA, to be a calm guy. But when he called me in early November 1989, less than six months after Larry died, I heard agitation in his voice. He wanted to come up from DC to see me the very next day.

The football players had just suffered a devastating defeat in their Minnesota antitrust free agency lawsuit against the NFL. The case, modeled after our *Bridgeman* lawsuit against the NBA, had originally been filed in October 1987. Back then, I had spent several hours on the phone in the Pittsburgh airport reviewing our just-filed *Bridgeman* complaint with Dick and his Minneapolis lawyer, Ed Glennon.

But the NFLPA had gotten a very different result. An appeals court sitting in St. Louis had effectively gutted their case, holding that the football players' antitrust claims were barred by the NFL owners' labor defense. The case had been scheduled to go to trial in mid-November in Minnesota, but the ruling had left the players with no viable legal options.

Dick was in my office early the next morning. He wanted a crash course in decertification and its legal ramifications. As he and I were talking, I looked up and saw a tall hulking figure in the doorway, whom I recognized immediately: Gene Upshaw, all-time great left guard for the Oakland Raiders and now NFLPA executive director. In his booming voice, he bellowed, "Quinn, how the hell are you?"

In the more than 20 years that I knew him, Upshaw never called me anything but Quinn.

I had met both Gene and Dick at the periodic joint meetings we held among the four players associations, and though I didn't know either of them well at that point, I felt from the start that they were kindred spirits.

Gene and Dick had been fighting the NFL owners together for more than a decade, but they were polar opposites. Dick Berthelsen was a burly, small-town midwesterner, extraordinarily courteous, with a quiet demeanor and an encyclopedic grasp of sports and labor law. After graduating from Wisconsin Law School in the late 1960s, he spent a couple of years at a Madison, Wisconsin, law firm before being convinced by Ed Garvey, head of the NFLPA and a law school classmate, to join the union's legal department. He spent the rest of his career at the NFLPA, eventually becoming the union's top lawyer.

Gene Upshaw, by contrast, had grown up in South Texas, picking cotton in the summers to make money. He hadn't even played football in high school. He liked baseball better, but he made the football team as a nonscholarship player at a little-known all-black school called Texas A&I (now part of Texas A&M). He played several positions before settling at offensive left guard, which is where he would distinguish himself as the greatest of all time. He was a perennial NFL All-Star with a couple of Super Bowl rings to his name. Upshaw was inducted into the NFL Hall of Fame in 1987.

Upshaw's personality was as huge as his trophy case. He filled a room with charm, laughter, and a keen intelligence; he was a natural-born leader. As a player, he was elected president of the NFLPA, then at age 36, the year he retired from the Raiders, he became the executive director of the union following the failed 1982 strike. Al Davis had wanted Upshaw to join the Raiders' front office, but as much as he respected Al, Upshaw had a different vision for his next career.

When Upshaw took over the union, it was nearly broke. After the ruling on the 56-day *Mackey* antitrust trial in the mid-1970s struck down the old Rozelle Rule on free agency compensation, the union had fumbled its gains through a series of strategic blunders.

Garvey, a socialist trade union leader, mistakenly bargained away free agency in 1977 in exchange for improved pension and other benefits, agreeing to restrictions more onerous than the Rozelle Rule and thereby tacitly accepting the league's paternalistic approach to its players.

When that labor agreement was up in 1982, Garvey still neglected to pursue free agency, choosing instead to seek a percentage of the NFL's gross revenues for the players. It was a fool's errand. When the NFL owners disdainfully rejected his proposal, Garvey called a strike, compounding his error. Of the four major sports, football players have the shortest careers and thus the most to lose in a work stoppage. Most players simply couldn't sacrifice paychecks for more than a few weeks; staying on strike for a whole season was simply out of the question.

Garvey's strike collapsed after 57 days, with the players accepting another five-year labor agreement that offered no improvement in free agency. At this point, Garvey departed to go into politics in Wisconsin as an unrepentant liberal firebrand. He wasn't any more successful than he had been as a union leader, losing a bid for the Senate in 1986 and one for governor in 1998.

When the next deal expired after the 1986–87 season, football players were determined to finally cash in on some form of free agency. They had seen the massive paydays in basketball and baseball and couldn't understand why they got nothing but stagnation.

The owners still thought they held all the cards. They were led by the mean-spirited Hugh Culverhouse, Tampa Bay owner and head of the NFL's management council. The idea of free agency made him "physically ill," he once told Upshaw. Another time, he told Upshaw, "You won't get free agency in a year, not in five years, not in ten years, not ever."

This is how nearly all the owners thought, we would learn. Culverhouse was just one of the few who would come right out and say it to your face.

For the second time in less than a decade, negotiations went nowhere, and the players called a strike, walking out after the second game of the season. The NFL then did something audacious—they filled out their rosters with scabs, or what they called "replacement players," and played three weeks of the season with some of the worst professional football ever seen. The games were unwatchable. I remember Fleisher saying that this could never happen in basketball. "The players are too recognizable," he'd said. But it had the desired effect in football: the union buckled, and the strike was called off after 24 days.

But if the players couldn't afford to walk the picket line, they were prepared to fight it out in court again. On the day the strike ended, October 15, 1987, the players filed their antitrust lawsuit in Minneapolis, the same place where *Mackey* had been decided in their favor a decade earlier. The case, with Marvin Powell, All-Pro offensive lineman for the Jets and newly elected president of the NFLPA, as the lead plaintiff, mirrored the one we had filed two weeks earlier in our battle with the NBA in the *Bridgeman* case.

The *Powell* case had been assigned to a brand-new judge, David S. Doty, a former marine appointed to the bench by President Reagan in 1987. *Powell* was one of his first cases. Doty was a true gentleman, white-haired and amiable. As I would soon learn, he had a warm sense of humor and an extraordinary sense of fairness. A lifelong Minnesota Republican, he was your typical midwestern Rotarian. He was the best trial judge I ever had. A judicial maestro, he conducted a jury trial with the skill and precision of a master musician.

Following the NBA's game plan in *Bridgeman*, the NFL lawyers, led by Paul Tagliabue, filed a motion to dismiss the *Powell* case based on the labor defense. Ed Glennon, the same lawyer who had tried and won the *Mackey* case 10 years earlier, took the lead for the NFLPA, but Ed's partner, Carol Rieger, argued the motion. An experienced trial attorney, Rieger pointed out that the NFL's labor agreement had expired more than a year ago and that the parties had reached an impasse on free agency and other issues months earlier. That meant, she argued, that the labor defense had long since ended and that antitrust laws now applied.

In late January 1988, Doty ruled for the football players, holding that since the parties were at an impasse, the labor defense no longer applied. The NFL owners, Doty declared, were in fact now at risk under the antitrust laws. The NFL immediately appealed to the Eighth Circuit Court of Appeals in St. Louis, which oversaw the Minnesota federal court.

In an ironic twist, I had been asked by Berthelsen and Ed Glennon to serve as an expert witness in the *Powell* case to talk about free agency in the NBA. My testimony was supposed to demonstrate the fact that a decade of free agency had not harmed the NBA at all—that in fact, the league was flourishing with new revenue and fan excitement precisely *because* there was more competitive balance than ever before.

On September 19, 1989, Jeff Pash—a man I would come to know well but not always love—took my expert deposition in the *Powell* case. This was our first of many run-ins over the years. At the time, Pash was a young partner at the Covington firm in DC and a protégé of Paul Tagliabue, who by then was a senior Covington partner. I testified, "What I'm really saying is that it's fairly obvious that there is no basis, at least in the NBA's experience, to believe that free agency in some form or another is going to lead to Armageddon and perdition, that at least in the NBA's experience, and my understanding is the same is true in baseball, the opposite is true, that the freer the agency, the more profitable the leagues."

This didn't make Pash and the other NFL lawyers happy.

The NFL owners recognized they were at risk for hundreds of millions of dollars in potential damages if they lost their appeal. At Tagliabue's suggestion, they embarked on a new line of argument, touting a new system of free agency they called "Plan B." It was a sham.

The idea behind Plan B was that each team would restrict 37 players on their roster, leaving a handful of fringe players supposedly "free" to negotiate with any team they wanted. The Plan B system, of course, kept in place all the prior restrictions preventing free agent movement, exempting only a few of the least desirable players. By restricting all the top players in the league, the NFL owners could continue to illegally hold down all player salaries. It was the legal equivalent of a trick play.

We didn't fall for it. As time went on, Plan B would become the focus of our attack.

The NFL's appeal went forward, and on November 1, 1989, the St. Louis appeals court reversed Judge Doty's decision. The court made it clear that so long as the NFLPA remained a union, NFL players would be barred from suing for free agency. Two days later, Berthelsen and Upshaw were sitting in my office.

I asked Jeff Kessler to join us, and the meeting quickly evolved into a brainstorming session. We talked about decertifying the union, which would effectively remove the NFL's labor defense. The only other option was an appeal to the Supreme Court—the legal equivalent of a Hail Mary pass. After several hours of discussion, Upshaw asked us to represent the football players in a new decertification effort.

By now we knew the drill. We had to obtain decertification authorizations from a majority of NFL players as quickly as possible and then file a new lawsuit to eliminate the league's labor defense. Berthelsen initially expressed reluctance about hiring a big New York law firm because of what he feared would be the huge expense. Upshaw dismissed his concerns, telling him, "We can't count bullets when we are in the middle of a war."

After returning to NFLPA headquarters in DC, Gene and Dick consulted with Doug Allen, the NFLPA's assistant executive director and third member of their leadership team. Allen had played linebacker at Penn State and then with the Buffalo Bills for several years. Allen was so intense on the field that he retired early because, as he once told me, he was afraid he might kill somebody out there. Allen organized the troops, and on the following Monday, Upshaw faxed a letter to Jack Donlan, the NFL's lead labor negotiator:

November 6, 1989

Dear Jack:

The NFLPA Executive Committee has voted to abandon bargaining rights and begin the decertification process. This action was made necessary by the 8th Circuit decision which purports to extend the NFLPA's labor exemption to your illegal activities.

We did not form our union to allow you illegally to restrain trade in the market for player services. The players would rather protect their rights as independent contractors than to subject themselves to the monopolistic whims of the NFL and its clubs.

s/Eugene Upshaw

Donlan was a tough bastard, a quick-witted Irishman whose pro-management philosophy had been fire-tested in the airline industry, where he had overseen countless strikes and lockouts. He immediately shot back at Upshaw's letter, calling the move "a parlor trick." He asked, "Are they saying this is some new kind of strategy or do they really mean it? Either way, we will find a way to deal with it."[40]

We obviously expected the NFL to respond skeptically, but it was disheartening to see so much of the media fall right into line with them. "In a surprising and not totally convincing move, the NFL Players Association has informed the league ownership that it is going to disband, and it further claims that action would eventually turn all the players into free agents and do away with the college draft," went a typical story from the *Orlando Sentinel*.[41] Back then, most sportswriters, particularly in football, tended to parrot whatever line the NFL's PR juggernaut was feeding them. In an almost literal sense, their philosophy was, "Don't bite the hand that feeds me."

By the end of November 1989, an overwhelming majority of NFL players had signed the decertification authorizations. The NFLPA was officially converted to a professional association at the NFLPA Board of Player Representatives meeting in Dallas on December 5, 1989. The organization abandoned all collective bargaining rights but remained in place as a professional organization protecting player rights. It would be funded largely by licensing revenues from trading cards and other player paraphernalia. The NFL attacked these actions, calling the NFLPA a "union in hiding."

In the intervening weeks, I pulled together a new legal team to represent the football players. Jeff Kessler was my number two, and Bruce Meyer led a new group of younger lawyers like Jon Weiss and David Feher, all determined to fight the mighty NFL and its vast, multifirm legal team. We put together a new antitrust complaint focused on the NFL's Plan B as an illegal group boycott and an unlawful restraint of trade. Dick Berthelsen was charged with the unenviable task of recruiting players willing to challenge the NFL's illegal rules and put their careers on the line.

As I've mentioned, job security is a much greater worry for football players than those in other sports. But it's not simply that the average career is shorter. It's also that the NFL has historically been ruthless at weeding out nonconformists. Unless you're a huge star, you abide by their strict rules of conduct or find yourself on the waiver wire. And NFL player contracts were not guaranteed.

Over the next several weeks, Berthelsen scoured team rosters and contacted dozens of players and agents. We needed at least a half dozen or more players who would be free agents as of February 1, 1990, and had the guts to fight for their freedom. The NFL had been the only league in the history of pro sports to bring in scab players to play in phony games, for the sole purpose of breaking the 1987 strike.

Two player agents, Randy Vataha and Tom Condon, both former union leaders, were particularly helpful in our recruiting efforts. Berthelsen eventually came up with a formidable group: Mark Collins, an All-Pro New York Giants cornerback and strong union supporter; Don Majkowski, the Green Bay quarterback, All-Pro in 1989 and a Vataha client; Dave Richards, starting offensive guard for the San Diego Chargers, another Vataha client; Frank Minnifield, All-Pro cornerback for the Cleveland Browns; and Tim McDonald, an All-Pro defensive back for the 49ers. Those were the stars. Dick also added a couple of journeyman players: Niko Noga, backup linebacker for the Lions, and Lee Rouson, backup running back for the Giants. It was a true cross section of NFL players.

Just weeks before we were preparing to file the lawsuit, Berthelsen came up with another name: Freeman McNeil, a onetime superstar running back for the New York Jets who was approaching the end of his career. Dick called Tony Curto, a Long Island entertainment lawyer who represented McNeil, and asked if McNeil was willing to be a plaintiff. A few hours later, I got a call from Curto asking about the lawsuit. He wanted to know what would be involved, and would Freeman have a prominent role?

I explained the case and assured him that Freeman would have a major role if that was what he wanted. Curto said OK and hung up. A few hours later, I got a call from Berthelsen, who said that McNeil was in, with one proviso: his name had to be listed first on the complaint so that the case would be (Freeman) *McNeil v. National Football League*. Dick thought the name "Freeman" was perfect. I agreed. We also appreciated that McNeil saw his role in historic terms. "I just want to leave something to the game I got so much out of," he told Dick. "If it is a matter of standing up for something that I believe in, then that is what it takes."

Our player group, which became known as "the McNeil Eight," was now complete. Following our *Bridgeman* strategy, we filed the *McNeil* case in New Jersey, expecting the NFL would try to move it back to Minnesota and the friendly Midwest appeals court that had reversed Judge Doty's decision in the *Powell* case.

Everybody prefers a home-field advantage. Because two of our plaintiffs, Collins and Rouson of the Giants, lived in New Jersey, we thought we had a fighting chance of keeping the case there. We also decided to file it only on behalf of the eight individual players and not as a class action. This was a new strategy. The benefit of a class suit is that it has greater impact if you win. The downside is that if you lose, it bars other players from suing, which is what happened in the *Powell* case.

We were ready for a long war. If we lost the first case, we would file suits on behalf of other players in other jurisdictions all around the country. That way, I told Paul Tagliabue, you may beat us once or twice, or even three times, but eventually we will win. Once we do, I told him, "You guys are screwed."

As long as our money held out, we were going to come after the NFL like waves of blitzing linebackers. Upshaw was all for it. The players had acquiesced for long enough. It was time to break the powerful psychological and economic grip that the NFL held them in once and for all. This was going to be a no-holds-barred fight to the finish, and both sides knew it.

We filed the *McNeil* case in Newark, New Jersey, on April 10, 1990. True to form, the NFL moved to transfer the case to Minnesota, arguing that the case was a follow-on to the *Powell* case and therefore should be heard by the same judge, Judge Doty. Our New Jersey complaint was assigned to Judge John W. Bissell, who took an immediate dislike to the plaintiffs and particularly their lawyers—Kessler and me. He thought we were just two clever lawyers trying to get out from under a bad decision in *Powell*. On June 12, 1999, in a decision that turned out to be a godsend to the players, Judge Bissell ordered the case transferred to Minnesota and Judge Doty. The NFL would regret that decision for the next 25 years.

As this was happening, the NFLPA also sponsored a little-noticed lawsuit regarding the fixing of salaries of players on the NFL's "taxi squads," where teams sometimes stashed extra players. This case, which came to be known as *Brown v. National Football League*, was filed in Washington, DC, federal court by another NFLPA lawyer, Chip Yablonski. The case would loom large some years later when it reached the Supreme Court, which would lead to a definitive ruling on the labor defense issue.

Meanwhile, as we were preparing to file the *McNeil* case, Kessler and I also filed our own Hail Mary petition to the Supreme Court seeking to have the *Powell* appeals decision reversed. We got the three other players' associations (NBPA, MLBPA, and NHLPA) to back our petition, and we even convinced the right-wing solicitor general, a man by the name of Kenneth Starr—yes, that Ken Starr—to support our petition. Despite our efforts, the Supreme Court denied our petition, which only reinforced our decision to decertify the NFLPA because, as a nonunion, the labor defense would be irrelevant.

The NFL was not content to sit back and play defense. They went on the attack. Some of their moves were out in the open and aboveboard; others were sneaky. One of the sneakiest involved licensing income. Back in the 1980s, a wily marketing genius named Frank Vuono had turned NFL Properties, the league's licensing arm, which made deals with manufacturers to use team logos on apparel and other merchandise, into a tremendous cash cow. The NFLPA had carved out its own licensing arm for player likenesses, and though it was much smaller than the league's, it provided the union's main source of funding for operations and, critically, our legal assault on the league. Without this cash, we didn't stand a chance against the NFL's deep pockets.

So what did the NFL do? Under Vuono's direction, it tried to lure star players away from the union's program and into the league's program—in other words, to turn the players against one another. You almost have to respect it in a Darth Vader, evil-shithead kind of way. Several players, including Roger Craig and Jerry Rice of the 49ers and Randall Cunningham of the Eagles, originally opted to take the deal with the NFL.

Vuono also came up with something he called the "Quarterback Club" and paid a number of top quarterbacks up to $300,000 to abandon the NFLPA. Charter members included Cunningham, John Elway, Dan Marino, Warren Moon, Boomer Esiason, Troy Aikman, Jim Kelley, Joe Montana, and Phil Simms—several of whom had been strong union supporters in the past. Lawsuits began flying. In June 1990, shortly after the *McNeil* case was sent to Minnesota, we filed a lawsuit against NFL Properties in New York, seeking to stop the league from gutting our licensing program.

Then along came Larry Csonka, a Hall of Fame fullback for the Miami Dolphins and a reality TV star of sorts, hosting shows like *American Gladiator* and *North to Alaska*. Csonka declared his intention to replace the NFLPA with a new union. Paul Tagliabue, the new commissioner, signaled the league's support for the new venture, saying, "If Larry Csonka is willing to step up to the bargaining table, it makes sense to me."[42]

Upshaw called Csonka "a pawn of the NFL."

With Tagliabue's approval, NFL teams aided Csonka's effort by allowing him free access to their training camps to meet with players. Csonka promised to kick-start collective bargaining, and he assured players that he would get them free agency and lots more. The players weren't fooled. Csonka was met with icy stares and unfriendly questions. He got only a handful of union cards signed, and the NFL's cynical effort to create a company-approved union fizzled and died before the start of the 1990 season.

By now, it was clear that this had become a war of attrition. As Jeff Kessler told *USA Today*,[43] "The NFL's ongoing plot is to destroy the licensing business of the players association and indeed the association itself." The licensing wars heated up throughout the summer of 1990 and well into the fall of that year. At one meeting between NFLPA representatives and several members of the NFL's Quarterback Club, Boomer Esiason and Kessler got into a screaming match that almost got physical. Luckily for Kessler, 300-pound NFLPA president Mike Kenn, along with Upshaw and Doug Allen, stepped in to protect our antitrust genius from bodily harm.

I sat quietly next to Upshaw, contemplating the absurdity of the situation: the NFL had successfully stirred up dissension in our ranks and put the players at each other's throats. After a series of "fuck yous" were exchanged, I leaned over to Upshaw and said, "Tell them what free agency has done for the players in basketball and baseball; it's been a bonanza."

Upshaw proceeded to explain in great detail the enormous economic benefits of free agency, using specific examples from recent deals, like Patrick Ewing's $4.25 million and Hakeem Olajuwon's $3.7 million in basketball and Robin Yount's $3.2 million and Kirby Puckett's $2.7 million in baseball. These contracts were all multiyear and guaranteed, adding up to tens of millions of dollars for each player. With few exceptions, top-paid NFL players, mostly quarterbacks, made only a fraction of those sums and only with short-term, nonguaranteed contracts. "Instead of taking the NFL's chicken feed now," said Upshaw, "wait a year or so, and you'll own the whole damn farm."

NFL Properties's scheme to undercut the players' licensing business eventually failed. Most players were persuaded to stick with the NFLPA. Upshaw and Allen, who ran the players' licensing arm, destroyed the NFL's Quarterback Club by convincing its "members" that they'd earn a lot more money in free agency. In the end, that is exactly what happened.

• • •

For most of his three decades atop the NFL, Pete Rozelle had been the golden boy of the old-guard owners. Whatever his detractors might say about him—and I usually counted myself among them—there was no denying that the NFL had become the dominant sports league on his watch. But from the mid-1980s onward, Rozelle faced labor strife, declining TV revenues, and an influx of troublesome new owners. It was time for a regime change. Rozelle announced his retirement in the spring of 1989. After a hotly contested election, Paul Tagliabue, the league's top lawyer, was elected to fill the shoes of his friend and mentor Rozelle; his first day on the job was November 5, 1989, one day before the union announced its decertification.

The son of Italian parents, Tagliabue was a big guy, at least 6′5″. He had been the starting center for the Georgetown Hoyas in the early 1960s, setting rebounding records that lasted until Patrick Ewing came along. He graduated from NYU Law School in 1965, had a short stint in the government, and then spent the rest of his legal career in Washington, DC, at Covington, where his principal client had been the NFL.

I first met Tagliabue at the outset of the NASL litigation nearly 10 years earlier. He was a low-key man, some would say laconic, with a brilliant legal mind. While he was a skilled litigator, he was not a street fighter. He instinctively sought consensus and conciliation, which were not always highly valued by NFL owners. From the moment he ascended to the commissioner's office, he faced a difficult, institutional problem. Years earlier, Rozelle had ceded labor relations to the NFL Management Council as an independent body. Tagliabue's mission was to rein in the NFL Management Council and bring labor relations back under the auspices of the commissioner's office.

There was plainly no love lost between Tagliabue and Jack Donlan, the NFL's number one hardliner. Donlan had supported Tagliabue's chief rival for the job of commissioner, Jim Finks, president and general manager of the New Orleans Saints. Nor was Tagliabue a friend of Hugh Culverhouse, who had engineered Rozelle's early retirement. Tagliabue told me early on that his highest priority was to solve the league's labor problems. Given that Tagliabue was the chief architect of the NFL's legal strategy in the *Powell* case (the very case that forced the NFLPA to abandon collective bargaining) as well as the creator of Plan B (the player restriction plan we were challenging in *McNeil*), I was not sure I could take him at his word.

Negotiations under the Culverhouse-Donlan regime had been a nightmare.

Donlan and the volatile Doug Allen went after each other mercilessly on every issue from pension to free agency. Donlan's sarcasm was not endearing. Upshaw simply abhorred being in the same room with Culverhouse. Then there was Tex Schramm, the powerful president and general manager of the Dallas Cowboys in the pre–Jerry Jones era.

Schramm was known to show up at negotiating sessions with a drink or two under his big Texan belt, and when he drank, he got confrontational and sometimes just plain nasty. At one unforgettable labor meeting during the 1987 player strike, in the midst of a heated exchange on the subject of replacement players (a.k.a. scabs), Schramm had looked at Upshaw and said, "The players are just cattle and we're the ranchers. We can always get more cattle."

It's hard to think of a stupider, more inflammatory thing to say to a proud man like Upshaw—as if it could do anything other than deepen his resolve to win. Schramm would eat those words before it was all over.

Now in charge of the league, Tagliabue was desperate to get negotiations restarted. There had been no face-to-face meetings between player representatives and owners in nearly a year. Throughout the summer of 1990, Herb Dym, a partner at Covington and now the lead lawyer for the NFL, called me repeatedly, assuring me that their side wished to resolve all the outstanding lawsuits and get the parties back to the bargaining table. I set a couple of conditions before agreeing to take a meeting: one, that the meetings be strictly confidential, and two, that they not be referred to by either side as collective bargaining. This second condition was especially serious. Sitting down to bargain with the owners could be used against us in the litigations as evidence of the NFL's contention that we were a "union in hiding."

Finally, I got a call directly from Tagliabue agreeing to my conditions. The two sides assembled on August 23, 1990, at Weil's offices in the General Motors Building. Joining lawyers from Covington and Faegre & Benson, the NFL's Minneapolis law firm, were Tagliabue, Donlan, Culverhouse, and Wellington Mara, whom I knew well from my prior NFL cases. Only Kessler and I represented the players.

The meeting was a disaster from the start. Donlan wisecracked and Culverhouse lectured. The owner of a team that had two winning seasons in 14 years of play, Culverhouse insisted on telling us how lousy our case was and assured us that the NFL would bury us in court. We told Culverhouse he was full of shit and then listened quietly and waited for an offer that never came. Tagliabue and Mara were clearly embarrassed by the behavior of their cohorts. Worse, as soon as Donlan walked out of the meeting, he told the press that we had been in collective bargaining, despite his signed pledge not to do so. We were outraged. I called Tagliabue after the meeting and told him, "Forget it, we are not meeting again. My orders from the players are to go full bore on the litigation." He was plainly disappointed and apologized for Donlan's breach of our agreement.

Within a matter of months, Tagliabue fired Donlan, and the management council came under his direct supervision. Culverhouse was asked off the council. Wellington Mara and Dan Rooney, the Pittsburgh Steelers owner, replaced him. After Donlan "resigned" in early February 1991, Tagliabue hired Harold Henderson, a career management labor negotiator who had spent most of his professional life in the railroad industry. Henderson, a graduate of Stanford and Harvard Business School, was tough but engaging and certainly no hardliner. He was the highest-ranking African American at the NFL at the time. Initially, Upshaw refused to meet with Henderson, though they eventually became good friends and golfing buddies. Upshaw's relationship with Tagliabue had always been adversarial, but eventually they too would become more friends than enemies.

The NFL soon filed a motion in the *McNeil* case asking Judge Doty to declare the NFLPA's decertification process invalid; their hope was that Plan B would continue to be protected by their labor defense. Without it, they knew they would have a hard time defending Plan B at trial. On May 23, 1991, Doty rejected the NFL's arguments in their entirety. In the first ruling of its kind, Doty declared that the decertification (a.k.a. disclaimer) process was valid and that the players had the right to give up bargaining rights in exchange for antitrust rights. Indeed, he pointed out that the NFL itself had, in the earlier *Powell* case, conceded that their labor defense would end "if the employees ceased to be represented by the certified union." He ruled that as of December 5, 1989, at the latest, the NFL's labor defense had ended.

"This proves that the players made the right decision when they voted to end the union," Upshaw told the press. "As I've always said, the NFL can run but they can't hide."[44]

The NFL owners were left exposed and would now have to defend Plan B on its merits. This meant only one thing: they would have to trot out "competitive balance"—their old shibboleth! It was the only play they had left.

A month later, on June 26, 1991, in a case arising out of Larry Csonka's failed union, the NLRB issued its own ruling on our decertification efforts. They separately reinforced Doty's ruling and held that "the fact that the disclaimer was motivated by litigation strategy, *i.e.*, to deprive the NFL of a defense to players' antitrust suits and to free players to engage in individual bargaining for free agency, is irrelevant so long as the disclaimer is otherwise unequivocal and adhered to." Within a single month, the door was twice slammed on the NFL's labor defense.

The litigation floodgates were now open. More lawsuits were filed, and discovery was also unleashed. Over the course of the year, hundreds of thousands of documents were exchanged, and dozens of players and agents were deposed by the NFL. We deposed league officials and NFL owners. Depositions were even taken of several people from baseball, including then baseball union head Don Fehr and commissioner Bud Selig.

The NFL took depositions of players and agents, presumably to show that players were making good money and didn't really need free agency. We took depositions of their side to show that their so-called competitive balance defense was nonsense. Much of this was pro forma; the real battle would take place at trial before a Minnesota jury, now scheduled for February 1992.

Meanwhile, the fighting on both sides continued to escalate. Tagliabue met with former union head Ed Garvey, who was leading a group of former NFL players against the NFLPA in a dispute over pension issues. Tom Condon, a former player and now a leading agent and Upshaw's close friend, accused Garvey of being "the owners' stooge." Meanwhile, Henderson, the NFL's new head of labor relations, spent his time trying to woo players back into the union fold with promises of a better tomorrow. He attempted to put together a settlement proposal to be made to anyone who would listen. No one did. He made several attempts to meet with Upshaw, all of which were declined.

On our side, we kept up the pressure, fulfilling my promise to Tagliabue by filing new lawsuits in both federal and state courts all around the country. We brought a new antitrust class action involving both free agency and players' health insurance before the Los Angeles federal court with Marcus Allen, the Raiders star running back, as the lead plaintiff. We filed another antitrust action in Washington, DC, over preseason pay with Mike Tice, the Seahawks tight end, as the lead plaintiff. We filed state court actions in New York on behalf of Joe Morris of the Giants and Mickey Shuler of the Jets over per diem payments. We brought yet another state court action in Indiana with Chris Chandler, the Colts quarterback, as the plaintiff in an arbitration dispute. These cases were filed throughout the summer and fall of 1991.

The only reason we were able to afford all this was because, in the early 1990s, licensing revenues for the NFLPA had doubled and then doubled again. Five trading card companies were competing with each other and pouring tens of millions of dollars into the NFLPA to use the players' pictures on their trading cards. Bubble gum had never tasted so good. The fact that we continued to play during this extended fight was also an enormous advantage—no missed paychecks, no immediate pressure.

I spent a lot of time keeping Gene and the players updated on the status of the various cases. We held player meetings everywhere from Daytona Beach to Maui to Tampa (during January, for the 1991 Super Bowl). Key player leaders—president Mike Kenn and NFLPA officers

Tim Brown, Dan Marino, and Dave Duerson among them—were instrumental in maintaining player solidarity. In Tampa, just as the first Gulf War began, dozens of players pledged to keep up their fight for freedom however long and at whatever cost. Then, with tears in our eyes, we listened to Whitney Houston's stunning rendition of the "Star-Spangled Banner" and watched my Giants eke out a 20–19 victory over Buffalo as Scott Norwood's last-second kick missed wide right.

As the months passed and we got closer to trial, Tagliabue and Henderson kept up their relentless attempt to get us "back to the bargaining table." We simply refused. After Donlan had breached our agreement to maintain secrecy, we would never take that chance again. Tagliabue knew that it was on him to rebuild the league's credibility, and he called me almost every other week. Slowly, we began to develop a relationship of mutual respect and trust.

Finally, Tagliabue and Henderson called to tell me that the NFL owners had approved a free agency proposal at their meeting in Dallas in the summer of 1991. We had heard rumors that Tagliabue and some less-hardline owners were looking for a way out, but we remained skeptical. Nevertheless, we agreed to meet at Weil's offices; once again, only Kessler and I attended on behalf of the players.

Gene, Dick, and Doug refused to participate, fearing another leak and another effort to undercut our legal position.

The meeting took place at Weil on October 9, 1991. Tagliabue, joined by Henderson and Pittsburgh's Dan Rooney, took the lead in discussions and outlined their proposal. They were trying to play good cop. But as polite and respectful as their tone may have been, their offer was no better than a slap in the face: Players could become free agents after *seven* years in the league—and only if they made less than $800,000 (plus other restrictions). For this major "concession," the owners wanted a salary cap and a rookie wage scale. Oh, and they wanted the NFLPA to reorganize as a union.

There was nothing about this proposal that was the least bit appealing. Their acceptance of free agency was purely nominal—with all the restrictions, exceptions, and exemptions, it would apply only to a handful of journeyman players. And the salary cap was a deal killer. It was clear that there would be no settlement in advance of a trial, which was set to start in a few months.

Throughout the fall of 1991, we locked horns on just about everything. We demanded to see the financial records for each team as part of discovery, and when they refused, Judge Doty ordered that the records be turned over. The owners were outraged. For the first time in the history of professional football, we would get a glimpse behind the curtain and find out for ourselves just how profitable the NFL really was.

As the trial approached, several prominent sportswriters slowly began to recognize that the NFL's propaganda about the dire potential impact of free agency was just that—propaganda. How come free agency hadn't ruined basketball or baseball? In fact, both were thriving. All of a sudden, NFL stalwarts like Will McDonough (*Boston Globe*), Thomas George (*New York Times*), and Peter Gammons (*Sports Illustrated*) were writing stories questioning the need for Plan B. I was on the phone with these guys and others, feeding them real facts about "competitive balance" and pointing to the recent dynasties of the Steelers, Cowboys, and 49ers, which flew in the face of the NFL's shaky narrative.

As it happened, Super Bowl XXVI was to be held in Minneapolis in January 1992, pitting the Redskins against the Bills, whose general manager was Bill Polian from the old USFL. By the time of Super Bowl weekend, Judge Doty had agreed to the NFL's request to postpone the trial until June 1992. The NFL's lawyers claimed they needed extra time to bring in additional counsel—who turned out to be none other than Frank Rothman, another USFL alumnus.

The day before the Super Bowl, Tagliabue, still working toward a pretrial settlement, announced that the owners were prepared to improve their free agency proposal. Rothman, now the public face of the NFL, couldn't constrain himself from spouting off to the media. "I don't know why it is so hard for people to understand," he told the *San Francisco Chronicle*. "Go to total free agency, and Los Angeles,

DON'T BE AFRAID TO WIN

San Francisco, New York and Chicago are going to buy all the players." Rothman also told the *San Francisco Chronicle*, "If you want to eliminate all player restraints now, what you are doing is you're tampering with the game that has proved to be the single most successful sporting enterprise in the world. I don't see any players suffering."[45]

When it came to playing the media, Rothman was a maestro. In response, I told the *New York Times*, "The NFL doesn't need Plan B for competitive balance, they want Plan B for two reasons: greed and power."[46]

As the weeks passed, the rhetoric heated up. In March, I described the NFL as "the last bastion of communism in the world" in *USA Today*.[47] OK, a bit of an overstatement, but they were the ones who set the bar!

As the trial approached, we decided to test the strength of our case before typical Minnesota jurors. We had heard all about "Minnesota nice," but we wanted to find out just how nice Minnesota jurors were going to be to our players. By then, there were jury research companies who specialized in this. We hired a pair—Ann Cole Associates and the National Jury Project—to run mock trials, in which the best case for both sides was presented to groups of potential jurors, who then deliberated over what they had heard, closely watched by the lawyers and clients from behind one-way mirrors. It is a fascinating and sometimes scary exercise.

In the spring of 1992, we held a series of jury simulations in a suburb of Minneapolis. Kessler presented the NFL's case, and I presented for the players. We went hard at it for several hours, then repeated the process three times over the next six weeks, presenting our case to nine different "juries," with a total of almost 100 mock jurors listening and deliberating. The whole thing was exhausting.

It was during these exercises that someone on our side used the term "chucklehead" to describe a mock juror who was a rabid sports fan with a predilection for believing the bullshit mantra of team owners: free agency destroys competitive balance, causes teams in smaller markets to go bankrupt, and otherwise hastens the downfall of our great nation. The problem with these chuckleheads, we found, isn't

Larry Fleisher prepares to file the Oscar Robertson lawsuit.
APRIL 1970

Fleisher at Madison
Square Garden.
CIRCA 1980

ITINERARY

Wednesday, July 7	Arrive San Francisco Overnight at Hyatt Embarcadero
Thursday, July 8	Leave hotel by bus for airport 1:00 p.m. - Japan Airlines flight leaves for Tokyo
Friday, July 9	3:30 p.m. - Arrive Tokyo Overnight in Tokyo
Saturday, July 10	10:40 a.m. - Leave Tokyo 2:40 p.m. - Arrive Beijing
Sunday, July 11	Sightseeing to be arranged by Chinese 2:50 p.m. - 10 players leave for exhibition in Shenyang, arriving at 4:00 p.m. on CAAC Flight 6202 7:30 p.m. - Competition in Shenyang
Monday, July 12	9:15 a.m. - 10 players return to Beijing from Shenyang, arriving at 10:30 a.m. on CAAC Flight 6303 Light sightseeing in the morning 3:00 p.m. - Practice at the Stadium; women's exercise class 6:30 p.m. - PRC Basketball Association will host a Peking Duck banquet, followed by a visit to a disco
Tuesday, July 13	Trip to Great Wall and Summer Palace 7:30 p.m. - Exhibition game of NBA Players (East vs. West) at the Stadium Post-game dinner at the hotel
Wednesday, July 14	Mao's Tomb, Forbidden City, and Imperial Palace 7:30 p.m. - Competition at Stadium (NBA vs. PRC National Team); half-hour exhibition between NBA Players will precede the game Post-game dinner at the hotel
Thursday, July 15	Sightseeing (underground shelter and/or subway) in the morning Shopping in the afternoon - downtown or at the Friendship Store 6:30 p.m. - NBA will host a banquet at the Great Hall of the People

Itinerary for the NBPA "China Tour."
JULY 1982

Fleisher, Bob Lanier, Freddie Brown, Paul Silas, myself, Rita Satz, and Beth Havlicek at the Ming Tombs.

JULY 1982

Maurice Lucas and
Kareem Abdul-Jabbar at
Beijing's Forbidden City.
JULY 1982

Myself and the "Big O" at the Great Wall.

JULY 1982

Gene Upshaw, all-time great left guard.
CIRCA 1978

Pretrial "trash talk" as players
get ready for the *McNeil v. NFL* trial.
MARCH 1992

Bruce Meyer and
myself on break at
the *McNeil* trial.
JULY 1992

Upshaw gives his trial team a pep talk during the *McNeil* trial.

AUGUST 1992

Card game waiting for the *McNeil* verdict.

SEPTEMBER 1992

The $35 Million Hat.

NOVEMBER 1992

Upshaw, myself, and NFLPA president Mike Kenn celebrating victory in Hawaii.

MARCH 1993

Myself and NFL commissioner
Paul Tagliabue at Dan Rooney's
American Ireland Fund dinner.
MAY 1995

September 26, 1995

Dear Jim:

Ernestine and I are very disappointed we won't be there to help you
bring in this landmark birthday! And what a landmark it is. I'm looking
forward to turning 50 in about 8 years.

As your family and friends gather in this celebration, know that
Ernestine and I are sending you our very best wishes. We raise a glass in
toast for you on this special day.

Sincerely,

Bill Bradley
United States Senator

Jim Quinn
1 Maple Way
Armonk, New York 10504

*Jim —
Happy Fifty!
Tell me how it
feels. I'll be there
in about seven years.
Bill*

NOT PRINTED AT GOVERNMENT EXPENSE

Note from Senator
Bill Bradley sending
best wishes on my
50th birthday.
SEPTEMBER 1995

John Havlicek and
Dave and Gerri
DeBusschere
at my surprise
50th birthday party.
OCTOBER 1995

NFLPA Annual
Meeting in Hawaii
with Katy, Tierney,
and Kerrin Quinn, plus
Dick (a.k.a. Richard)
Berthelsen and Jeff
Kessler.
MARCH 1998

Myself, Berthelsen,
and Kessler in Hawaii,
relieved that Upshaw's
successor, DeMaurice
Smith, has been
unanimously elected by
the NFL players.
MARCH 2009

just that they're wrong—it's that they can't be reasoned with. As much as they love watching football, they believe that the sanctity of the sport is threatened by the greed and selfishness of the players, not the owners. And these chuckleheads are going to the grave with that conviction.

So one thing we learned from these mock trials was to keep chuckleheads off our jury at all costs.

Fortunately, the chucklehead rule had a flip side. On our mock juries, we found that women consistently voted in favor of the players. Though they generally didn't award big damages, women almost universally expressed the belief that players should have the right, just like everyone else in America, to choose where they worked and for whom. The results were astonishing: 90 percent of the women voted in favor of the players in these mock exercises. As a result, we won all nine mock juries. We walked away from this confident that if we had enough women on the jury, we would get a winning verdict for the players.

Much later, I learned that the NFL had also run similar jury simulations and discovered the same thing, although not to the same degree as had shown up in our exercises. It turned out that the NFL's lawyers were more focused on union membership—the fear that workers of the world might unite in the jury room and penalize the plutocratic owners. So their emphasis was on preventing union members from sitting on our *McNeil* jury, a catastrophic misstep.

Throughout the first half of 1992, the NFL kept up the pressure to get back to the negotiating the table. Following a series of one-on-one meetings and telephone calls between me and Tagliabue, we held confidential meetings in May and June with Tagliabue, Harold Henderson, and Dan Rooney. For the first time, Gene, Dick, and Doug participated but only as "consultants" to Kessler and me. Tagliabue and his team had agreed that there was to be no collective bargaining. The discussions were only about the settlement of the pending lawsuits.

By this time, Bill Polian had joined the NFL's team as their "football man." Polian was fiery, opinionated, smart, and funny, and even though we disagreed on everything, I came to like him. With wiry red hair and a face that expressed the map of Ireland, he approached everything with high energy and even higher hyperbole. At one point, Polian exclaimed that if we won, "the golden age of football is gone."

These meetings continued until the week before the trial was set to start. All that their side wanted to talk about was a salary cap, and they were insisting on a so-called hard cap with no exceptions. We told them we didn't want any cap, just free agency, pure and simple. We got nowhere.

Finally, after one last frustrating session, this time in a Minneapolis hotel room just before trial, we all shook hands and departed. When we got to the hotel lobby, Upshaw looked down at Kessler and me and said simply, "Buckle your chin straps, we're going to trial."

CHAPTER 14

"God Almighty Free at Last"

IN EARLY JUNE 1992, THE WEIL TEAM MOVED LOCK, stock, and barrel to Minneapolis. We had a tough summer ahead of us. When you're from New York, you don't necessarily know how unbearably hot it can get in Minnesota. We rented suites of rooms at the Radisson Hotel downtown and set up shop with our own mini-office a few blocks down the street, in the city's tallest structure, the IDS Center. I was lead counsel, with Kessler as my sidekick along with our dedicated team of associates: Bruce Meyer, David Feher, and Jonathan Weiss. Ed Glennon and his partner from the Lindquist firm, Carol Reiger, both of whom would play roles at the trial, were just a couple floors below us in the same building. Gene, Dick, and Doug moved out from DC as well. The whole enterprise was overseen by my no-nonsense assistant, Brenda Young, a woman with a tough veneer and a heart of gold. She was aided by her good friend Sharon Adams. Only Upshaw could crack that cool exterior and make Brenda smile even in the toughest of times. That was Upshaw's way. He was the type of guy who would walk into the kitchen to talk to the staff whenever he went to a restaurant. He loved people, and he always had to know what was going on.

The NFL lawyers also showed up in force. There was the inimitable Frank Rothman and his young partner, Shep Goldfein, along with a corps of Skadden Arps associates. Herb Dym and Jeff Pash from Covington and a bunch of their young lawyers were on hand, along with several lawyers from the NFL's local firm of Faegre & Benson. I could not have cared less how many lawyers they had arrayed against us. This wasn't about numbers or power; it was about making a jury of midwesterners see through the NFL's legal smoke screen and recognize a greedy attempt to suppress players' salaries while taking away their freedom to choose where they wanted to work and live their lives.

The trial was now scheduled to start on June 15, 1992, in the old Minneapolis federal courthouse, directly across the street from a gentlemen's club by the name of the Solid Gold. As a newly appointed judge, Doty had the least seniority in the courthouse; hence his was the smallest courtroom in the building. A large pole in the middle of the courtroom partially blocked the view of spectators. The morning the trial was to begin, with jury selection, the gallery was packed with media, players, owners, officials, and potential jurors, as well as a handful of onlookers. Standing room only. The tables for the opposing lawyers were literally right next to each other. To my left was Frank Rothman; to my right, Jeff Kessler; and directly behind us sat Gene, Dick, and Doug, with our various assistants spread all over. It was chaos from the start, and we knew it would be like this for many months.

A portion of the gallery had been set aside for potential jurors. Over a hundred people had been summoned and asked to fill out a lengthy questionnaire. This allowed both sides to winnow the group down to a few dozen. Most of them were dressed informally, although some had dressed up for the occasion—suits and ties for the men, skirts and blouses for the ladies. From their demeanor, a few seemed excited and interested in being there, but most looked glum, fearful of being stuck on a months-long antitrust case, which would surely ruin their summer.

The bailiff then brought back into the courtroom the remaining potential jurors: white, mostly middle-aged, with a pretty equal split between men and women. For the next several hours, we went through the arduous task of questioning each of them individually, our sights set on finding nine acceptable candidates (for a six-person jury with three alternates). In an unusual move, Judge Doty let the lawyers question the jurors directly, a process known as voir dire. Typically, in federal court, only the judge asks questions of the jurors.

When we got down to 20 potential jurors, Judge Doty told us to begin to use our strikes. Each side had six that we could use for any reason to excuse a candidate. The process began. We didn't over-think it. We had only two goals: as many women as possible, and no chuckleheads.

We used all our strikes on men and watched, to our delight, as the NFL did the same. We were trying to eliminate chuckleheads; they were trying to eliminate union members. When all the strikes were done, Upshaw and I smiled at each other.

"Upshaw, it is all women," I whispered. We were ecstatic. Nine women (eventually eight because one juror was excused several days into the trial), all non–sports fans except for one, would decide the fate of the NFL. How delicious. How delightful. How ironic.

At this point, we were ready for the opening statements.

We had worked on the opening for weeks, honing our themes and anticipating the NFL's response. As I stood up, with the usual butter-flies in my stomach, I thought to myself, this may be the biggest case of your life—don't fuck it up.

I went first and outlined the players' case, conceding that football players are highly paid but emphasizing just how risky their profes-sion is due to injuries and intense competition for jobs. I pointed out how highly profitable the NFL clubs were and that Plan B was about not competitive balance but holding down player salaries, plain and simple. I described Plan B as a "dodge, just a slick way around the antitrust laws."[48] Most importantly, I told the jury that these play-ers were like anybody else: "They have the right to work where and for whom they want, just like anybody else in America." I said this case was about "freedom" and asked the jury not to be fooled by overblown rhetoric and fancy footwork from the NFL's highly skilled lawyers, pointing directly "at that nice Mr. Rothman sitting over there."

Rothman got up and, in his most stentorian voice, predictably labeled the eight plaintiffs as "selfish ingrates." He went after Freeman

McNeil and Don Majkowski in particular, referring to McNeil as a "multimillionaire" and Majkowski as an "abysmal failure." He then went on to warn the jury that tampering with the NFL's system, specifically Plan B, could lead to disaster, hinting—absurdly—that the league might actually collapse. It was a tour de force of nonsense, but it was well delivered, and it certainly made us nervous.

I later learned that the day before the opening statements, Rothman realized he had not brought his "lucky shoes" with him—special shoes that he apparently wore during all his trials. A young lawyer from Skadden Arp's Los Angeles office was directed to pick up Rothman's shoes from home and fly them to Minneapolis on a redeye flight so he would have them for the start of the trial. He was forever after known among us as "Lucky Shoes Frank."

After hearing the opening statements, Commissioner Tagliabue told the media, "Whatever reason we had to settle has gone by the boards. We are going to win."[49] He would eat those words.

The media was all over the trial. Reporters from the *New York Times*, *Sports Illustrated*, *Washington Post*, Minneapolis's *Star Tribune*, and *Philadelphia Inquirer* were there almost every day throughout the three-month trial. Even the *National Law Journal* got into the act:

> Accusations of indentured servitude and fakery. Glitz. Cheap shots. Power. Intimidation. Big money and guys in dark suits. Hero worship, humility and broken Sunday dreams.
>
> Welcome to the courtroom of U.S. District Judge David S. Doty, which has turned into what might as well be called the National Football League Laundromat, a place that carries no guarantee of wiping clean stained images.
>
> After the spin cycle is through around here and they air the place out, the fabric of professional sports in America will likely be forever changed.
>
> On its face, the case centers on the question of whether a professional football player is free to play for whoever pays him the highest price; and whether the NFL's Plan B "protection" system,

set up in 1989, is in violation of the nation's antitrust laws that are, as plaintiffs' attorney James W. Quinn, of New York's Weil, Gotshal and Manges put it, "our economic bill of rights."

Mr. Quinn has been blunt in the courtroom before the eight women jury: "The players are the game. Without the players, there is no game. There are no profits. The talk about salaries is a diversion. This is about economic freedom, not high salaries. This is the entertainment business."[50]

The coverage throughout the trial was generally favorable to the players. The football writers were finally beginning to see through the NFL's bombast; the sky was not about to fall, and civilization as we know it would not end if some football players were allowed to sell their services in an open market.

As our first witness I called Randy Vataha, our old friend and ally. He knew the game as a player, an agent, and (briefly) as part owner of a USFL franchise. He had truly seen it all. We were counting on him to be both likeable and knowledgeable on the stand, and he did not disappoint. He was excellent at explaining many of our key themes, including the risk of injury, the players' short careers, and the fact that players had all sorts of different reasons for where they wanted to play. "My experience is some players say, 'Hey, I want to be in a small city; I hate to be in New York,'" he said, "and other players say, 'I love the big city.' It varies all over the place."

This undercut the NFL's "flocking" theory that all players wanted to play in warm weather cities or in big markets where they could earn extra income from endorsements.

Plan B, Vataha went on to say, was actually "anticompetitive balance" because it allowed good teams to hoard talent and keep the best players away from bad teams that needed them to improve. This tore the legs out from under the NFL's competitive balance argument because it showed that if players were able to freely sign, they would go where they would be most productive, whether it was in Los Angeles or Green Bay, Chicago, or Tampa Bay.

Seeing how much the jury liked Vataha, Rothman did very little on cross. He just wanted to get him off the witness stand.

We followed with an array of our plaintiffs, starting with Dave Richards, a massive offensive lineman for the San Diego Chargers (and a Vataha client). Despite his size and profession, Richards had a gentle disposition, and he told a compelling story about what happened when he complained to his coach about making less money than players he had beat out for a starting position. If he didn't like it, the coach told him, he could always "go back to bagging groceries at Vons supermarket." He also testified that, given the chance, he would like to play somewhere in Texas where he grew up. When I asked him why this was so important to him, he looked directly at the all-women jury and said, "Because that is where my mom lives."

It was shameless stuff. I looked over at the women on the jury, and every one of them was smiling. They fell in love with Dave Richards. Rothman saw it too and had no choice but to go easy on him on the cross.

Next came another Vataha client—Don Majkowski from Green Bay. This one did not go so well. Majkowski, a quarterback, was a cocky, good-looking guy, the type who left homecoming queens in tears in high school. I tried to soften his image a bit by emphasizing his involvement in local charities in the Green Bay area, but I couldn't do much about his flashy smile. Rothman was licking his chops, and when he got his chance, he went after Majkowski with a vengeance, pointing out that he had just been paid $1.5 million for an "abysmal" performance in the 1990 season. Rothman implied that what Majkowski really wanted was to ditch Green Bay for a big market like Chicago or New York where he could get more endorsements.

As it happened, the one juror who liked football was a Green Bay fan—we had nicknamed her the "Packer Backer." Rothman played a tune just for her, slicing and dicing Majkowski like a salami. It reminded me of what great trial lawyering is all about, and there is nothing worse than seeing it done to one of your star witnesses.

After Majkowski limped off the witness stand, we took him out for a few drinks and assured him he'd done great. I don't think he bought it.

We followed Majkowski with Freeman McNeil. At his deposition, McNeil had testified that he was satisfied with his own situation in New York, and that seemed to present a nice opening for Rothman. It made me nervous. We had no choice but to put him on the stand—the case was called *McNeil v. National Football League*, after all—but I hoped to make it as brief as possible. I finished my questions in less than 15 minutes and then held my breath as Rothman rose from his seat and approached McNeil.

Rothman, in his typical style, banged Freeman around for a while over his multimillion-dollar contract and the fact that he said he was happy with the Jets—so there was really no reason for him to be in this courtroom, was there? But then Rothman stepped over the line: he accused McNeil of being greedy.

There was rapt silence in the courtroom as McNeil began to testify haltingly with tears in his eyes. "Well, Mr. Rothman, let me put it like this: If you think giving a person money will make up for restricting that person—do you think that is fair, sir? I don't. I am asking for the right to make a choice." It was electric, a true emotional tour de force. The jury glared at Rothman, who had not much left to say. Minutes later, he returned to his seat. I had no further questions for Freeman. He had said it all.

McNeil's attorney, Tony Curto, was the next witness. When Rothman asked him on cross-examination about the individual negotiations for restricted players being "a two-way street," Curto responded, "It's a two-way street with four lanes in one direction and one in the other." Another shut-down answer. Rothman had no further questions for Curto either.

We then called Tom Condon to testify about Irv Eatman, one of the original *McNeil* plaintiffs, who withdrew from the case after the president of the Kansas City Chiefs, Carl Peterson, threatened to blackball him from the NFL. Condon, Eatman's agent, testified that Peterson had told him that if Eatman didn't drop the lawsuit, he would never play in the NFL again. Condon's testimony ended the second week of trial.

Throughout that long, hot summer, Upshaw embraced the role of master of ceremonies. He kept everyone loose, assigning nicknames and peppering everyone with good-natured jibes and occasional hijinks. Our Weil associate Bruce Meyer earned the nickname "the Cloud" from Upshaw because Bruce was always worrying about the outcome. This offset Kessler's overbrimming optimism, which often needed to be reined in. Upshaw gave Kessler the name "Lead Dog" and kept a tight leash on him. Luckily, I remained just "Quinn."

After trial each day, the team would return to our makeshift offices, briefly review the proceedings, and then spend several hours preparing for the next day. Upshaw took charge of our food requirements, always selecting from among his favorites: Manny's, Murray's, Matt's, Morton's, and McCormick's, with an occasional sojourn to Al's Eatery for a late-night breakfast. I had to run even harder along the Mississippi every morning just to avoid the extra poundage.

The trial droned on for another week as the remaining five plaintiffs and several agents testified one by one. During this part of the trial, dozens of players flew in from around the country to watch the trial. Whenever a player asked directions to the courthouse, we invariably told them that it was across the street from The Solid Gold. Every one of the players made it to the courthouse without further assistance.

On June 29, we called our free agency expert, my old friend Don Fehr, who was the executive director of the MLBPA at the time. I asked him to testify specifically about competitive balance in baseball in the wake of free agency. Don had the data at his fingertips; in the 15 years of free agency, 17 different teams had won league pennants and 11 different teams had won the World Series—virtually all from small- and midsized markets. In fact, teams from New York, Chicago, and Los Angeles had mostly ranked at the very bottom of their respective divisions. Fehr reinforced Vataha's testimony with his observation that "far and away the most important thing for most players, and I say players are like anybody else, there is nothing that is universally true, is that they want to have a chance to try and be on a team that wins and they want to play. And when I say they want to play, they want to play every day and as often as they can."

Fortunately for us, everyone in the courtroom was well acquainted with the recent fortunes of one small-market baseball team, the Minnesota Twins, who had won the 1991 World Series. When Rothman cross-examined Fehr, he tried to incite fear in the courtroom by pointing out that because of free agency, Twins star Kirby Puckett might abandon Minnesota. Puckett, said Rothman, was a "public asset."

"Mr. Rothman, you understand that Kirby Puckett is not a monument, he is not a building, he's a person," responded Fehr.

That put Rothman right back in his seat.

When we broke for the long July 4th weekend, I made a quick trip over to Madison, Wisconsin, to visit my eldest daughter, Kellianne, whose husband, Chris, was studying for his PhD at the University of Wisconsin. After dinner, we watched the holiday fireworks display over scenic Lake Mendota. Watching the fireworks, it struck me that we were fighting for the same kind of freedom that our Founding Fathers had in mind two centuries ago. The players wanted economic independence and the opportunity to exploit their individual talents in a free and open marketplace.

The following morning, I flew back to the Twin Cities to prepare our next witness: Gene Upshaw. I expected his testimony to be critical; he had spent a decade being stonewalled by the NFL owners about free agency. He could testify firsthand as to their stubborn refusal to grant their players even a smidgen of dignity.

Upshaw took over the courtroom the same way he took over a football field. He was smart, engaging, funny, and the jurors loved him. I quickly established that under the NFL's free agency restrictions, only 1 in 3,000 players had actually been able to move from one team to another in the last 10 years. I asked Upshaw during that same period how many teams had actually switched cities. He testified that three teams had moved in that same time frame: the Raiders, from Oakland to Los Angeles; the Colts, from Baltimore to Indianapolis; and the Cardinals, from St. Louis to Phoenix. "There were more teams that moved during that period of time than players," he said, "and there were several other teams that also threatened to move." He called it "franchise free agency."

Upshaw next recounted various statements made to him by Schramm and Culverhouse during negotiations for free agency. They had told him, "We are not going to bid against each other, so just forget it." Schramm, like Culverhouse, had also told Upshaw that "there would never be free agency for players, not in five years after ten years or fifteen or even thirty." That was how nasty and condescending they had been. I looked over and could see the reaction of the NFL's lawyers. They weren't happy. When Upshaw referenced Schramm's comment that players were like cattle and the owners were the ranchers, Rothman exploded and asked for a mistrial. Judge Doty calmly instructed the jury to disregard the cattle testimony because he had previously ruled it was too inflammatory. But as they say in Texas, "You can't take the skunk out of the jury box." Our eight jurors heard the cattle testimony, and no matter what the judge told them, they were not likely to forget it. No one from the NFL ever came into the courtroom to deny it.

We then called Bobby Hebert, the Saints quarterback and former USFL star. His story was unique, and we hoped it would score us points with an all-female jury. Hebert was by then a backup quarterback, and he had wanted to be traded. Instead, the Saints cut his pay in half. He and his wife, who often advised him on his career, went in to see Jim Finks, the president of the Saints. When Mrs. Hebert protested that the Saints were treating her husband unfairly, Finks called her a "hard-headed redneck"—yet another reason for the all-female jury of Minnesota to turn against the NFL, if they hadn't already.

After Hebert, we called our expert economist, Roger Noll, a leading authority on the economics of professional sports. Even Buffalo and Green Bay, the smallest markets in the NFL, were tremendously profitable, Noll testified, adding that many owners actually paid themselves salaries, a not-so-clever way to hide real profits by charging these "salaries" as expenses. Between 1987 and 1990, owners paid themselves as much as $60 million, accounted for as general expenses. Philadelphia's Norman Braman paid himself $7.5 million a year to "own" his own team.

Noll was the last witness before Judge Doty recessed the trial on July 9 for a two-week period. I flew off to see my family in Cape Cod to relax and prepare for cross-examination of the NFL's witnesses. During our so-called vacation, we invited Jeff Kessler and his wife, Regina, to visit us for a few days at the Cape. One sunny afternoon, sitting on our deck overlooking the Atlantic, we created a chart for Jeff to use on cross-examination of the NFL's expert economist. It read:

Unrestricted	Restricted
NFL Owners	NFL Players
NFL Employees	Prisoners
NFL Coaches	Little Children
The Rest of America	Slaves

During that same week, I received a message from Tagliabue, eager to get settlement negotiations restarted. I returned the call message from a pay phone at the Barnstable County Fair, watching from afar as my family enjoyed the last day of the festivities. It was a hell of a place to discuss free agency. I finally agreed to come down to New York the next day to meet Tagliabue, Mara, and Dan Rooney for dinner to see if we could settle the case before it went to the jury. I told Paul that I was feeling pretty good about our chances with this jury but that I was always willing to listen to what they had to say.

We met in an Italian restaurant on the East Side. Their intentions weren't hard to read—they knew as well as we did what direction the trial was heading in, and they wanted to get out in front of it and settle. Unfortunately, they brought no new ideas to the table. They stuck to their position that players only become eligible for free agency after seven years. They also hadn't relented on the salary cap. It was a pleasant enough dinner. By this time, I had gotten to know and like all three of them, particularly Dan Rooney. But it wasn't hard for me to separate my feelings for them as people from my responsibility to my clients. I said thanks for dinner and flew back to the Cape the next day to prepare for the rest of the trial.

On July 27, we were back in Judge Doty's cramped courtroom. Our last witness, Mike Glassman, an expert in damage calculations, took the stand. Glassman had helped baseball players secure a $300 million settlement when the owners conspired not to bid on baseball's free agents. Our eight football plaintiffs, Glassman assessed, were entitled to damages of $4 million. Extrapolating that amount across all 1,500 football players could lead to hundreds of millions of dollars in potential damages on a league-wide basis.

Rothman went after him hard on the cross. He questioned Glassman's assumptions and accused him of just making things up.

Then we rested our case and sat back to watch Rothman pull off the impossible—defend Plan B.

The NFL's first witness was the architect of Plan B, Commissioner Tagliabue. Just two years into his job, he didn't testify so much as argue his case from the stand, like any good lawyer would. He talked about the NFL's supposed need for competitive balance and continuity; in other words, the typical nonsense.

On cross-examination, I attacked the premise that Tagliabue was a witness—wasn't he really a lawyer there to defend his own Plan B?

The NFL then called a string of club general managers, including Chuck Schmidt from the Lions, Carl Peterson from the Chiefs, and Eddie Accorsi from the Browns. It wasn't hard to see why they liked Plan B. It made their jobs infinitely easier, to say nothing of the major bucks it saved their teams. As a lawyer, you know you're in good shape when the witnesses don't say anything remotely unexpected. I could've scripted the GMs' testimony. It was all about the continuity of the league, competitive balance, and their bullshit "flocking" theory.

It was easily debunked on cross-examination by pointing to basketball and baseball, where free agency had actually improved competitive balance and free agents had signed with teams in cities big and small, cold and warm.

The NFL did have one standout witness—George Young, the general manager of the New York Giants and the man who had turned the moribund Giants into two-time Super Bowl champions.

Young was a real presence: a jovial man weighing close to 300 pounds, chockablock with football wit and wisdom. Young did yeoman's work trying to defend the indefensible. At one point, he joked in response to a question about how he went about picking talent that "I wouldn't hire anyone fatter than me." The entire courtroom, including the jury, burst out in laughter.

During a break, before starting my cross-examination, Young and I got into a conversation about who was going to start at quarterback for the Giants. I had been an avid fan of the team since the Charley Conerly days of the 1950s, and I mentioned that my 10-year-old daughter, Kerrin, was a huge fan of Phil Simms. At training camp, which had just started, Simms was battling Jeff Hostetler for the starting QB job. Young wouldn't tell me who had the inside track, but months later, after the trial had ended, a package showed up at our house in Armonk addressed to "Kerrin Quinn." Inside was a framed Phil Simms jersey, autographed, "To my friend Kerrin Quinn, All the Best, Phil Simms." That's what kind of guy George Young was.

Which is exactly why I got him off the witness stand as quickly as possible. I tossed him a couple of softball questions, laughed heartily at his answers, virtually blew him a kiss, then said, "No further questions." When you see that the jury likes a witness, your job as a lawyer is to like them too, no matter what side they're on.

Not all the NFL's witnesses were so winning. Chuck Noll, the great coach who had led the Pittsburgh Steelers to four Super Bowl victories, testified that for a player to leave his team was "worse than a divorce"—it was "a breach of trust." He also railed against the idea of guaranteed contracts, saying they could actually cause players to have injuries. He referred to Rufus Guthrie, an obscure player who allegedly had a guaranteed contract and then went down with an injury on a kickoff. Noll was clearly a man hopelessly stuck in the past, unable to accept that players no longer had to submit to autocratic coaches and demeaning rules. It was an embarrassment. Even the jurors were rolling their eyes.

Ed Glennon, the tough-nosed trial horse and winner of the *Mackey* trial, went after Noll with a vengeance. Glennon asked if it was a "breach of trust" for a coach or general manager to move to another team. As for the tale about poor old Rufus Guthrie, Glennon asked, "What happened, did he trip over his guaranteed contract?" Noll looked foolish; he looked even worse when Glennon pointed out that Noll himself had a 10-year guaranteed contract. "Mr. Noll," Glennon said, "it didn't apparently cause you any injuries, did it?"

In mid-August, my wife and two of our three daughters, Tierney and Kerrin, flew out for a week-long visit. They got to visit Mall of America on its opening day. They also watched the trial for several days. Kerrin sat next to Upshaw, the best seat in the house.

The NFL's next witness was Neil Austrian, their recently hired CFO and Tagliabue's number two, who attempted to counter Roger Noll's devastating testimony about the enormous profitability of the league and its wealthy owners. He presented calculations that purported to show NFL teams as break-even businesses. It was a messy, unconvincing job. Austrian referred to financial documents that the NFL had not given to us despite Judge Doty's order months before. At Doty's request, Magistrate Floyd Boline investigated the matter and concluded that the NFL lawyers had "bushwhacked" our side; he ordered that the NFL be fined $15,000. As it turned out, the "bushwhacker in chief" was none other than the NFL's future general counsel, Jeff Pash.

Once we had access to the new financial information, Kessler cross-examined Austrian vigorously. Austrian was forced to admit that the $7.5 million "salary" that Eagles owner Braman paid himself amounted to hidden profits. The NFL's internal financial documents also showed that owners Al Davis (Oakland), Pat Bowlen (Denver), Ralph Wilson (Buffalo), and Bill Bidwill (Arizona) also paid themselves tens of millions of dollars that they improperly charged as expenses to their teams. Austrian was too honest of a guy to do this type of dirty work. His testimony was devastating for the NFL.

As the NFL's case dragged on through August, tedium set in. Since Rothman and I were sitting next to each other, we would often exchange pleasantries as other lawyers examined witnesses. One day I leaned over to Rothman, who was approaching 70 and still actively trying cases all over the country, and I asked him, "Frank, why do you keep doing this? Doesn't your wife [Los Angeles federal judge Mariana Pfaelzer] object?" He looked over at me with a big smile and said in a stage whisper, "Jimmy, I just love it." In the years to come, I began to know exactly what he meant.

As the trial ground on, I could see the toll it was taking on Upshaw. His morning workouts became more intense, his patience shrunk, and he had that extra glass of wine at dinner. Despite his outward demeanor of jocularity and confidence, the strain was plainly eating at him. He was the one who chose this all-out, take-no-prisoners strategy; he was the one who would take the brunt of the criticism if the strategy failed. This is what it was like to go up against some of the richest, most powerful men in America. They had the resources to wear you down.

One night in mid-August, we sat alone in the hotel bar nursing an after-dinner drink. "Are you all right?" I asked Gene.

He looked at me and smiled. "Just win the case, Quinn," he said with a laugh. "Just win the fucking case."

"That's the plan, Upshaw," I replied. "That's the fucking plan." He laughed again, and I knew everything would be OK. I felt our case was going well, but in a jury case, nothing is for sure.

The NFL closed its case with two experts: Professor George Daly, who taught economics at the University of Iowa, and an ex-government economist named Bruce Owen. During Daly's testimony, Kessler busted out the chart that we had created on our Cape Cod sundeck. After going through the various unrestricted categories—owners, executives, coaches, the rest of America, and so on, Kessler reviewed the people in the restricted category, including players, prisoners, and little children. First, Daly agreed that NFL players were restricted. Next, he had to agree that prisoners were restricted as well. Then came little children. Daly once again agreed that little children are restricted.

When Kessler got to the word "slaves," the logical follow-up to little children, the NFL lawyers erupted. Rothman started screaming again about a mistrial. Kessler feigned surprise and accepted Judge Doty's admonition to move on to another subject. But the punch had landed.

As for Bruce Owen, he testified that the eight plaintiffs had not been damaged at all, and if there actually had been bidding for these players, their salaries would have gone down. Owen was not a serious witness. He was a hired gun willing to stake his reputation on pretend facts. Kessler had little trouble making him look ridiculous.

The witness testimony ended on September 1, 1992. Not a single NFL owner took the stand.

We spent the next few days pulling together the testimony and arguments I would use in my summation. Seldom do you have a full week to prepare, but this case was unique—the future of an industry was on the line. We had no idea what the jury was thinking; they had shown little emotion over the last three months. Upshaw remained upbeat, making wisecracks and dinner reservations.

Closing arguments were set for September 8, the day after Labor Day. Rothman went first. Not surprisingly, he emphasized the players' "astronomical salaries"—that's always been a vulnerable issue for players. Fans rarely consider the full economic picture of professional sports; they tend to object to the size of individual salaries without considering the revenues that these players make possible. It's human nature.

Rothman insisted the case was not about freedom. "What they're talking about is more money and that's all they're talking about," he said, then ramped up his scare tactics, predicting "the destruction of the National Football League as we know it today" if the jury struck down Plan B. He ended on this hyperbolic note: "If you find the rules don't fit, you might be taking a decision which is going to affect a whole lot of people, including these players. You might be bringing my words to truth, which is that you will destroy professional sports."

After Rothman's apocalyptic sermon, the courtroom fell silent. We'd heard this bullshit a million times, but of course, the jury hadn't. Rothman had burdened them with the very future of the league. This was tough stuff. Regardless of whether or not they liked football, nobody on that jury wanted anything to do with killing the NFL.

I was up next. As I rose to speak, Upshaw leaned over to me and said, in words I will never forget, "Don't be afraid to win."

I knew it was something football players say before the big game, but I'm not sure I can actually explain the logic of that message—afraid to win? Why in the world would I be afraid to win? But in that moment, I didn't parse the logic. I just felt the emotional surge of Gene's optimism and his faith in me. Upshaw could have done a lot of things with his life after playing football—he could've been a great coach, a great general manager, maybe even a great owner. But he chose instead to correct an egregious imbalance that had taken root in the game. It was a cause he truly believed in. When I heard him say those words, I understood more clearly than ever what was at stake.

Bruce Meyer and I had worked carefully for several weeks on my closing argument. I went on the attack from the beginning, calling the notion of the destruction of professional sports "a lot of nonsense." I told the jury repeatedly that they were being fed "the big lie" that without Plan B, the NFL could not survive. "It doesn't mean there wouldn't be other rules that the NFL may come up with," I said. "They probably will. And, at the appropriate time, people will either agree to them or not. Mr. Tagliabue will decide, others will decide, but this rule is the only rule you have to look at."

Then I went after the rank unfairness of their system, telling the jury,

> The reality is that this system is about the dehumanizing of play-
> ers. You heard the testimony about people like Mr. Rouson, who
> was told that he had to fake an injury in order to make the team.
> Frank Minnifield was told that if he went home for his grand-
> mother's funeral, he might not have a job. You also heard the
> testimony from Mr. Richards about how every Monday after a
> game, his coach was yelling in his ear that he was going to be fired
> if he kept this up; he was going to be bagging groceries.
>
> You heard testimony from Mr. McDonald, who was told that
> he couldn't go home and visit his family even though he had free
> time, and after that, he was fined just for wearing a hat.
>
> This is what the system is about: it's about control, it's about
> money, and it's about greed—but it's the owners' greed, not the
> players' greed. That's what the system is all about.

Much to my glee, I noticed that the NFL had actually brought a half-dozen owners into the courtroom for the closings. Sitting in the front row under a sign saying "reserved" were Pat Bowlen from Denver, Dan Rooney from Pittsburgh, Art Modell from Cleveland, Wellington Mara from the Giants, and even my old client, Lamar Hunt, from the Chiefs. They made for perfect props. Pointing directly at them, I said:

> Now, there are a bunch of owners sitting out there now, but not
> one of them made that, what is it, forty-, fifty-, sixty-foot walk up
> to that witness stand. Do you know why? Because if you sit out
> there [in the gallery], you are not under oath. If you are up there
> [on the witness stand], you are under oath. And they didn't bring
> in a single NFL owner to tell why this Plan B is so important,
> why they had to have only a Plan B and nothing else. I suggest to
> you they didn't because they couldn't possibly defend it.

As I made these remarks, I pointed to our eight plaintiffs also in the front row, all of whom had testified, all of whom had withstood the heat of cross-examination. As I was saying these words, a young child began to cry. It was Giants player Lee Rouson's two-year-old daughter, who was sitting on his lap. I thought to myself, "From that child's mouth to this jury's ears."

I then argued that it was important that the jury find damages for these players so that the NFL suffer tangible consequences and therefore be less likely to try to restrict these players in the future. I left the jury with these words:

So I ask you, members of the jury, when you go back in that jury room you remember what Dave Richards said as to why he became a plaintiff here. I asked Mr. Richards to tell us why he decided to become a plaintiff in this lawsuit. This is what he testified: "I felt that the restrictions being placed on me as a player were degrading and unfair, and I didn't feel it was right to be treated as a commodity that could be bought and sold and traded without my wishes considered." I didn't think it was right, he said.

Well, it's up to you, members of the jury, and I'm confident that you'll right that wrong.

And one way to do that is to find for the players and find damages and in doing so you will strike a blow for competition and for freedom of choice for all of these players. Thank you very much.

I knew I nailed it.

Closing arguments had lasted for several hours. Judge Doty then gave the jury his legal instructions, and at approximately four o'clock, the jury of eight women retired for the day, agreeing to begin their deliberations at nine o'clock in the morning on Wednesday, September 9.

Waiting for a jury verdict is always excruciating. Our group retired to our temporary offices in the IDS Center to wait and hope. My wife Katy had come out to watch the closings. She joined the rest of the team: Upshaw, Berthelsen, Allen, Kessler, and our associates Bruce Meyer and Jonathan Weiss, as well as Tony Curto and former player and NFLPA regional director Dave Meggyesy. Back in the 1970s, Meggyesy had become famous for being the first former NFL player to write an exposé on the NFL's horrendous treatment of its players, entitled *Out of Their League.* The mood of our group was subdued, although we did spend time trading funny highlights from our three-month sojourn in the Midwest. We had an early dinner at Murray's, Upshaw's favorite Minneapolis restaurant, then returned to our offices early Wednesday to continue our wait.

It's impossible to think of anything else when you're waiting for a verdict. We played Frisbee and whiffle ball, and finally, sometime early Wednesday afternoon, we started a low-stakes poker game. We also had a pool on how long the jury would be out, with guesses running from midday Wednesday to sometime late Friday afternoon. As the hours slowly ticked by, no one could work; we just kept waiting for the phone to ring. At five o'clock Wednesday evening, the jury went home for the day, vowing to continue deliberations the following morning. We had another subdued dinner that night, this time at Manny's. We all held our collective breath.

The next morning, another warm Minneapolis summer day, deliberations continued and so did the card game. Brenda and Sharon, our key staffers, packed up to go home; the card game continued. I wasn't really worried. In this kind of complex case, a quick verdict is usually bad for the plaintiffs. And I felt that our lady jury was likely to be both diligent and thoughtful in figuring out what the damages should be and who should get how much.

Finally, just before three o'clock in the afternoon, with several hundred dollars in the pot (the biggest of the day), the phone rang; Doty's law clerk Barbara Berens told me that there was a verdict and that we should come to the courthouse immediately. We all jumped up and sprinted the four and a half blocks to the courthouse. Apparently you don't see people running down the street in downtown Minneapolis very often. The local citizenry looked at us like we were lunatics. In less than 10 minutes, we had taken our places in the courtroom to hear the verdict.

There's nothing like waiting for a jury verdict to be read. Every time, I've felt like I'm stuck in that famous Edgar Alan Poe short story "The Tell-Tale Heart," where the narrator is overwhelmed by the loudness of his own beating heart. This was no exception. Barbara handed the verdict form to Judge Doty. His poker face gave way to the slightest of smiles as he read the verdict.

The jurors had been asked to rule on four questions. As to Question No. 1: Did the Right of First Refusal/Compensation Rules in Plan B have a substantially harmful effect on competition in the relevant market for the services professional football players? The jury answered "YES."

As to Question No. 2: Do the Right of First Refusal/Compensation Rules in Plan B significantly contribute to competitive balance in the NFL? The jury answered "YES." Our hearts fell, but only slightly.

Question No. 3 was key: Are the Right of First Refusal/Compensation Rules in Plan B no more restrictive than reasonably necessary to achieve the objective of establishing or maintaining competitive balance in the NFL? The jury answered "NO."

We knew we had won. Kessler and I shook hands under the table. The remainder of the verdict related to damages. The jury awarded money to only four of the eight plaintiffs—Mark Collins of the Giants ($178,000), Frank Minnifield of the Browns ($50,000), Dave Richards of San Diego ($240,000), and Lee Rouson, also of the Giants ($75,000)—for a total of $543,000, which, when trebled under the antitrust laws, became approximately $1.6 million.

We did the quick math: extrapolated to all 1,500 active NFL players, damages would total well over $200 million. I turned around to Upshaw, who gave me a big hug. Then I hugged my wife, Katy, and then we were all hugging. This was the highest of the highs.

Right after the verdict, Judge Doty invited the jurors into his chambers and asked them if they wanted to speak with any of the folks involved in the trial. All eight requested Upshaw; Gene and I went back to the judge's chambers and individually met with them. It got quite emotional. We gave our hearty thanks to Helen, Wendy, Bonita, Therese, Alice, Rosemary, Sandy, and Marie. I can recite their names from memory even now—the solid citizens who helped us break the tyranny of NFL owners.

The verdict was front-page news around the country. The *New York Times* reported, "The National Football League's system of free agency, under which teams retain the rights to their best players, was rendered illegal today by a Federal jury in an antitrust lawsuit brought by eight players. The case was widely viewed as a key to the financial future of the N.F.L."[51]

Upshaw said it best: "It's a huge victory. Today, a jury gave players something that the league had denied them for years—some freedom over their lives."[52]

As Freeman McNeil told the *New York Times* the day after the verdict, "I didn't get into this thing to hurt anyone or get anything from anyone. I got into it to stand up for something that is right and have it be a fair arena."[53]

The *Minneapolis Tribune* called it "the owners' worst nightmare."[54] The next day, Leigh Steinberg, the so-called superagent that the movie *Jerry McGuire* was supposedly based on, told *USA Today*, "What a wonderful day. Gene Upshaw and Jim Quinn deserve the players' Nobel Prize for conspicuous achievement. I wish Gene Upshaw was here so I could hug him."[55]

Naturally, we were ecstatic as the TV cameras followed us from the courthouse back to our offices on this lovely, hot Thursday afternoon in Minneapolis. As we walked along, at one point I looked up at the deep-blue sky and thought to myself that there is something unique and beautiful about a midwestern summer sky. At that moment, I was the happiest man in America.

There was, however, one shock. When we got back to the office, the pot from the poker game was gone. I always suspected Upshaw and accused him of it many times over the next 15 years. He never confessed.

When we assembled that night at Morton's Steakhouse for a celebratory dinner, we noticed a long table set up for another large group that hadn't yet arrived. Guess who that was for? When Rothman and his team showed up at Morton's, they turned right around and decided to find another place to eat. Another little victory for us! We went dancing at a local disco after our feast. Our entire team was there: the lawyers, the NFLPA people, our paralegals, our assistants, Brenda and Sharon, and of course my wife, who had put up with all this for years. We danced well into the night.

The NFL immediately tried to salvage some dignity from this disastrous defeat, with Rothman proclaiming "a terrible loss for the players"[56] because we hadn't gotten all the damages we wanted. Upshaw quickly pointed out to the press, "Losers always appeal, not winners. We're not appealing."[57]

The media continued to follow the story. A few days later, the *New York Times* predicted our trial victory would be "instrumental in helping change the face of major professional sports."[58] Another writer at the *Philadelphia Inquirer* pointed to Tagliabue's earlier prediction of victory after opening statements: "Three months and millions of dollars in legal bills ago, NFL Commissioner Paul Tagliabue stood outside the courtroom where *McNeil v. NFL* was getting under way and arrogantly predicted a take-no-prisoners victory for the league . . . Joe Namath, he ain't."[59]

Joe Browne, the NFL's senior mouthpiece, told the world that the NFL wasn't worried; they could always go on to Plan C or Plan D. Our response, of course, was that we'd continue to sue until we had real free agency. We knew we had all the leverage; it was time to think about moving toward settlement. To that end, we began to make more threats, including taking a shot at their next college draft. As I told the *Philadelphia Inquirer* a few days later, "The NFL definitely can expect a legal challenge to next April's draft. I don't think they really believe they're going to be able to hold that draft next year without facing lawsuits and big, big damages."[60]

Despite our big win in court, we were far from done in Minneapolis. The very next day, we were back in the IDS Center preparing new litigation. First, we needed to get Plan B enjoined once and for all so it couldn't affect any free agents not yet under contract. Second, since the case only technically involved these eight players, we had to file a class action on behalf of all the NFL players to take advantage of the *McNeil* verdict going forward. That way we could threaten the NFL with hundreds of millions of dollars in additional damages.

As to Plan B, Dick Berthelsen immediately rounded up a group of 10 free agent players who had not yet signed contracts and who would be free if not for Plan B. Kessler and Meyer quickly threw together a complaint and injunction papers over that weekend, with Keith Jackson, an All-Pro tight end for the Philadelphia Eagles, as lead plaintiff. Late Friday, my wife and I flew back to Cape Cod to enjoy a few days of peace. My legal team filed the *Jackson* lawsuit the following Monday, stating that the NFL was still restricting players despite the *McNeil* verdict's declaring Plan B illegal.

Less than two weeks later, Judge Doty put Plan B out of its misery. By that time, the original 10 plaintiffs had been winnowed down to what became known as the Jackson Four—Eagles tight end Keith Jackson; Webster Slaughter, a Browns wide receiver; D. J. Dozier, a running back for the Lions; and Garin Veris, a Patriots defensive end. The other 6 players had either been released or had already signed contracts.

On September 24, 1992, Judge Doty ordered "all defendants enjoined from enforcing the rights of first refusal/compensation rules of Plan B" against the Jackson Four. Within days, Keith Jackson had signed a huge contract with the Miami Dolphins. Slaughter signed a multimillion-dollar deal with the Houston Oilers, Garin Veris signed a new contract with the San Francisco 49ers, and D. J. Dozier went off to play baseball for the New York Mets.

Meanwhile, we kept busy. On September 21, 1992, just 11 days after the *McNeil* verdict, we filed a class action lawsuit entitled *Reggie White v. The National Football League* before Judge Doty. This time, all 1,500 players would be in play, and we could rely on the *McNeil* verdict to hammer the NFL into submission. The NFL owners would either agree to free agency on our terms or face hundreds of millions in damage claims, plus the possibility that hundreds of players would become free agents at the end of the 1992–93 season.

In the end, our unorthodox and much-maligned strategy of blowing up the union worked as well for football players as it had for basketball players. Stripped of the labor defense, the 28 NFL "emperors" had no clothes, no way to defend their illegal system, and no way to prevent NFL players from becoming "free at last."

CHAPTER 15

The Sword of Damocles

WITH THE *MCNEIL* AND *JACKSON* WINS BEHIND US, it was time to bring our war against the NFL to an end. We had more leverage over the owners than we'd ever had; now we needed to turn that advantage into concrete gains. The players had been without a union for nearly three years, forgoing tens of millions of dollars in pension and other benefit improvements. Absent a settlement, we could remain bogged down in litigation for years. There were a dozen pending cases and more to come. Litigation costs for both sides had spiraled into the tens of millions of dollars. The lawyers were making out like bandits, and everybody else was miserable.

To get a fair settlement, however, we had to act as if we were willing to go on fighting forever. That's why we had filed the class action suit, relying on the *McNeil* and *Jackson* rulings, which threatened chaos for the NFL—hundreds of totally free agent players, hundreds of millions of dollars in potential damages. The league, meanwhile, was threatening to impose a mysterious "Plan C"—a new set of restrictions that they claimed could withstand legal challenges, though they refused to provide any details.

Gene, Dick, Doug, Kessler, and I spent hours in conference rooms and over lengthy dinners and late-night drinks debating what the players really wanted. We boiled it down to three key elements. First, because of NFL players' short careers, there had to be free agency for all players after four years. Second, the players' overall share of league-wide revenues, which had traditionally hovered around

50 percent, would have to be at least 60 percent to make up for all the lost wages of the past. Third, the NFL owners would have to pay at least $250 million in damages to the thousands of present and former NFL players whose salaries and benefits had been suppressed by the illegal restraints the NFL had imposed on the players over the last six years.

If we could achieve these three goals, we could probably live with some kind of salary cap.

Solidarity among the players was at an all-time high. The day after the *McNeil* verdict, Upshaw got a call from Reggie White, the All-Pro defensive end for the Philadelphia Eagles. He told Upshaw he would do anything to help the players. "Just tell me what you want me to do," he said. White, a giant of a man, 6'6" and 300 pounds, had started his pro career with the Memphis Showboats in the USFL. When that league collapsed, the Eagles took him in a supplemental draft, and he became one of the franchise's all-time greatest players—maybe *the* greatest. Fans called him the "Minister of Defense."

White was a Baptist preacher at heart. While still in college at Tennessee, he had become an ordained minister in the Evangelical Christian faith. Later he would be criticized for making controversial statements about gays and racial stereotypes, but in 1993, he was among the most popular players in the league. Critically for us, White was about to become a free agent at the end of the current season, making him the perfect lead plaintiff for a class action suit. On the phone with Upshaw, he agreed to be just that.

Four other players also stepped up to be class representatives—Hardy Nickerson, the Steelers linebacker; Michael Buck, a Saints reserve quarterback; Vann McElroy, a Seahawk defensive back; and Cardinals defensive back Dave Duerson. These players were all strong NFLPA supporters. Duerson sat on the NFLPA executive committee. Many years later, Duerson, suffering from chronic traumatic encephalopathy (CTE) brain damage, tragically committed suicide; he shot himself in the chest so that his brain would remain intact and could be donated to research to help other football players.

To ramp up the pressure on the NFL, we included a new claim in the *White* lawsuit—an attack on the NFL college draft as an illegal boycott. The NFL owners had always considered the draft sacrosanct, a core part of the league's very existence. The legality of the draft had been called into doubt in an earlier NFLPA lawsuit, but it had survived as part of a collective bargaining deal Ed Garvey had negotiated nearly a decade earlier.

We filed the *White* class action lawsuit on September 21, 2002, before Judge Doty. In early October, only days after Doty's late September ruling that freed the Jackson Four, I got a call from Tagliabue. The league had new proposals, he said.

We knew that the NFL labor chief Harold Henderson had recently formed a new committee of NFL executives, led by Bill Polian of Buffalo and Steve Gutman, the Jets president, to act as Tagliabue's "football people" in designing some kind of free agent system. We weren't too optimistic. The other members of the committee—Jim Finks (New Orleans), Carl Peterson (Kansas City), Jim Irsay (Indianapolis), Mike Brown (Cincinnati), and Chuck Schmidt (Detroit)—were mostly hardliners. It seemed unlikely that they'd come up with something we'd find acceptable.

By this point, we had a window into the NFL league office, courtesy of a confidential source Upshaw had cultivated whom he'd nicknamed "Deep Helmet." From this person (whose identity I never learned), we received a flow of valuable intelligence, sometimes including internal NFL documents, that revealed the deliberations of several league committees. Deep Helmet's first reports on their proposed new free agent system confirmed our skepticism—the hardliners were fully in control of the process.

Despite our misgivings, I called Tagliabue and told him we were willing to listen. Once again, Kessler and I attended for the players. Upshaw had made it clear that no one from the NFLPA would attend until the NFL got serious about their free agency proposals. Tagliabue, Austrian, Mara, and Rooney attended for the owners. The meeting took place at Weil.

The NFL outlined new proposals that weren't that different from what we'd seen before—all they'd really done was shave a year off the free agency requirement. Now it was six years. Big deal. I told the NFL representatives that six years was still too long and that, in the aftermath of the *McNeil* verdict, our ability to sell a cap to the players was virtually nonexistent. The meeting ended cordially but with zero progress.

Upshaw, knowing that Tagliabue and I had developed a good rapport, suggested I meet one-on-one with the commissioner. We started a series of informal talks, totally under the radar. Sometimes I would sneak over to the league office, which was just down the street on Park Avenue; sometimes Paul would walk up to Weil's offices on 5th and 58th Street. And there were many, many phone calls. Negotiating with Tagliabue was completely different than my dealings with other football executives and commissioners in other sports. Though his owners were as ornery, arrogant, and hidebound as any group of men you could imagine, Tagliabue represented their interests without a trace of animus and always sought out common ground. Over several weeks, we began to formulate the outlines of something workable. Tagliabue was well aware of the risks on their side and had been urging his owners to compromise. His problem was that he needed three quarters of the owners to approve any settlement—21 of 28 votes. That meant that a cabal of just eight owners could kill any deal.

Our side had real risks too. The NFL had already appealed the *McNeil* and *Jackson* rulings and, given the track record of the Eighth Circuit Court of Appeals, a loss on appeal was a real possibility. Either way, without a settlement, we were in for endless legal fights, which were not just expensive but also completely unpredictable.

Tagliabue and I continued to talk throughout October and early November. I reported back to Upshaw on an almost daily basis. I held the line on free agency after four years and also told Tagliabue that the cap issue had to be finessed, since Upshaw was on record as opposing it. A few days later, Tagliabue suggested the idea of a trigger—a salary cap would come into play only if and when the players had received, in aggregate, a certain percentage of designated gross revenues (DGR), consisting principally of all TV revenues, gate receipts, and related game-day income. The owners had previously offered to cap the players' share of DGR at 55 percent, but we considered that way too low.

After conferring with Upshaw, I told Tagliabue, off the record, that the players' share of DGR would have to reach 67 percent in a given year to trigger a cap, with a sliding scale starting at 64 percent in the first capped year and eventually landing at 62 percent of DGR by the third capped year. Upshaw thought he could sell this to his membership because the agreement would start out without a salary cap at least for the first year and perhaps longer. A few players raised objections to the notion of a cap, but most believed that getting free agency was more important. It was all optics. In reality, we expected that the 67 percent threshold would be crossed in the first year, putting a cap in place for the remainder of the four-year deal.

Two factors drove us to that conclusion. First, we knew the NFL was negotiating a new set of network TV deals rumored to be nearly double the size of their current contracts. Hence the owners would feel flush and start throwing around money.

Second, because player salaries had been artificially suppressed for so many years, the pent-up demand for talented players in a new competitive marketplace would be enormous. We didn't need an economist to tell us the obvious: owners want to win, and free agency in any form would lead to bidding wars just like in basketball and baseball. We turned out to be right on both counts.

With a trigger structure as a starting point, both sides began to meet regularly. There was still no union, so Gene, Dick, and Doug joined Kessler and me as "advisors," with Bruce Meyer coming along as our scrivener in chief. In addition to Harold Henderson and Dan Rooney, Tagliabue added Pat Bowlen (Denver Broncos owner), Al Davis, and 49ers president Carmen Policy to their side of the table. We welcomed the addition of Policy, who had told *Pro Football Weekly*, "We've got to stop this talk about going to Plan C or whatever. . . . We've got to get together with the players as David Stern has done in the NBA."[61] This was the kind of talk we wanted to hear.

Upshaw now took a central role in the negotiations, recognizing that we had reached a critical point. The players and the owners had been fighting about free agency for nearly 20 years, but for the first time, the players had significant leverage. Upshaw was adamant that he had to obtain real free agency for current players and substantial damages for players who were now at the end of their careers and not able to enjoy the benefits of free agency. Roger Noll, a sports economist and our trial expert, told *Pro Football Weekly* that these discussions were at a critical juncture because the players realized this might be "their last bite at the apple."[62] There was enormous pressure on Upshaw to get something done.

These were hectic times for our side. While we were in the midst of critical negotiations, we were also continuing to fight in court. Within days of filing the *White* class action, we requested Judge Doty to grant free agency to the nearly 600 NFL players whose current contracts would expire on February 1, 1993. In mid-November, we were back in Minneapolis, arguing the motion before Judge Doty. After an all-day hearing, the judge said he would rule promptly, but we had no idea when that would be.

A few days later, the *Boston Globe* ran a story under the headline "The Mighty Quinn—Players' Heavy Hitter." Chronicling my career from *Robertson* to *McNeil*, it was the puffiest of puff pieces. Stern called me "indefatigable and formidable," and Tagliabue said I was "obviously a very intelligent and persuasive attorney." Upshaw laid on even more hyperbole by saying, "When you bring Jim Quinn to the table, you let the owners know you're serious, you're not doing this as a lark. It sends the right message."[63] A fella could get a big head listening to such nonsense, particularly from your adversaries.

It was also about this time that Pat Bowlen, the Broncos owner, raised an issue similar to the one we had dealt with years ago involving Larry Bird and the Celtics.

Bowlen's star quarterback, John Elway, was among those players who, under the current proposal, would be free agents at the end of the season. Bowlen insisted that he have the ability to keep his star quarterback.

What we had done in the NBA was carve out the Bird exception—teams could exceed the salary cap to sign their own players. By giving owners this power, the players had actually scored a great victory, because it meant the cap could be circumvented. It was soft rather than hard.

The NFL, obviously, knew all about this. An escalation of salaries similar to that experienced by the NBA was precisely what they were trying to avoid. So we had to come up with a different rule to govern how they spent their own money, a pretty funny concept when you think about it. In football, it got very convoluted. We invented something called a "franchise player"—each team could designate one per year, presumably their quarterback, who would have to be offered a salary equal to the average of the top five salaries at that player's position. That solved Bowlen's problem, but then other worries popped up, like, What about my second-best guy, that fearsome pass rusher I can't live without? So now we had another new term: "transition player." That guy had to be offered an average of the top 10 players at their position. Thankfully that concept only lasted a year or two.

Once we started down this road, NFL owners couldn't help themselves. Despite their intention not to repeat the "mistake" of the NBA, they eventually blew larger holes in their cap than anything that existed in the NBA. The issue of signing bonuses was where they totally lost control. Up to this point, without competition for players, signing bonuses had been a rarity in the NFL, since there had been no need for them. In those few instances where clubs offered bonuses, the clubs accounted for them by spreading them out over the years of the contract, even if the bonus was paid in one lump sum up front.

During our negotiations, Steve Gutman, the Jets president, proposed that this custom be continued under the salary cap. If a player had a five-year contract with a $5 million signing bonus, only $1 million would be counted against the cap in the signing year, and the rest would be allocated over the remaining years of the contract. As a result of that structure, a team would have $4 million of additional room that they could spend "over the cap" that year.

In labor negotiations, nothing feels better than watching the other side take their eye off the ball and do your negotiating for you. Our side tried to hide our glee as we absorbed Gutman's proposal. We immediately realized that this allocation concept would be a huge benefit to the players. The NFL's negotiators had become so fixated on the accounting treatment of the signing bonuses that they were oblivious to implications for the salary cap. We felt no obligation to enlighten them. Over the next few days, we feigned opposition to the idea—which we began to call "cash over cap"—until "reluctantly" agreeing to it.

Over the next several years, two things happened. First, hundreds of millions of dollars of cash was spent over the cap in the form of bonuses. Second, a substantial portion of player salaries were now effectively guaranteed because they were getting their signing bonuses paid up front, which they were entitled to keep even if they were later cut or injured. Over the years, the NFLPA has sometimes been criticized for failing to secure the guaranteed contracts that abound in other sports. In fact, because of bonuses, the players now have much better protection than is commonly assumed. The very "nightmare" that Chuck Noll had preached against in his *McNeil* testimony—guaranteed money—became a reality. Before our deal, less than 15 percent of salaries in the NFL were guaranteed through bonuses or otherwise. Within a couple of years, over 50 percent of player compensation was guaranteed in the form of bonuses or otherwise.

When the deal was up in 1997, the NFL owners claimed that we had "tricked them" into the bonus allocation system. We reminded them, with smiles on our faces, that it was the NFL, not the players, who had insisted on the allocation system. But now that the "cash over cap" system was part of the status quo, we weren't about to give it up.

But I'm getting ahead of myself. Just because the NFL blundered by handing us the bonus allocation didn't mean we leapt into their arms and made everlasting peace. It was highly unlikely that the NFLPA could ever risk a strike again, so we needed strong safeguards built into the deal—things that would put a high price on attempts by the NFL to renege on terms. We insisted that Judge Doty retain jurisdiction over any antitrust settlement agreement. Upshaw made this an absolute deal breaker, telling the NFL owners at one meeting, "We just don't trust you guys." The NFL hemmed and hawed for weeks but finally gave in. They thought Doty was somehow in the players' pocket. It was nonsense. The reality was that Doty was a good and fair judge, and the last thing in the world the NFL owners wanted was fairness.

The talks continued at a heightened pace through Thanksgiving week and on into the first two weeks of December. We met in spurts two or three times a week, often late into the evening, breaking only for dinner. Some nights if we broke early, our side would head uptown to Upshaw's favorite Italian restaurant, Nicola's, for pasta, veal chops, and lots of hearty red wine. Meanwhile, I had commandeered several conference rooms at Weil. We spent many hours sitting around waiting for one side or the other to caucus.

Eventually we got $195 million in damages for our players, plus $20 million in legal costs—more than we expected—and the draft was cut from 12 rounds to 7, creating a more open market for players coming into the league. But as much progress as we were able to make, there remained a powerful constituency within the league that truly believed the viability and appeal of the game itself depended on the rules heavily tilting toward management. Owners instinctively fought any encroachment on their power, including minor regulations on training camp. "Jeffrey, you're going to ruin football as we know it," Bill Polian, his eyes bulging, screamed at Kessler one day. In a calmer moment, Polian lamented that "the golden age of football is over."

He must have meant the golden age for football *owners*. Although, you know what? Even that isn't true. A more equitable split of football's economic pie has proved to be good for everybody involved with the game. But we'll get to that later.

As we rolled toward peace, vicious firefights still broke out. At one point, Doug Allen came up with a new logo with "Players" overlaid by the letters "NFL"—hence "NFL Players," which he had somehow gotten registered as an NFLPA trademark. The league went berserk, claiming that we were infringing on their NFL shield. We disagreed, pointing out that the logo was merely descriptive because, after all, we *were* "NFL Players."

As part of the overall licensing settlement, the NFL agreed to pay the NFLPA $35 million over seven years *not* to use the "NFL Players" logo, something we had never intended to do in the first place. A few days later, a package arrived in my office; in it was an "NFL Players" hat. On the brim, Upshaw had written, "This is a $35 million hat!" It still sits on a shelf in my office.

By the second week of December, both sides were hopeful of a deal, at least in principle, by year's end. We now started looking ahead, thinking about how to reduce the risk of future hostilities. Tagliabue came up with the idea of a "stub year," which would be the last year of any agreement. If no agreement to extend the deal were reached by the start of the final stub year, that year would become uncapped, and free agency would go from four to six years. The theory was that neither side would want such an outcome—the owners would want a cap, and the players would want free agency at four years, creating a strong incentive to get going on a new deal. It was a form of mutually assured destruction. Both sides agreed.

It was in early December that Dan Rooney, a man I had come to like and trust over the many months of negotiations, handed me a book on the life of the Irish patriot Michael Collins, who had been murdered by his own IRA colleagues because they suspected him of being a traitor (later proved to be untrue). Rooney, an Irish history buff, wrote an inscription inside the book that read, "To Jim, from your friend Michael Collins." It still makes me chuckle. Rooney survived long enough to serve as the US ambassador to Ireland in the Obama administration.

It got a little blurry toward the end. After a long day of negotiations, a small group of us adjourned for dinner at Il Tinello on 56th Street just off 5th Avenue. We hoped to iron out a few final points. Tagliabue, Harold Henderson, and Rooney were on hand for the NFL; Upshaw, Kessler, and I were there for the players. After an excellent meal and several bottles of wine, we reached agreement on all key points, and the meeting broke up with handshakes and even a few hugs. All was well—until the next morning, when I called Tagliabue to confirm a few drafting points. Neither of us could remember exactly what had been agreed to. In fact, no one else could remember either. The third bottle of wine had done us in. It was back to the negotiating table.

As the holidays approached, we were so optimistic that Tagliabue and I issued a joint statement: "We have made progress on the remaining issues and have reached a tentative settlement agreement in principle. The parties will attempt to finalize that agreement on Monday, December 28 after the Christmas holiday."

And that's where it all came crashing down. When we convened that Monday at Weil's offices, Al Davis immediately started lobbing hand grenades, trying to reopen issues that had already been painstakingly negotiated. Free agent players could only be signed by a new team during a brief window, he argued, otherwise their rights would revert to their prior team. Other NFL hardliners added new demands on the college draft and more exceptions to free agency. It was as if the hours and hours of talks over the last several months had never happened. "Goddammit, Al, you don't understand!" Upshaw shouted at Davis. "Free means free!"

Davis was a truly vexing figure. He could be annoyingly argumentative one minute, utterly charming the next. He was a fantastic storyteller. He could give you a play-by-play recap of entire games—and not just football but baseball games as well, including decades-old Dodgers games he had watched as a kid growing up in Brooklyn. At breaks in our negotiations, Davis was the best guy to talk to.

But that December day, Davis turned into an ogre, churlishly rejecting any semblance of compromise. It was as if he had been playing all of us for weeks, waiting for the precise moment to strike. Our months of hard work suddenly looked shaky. All he needed was seven other owners in his pocket, and that would be enough to kill any deal.

So the meeting that we had talked ourselves into thinking would be mostly a formality went well into the evening and ended on a decidedly unpleasant note. As Upshaw explained to the *New York Times*, "Free means free, not free for a while. There are no such time limits on free agent players in baseball or basketball. If a baseball or basketball player becomes free, he remains free until he signs a contract."[64] I added, "The players have no choice now. This just proves that the only place players can secure the free agency they are legally entitled to is in Court."[65] I was pissed.

As the meeting was breaking up, Dan Rooney, always the gentleman, learned that Bruce Meyer had to be in Pittsburgh the next day for a meeting. Dan offered Bruce a ride on his plane, and Meyer happily accepted. Not a comfortable flyer, he was picturing a private jet with a pilot and crew. When they arrived at the airport that evening, Meyer discovered it was a four-seater prop plane and that Rooney was the copilot. As they flew across Pennsylvania in a snowstorm, Meyer held his breath, closed his eyes, and hoped to survive. Rooney kept telling him not to worry; he had flown like this for years. As Bruce later told me, "Rooney just sat there serenely as I feared for my life."

The next afternoon, I got a call from Minneapolis. News of our breakdown in negotiations had traveled fast. Judge Doty's clerk, Barbara Berens, told me the judge had ordered both sides to meet with him the following week.

So on Wednesday, January 6, 1993, the first-class section on a Northwest Airlines flight from New York to Minneapolis was taken up entirely by our two warring parties. We joked that if the plane went down, either the NFL was in big trouble or all their problems were solved.

Kessler and I appeared as counsel for the *White* class, and Gene, Dick, and Doug came along as our consultants. Commissioner

Tagliabue and Harold Henderson appeared on behalf of the league office, along with three owners: Rooney, Mara, and Davis. I had told Berens that Davis was the reason for the breakdown, so the judge specifically ordered Al to appear. Everyone knew that the owners were scheduled to meet the next day in Dallas to discuss the settlement.

Doty was his usual charming self. We sat around his big desk as the judge shared with us some of his memorabilia from his years as a marine, one of which was a huge ceremonial sword he had obtained in the Far East that hung over his desk.

Doty pointed to a one-inch-thick pile of paper on the corner of his desk and said, "Here, gentlemen, is my decision on the free agency injunctive request. I am prepared to issue this decision by day's end, but I am telling you right now that neither the owners nor the players are going to be entirely satisfied with it." Then he smiled, looked around the room, and asked, "OK, so what's the problem?"

Both sides explained their positions and after some back and forth, it became obvious that the problem was Davis's backtracking on free agency. The limits he was trying to impose were a deal breaker, we told Doty. He then asked us to step out of the room so he could talk with the owners' side.

Our group repaired to the anteroom. We were chewing over various ideas for bridging the gap when suddenly Kessler, our lead dog, had a brainstorm—free agents should have the entire off-season to sign with another club, a period of seven months instead of the two months that Davis had proposed. If they hadn't reached a deal by this point, players could only return to their old team. Doty eventually called us back into his chambers, where we offered Kessler's idea as a possible compromise—but only if the league dropped all other demands.

Over the next few hours, with Doty mediating, they finally agreed to our compromise. Davis had reluctantly caved. We told Kessler he was a genius, which he knew already.

Since the owners' vote was to take place in Dallas the following day, their group would be flying to Texas together. There was, of course, no love lost between Tagliabue and Davis, dating back to

Davis's Raider antitrust lawsuit against the NFL a decade earlier. They barely spoke throughout the entire day. At one point, Berthelsen overheard Tagliabue talking to Joe Browne from the league office. He said, "Whatever you do, make sure I'm not sitting next to Davis." The next day, the owners voted in favor of the settlement. A few days later, the players approved the deal as well. I never did find out exactly what was in Doty's free agency decision, although many years later, Berens told me that it would have been more favorable to the players than the owners.

Tantalizingly close to a settlement, the players now had to decide about re-forming their union. For months Upshaw had vigorously resisted the idea. He didn't trust the NFL owners to ever agree to anything without the threat of litigation. The NFL, however, demanded to have their labor protection back, or there would be no final deal. Upshaw finally relented, in exchange for a provision in the deal that would prevent the NFL from arguing that any future decertification by the NFLPA was a sham. Many years later, they would blatantly violate that solemn agreement.

And with that, we had a deal. In mid-March, the NFLPA held its annual meeting at the Grand Wailea in Maui. More than 100 current and former players attended. There were standing ovations, champagne toasts, Cuban cigars, and many margaritas. We had the time of our lives celebrating the end of what had been a six-year war. And on April 1, 1993, the NFLPA once again became the certified collective bargaining agent of NFL players.

There were a few brush fires to put out. More than 70 current and former players protested various provisions. Wilber Marshall, the star linebacker of the Washington Redskins, objected to being designated as their franchise player. Eagles owner Norman Braman, with his new lawyer, objected to the licensing settlement, even though he was no longer chairman of NFL Properties. Several college players had complaints about the draft, and even an agent objected on behalf of himself, Lord knows why. In the end, after a series of hearings, Judge Doty finally approved the entire deal on August 19, 1993, almost six years to the day since the players had gone on strike for free agency prior to the 1987 season.

Relative labor peace would reign in professional football for more than a decade and a half. Three times—in 1998, 2002, and 2006—both sides agreed to extend the basic deal with minimal revisions. Tagliabue's idea of mutually assured destruction in the last year of the deal—the uncapped year and six years of free agency—worked for a while. NFL owners lived in mortal fear of an uncapped year. Upshaw had established a strong base of power for the players, and we gradually built on it, culminating in the 2006 deal, which dramatically increased the players' share of revenues.

And then the next war erupted. But that's a story for another chapter.

The establishment of free agency in the NFL led to some interesting ironies. The first team to sign a free agent was none other than Green Bay, long the poster child for the frostbitten, small-fry teams that would never be able to compete for players in a free market. Well, it turned out to be good enough for the "Minister of Defense," Reggie White.

The players who benefited most from free agency were not the most glamorous—not the quarterbacks or running backs, not even the receivers. The recipients of the greatest pay increases were offensive linemen. The dollar value of their essential grunt work had long been underestimated and held in check by the unfair system. And because they had longer careers than other positions, they rated a wise allocation of capital. Upshaw, himself an offensive lineman, had predicted all this—though of course we had all thought he was full of shit. He enjoyed reminding us how right he had been.

The NFL today is among the most profitable enterprises in the country, if not the world; certainly, it is among the most powerful. This profitability and power is due in large part to the structural changes forced on the NFL owners by their players. It took the longest labor struggle in sports history to make it happen, but once the owners stopped worrying so much about sharing their precious pie, it grew larger than they had ever imagined. Everybody won—the players, the owners, and especially the fans. Not a single game was missed.

I can't help wondering, however, how this might have turned out had Judge Doty not hung his own Sword of Damocles over our heads. As Doty made clear that cold January day so many years ago when he gestured toward that big pile of paper on his desk under his treasured sword, the future of the NFL was hanging by a thread. Both sides had a great deal of power, and with power came responsibility. Each side had the responsibility to get something done that would be both lasting and fair. As in the ancient Greek legend, a wise man in a black robe knew how to use the paper sword to bring both sides together for the good of the game.

CHAPTER 16

Hockey Fights— from Slapshots to Slapstick

IN ALL THE WARS I FOUGHT ALONGSIDE PROFES-
sional athletes, I was fortunate to have been allied with some pretty
distinguished gentlemen. Larry Fleisher, Marvin Miller, Gene
Upshaw—they were unconventional characters, and they certainly
had their faults, blind spots, and idiosyncrasies, but on the issues
that mattered the most, they were exceptional people. I trusted them
implicitly and would have followed them into battle against anyone.

Alan Eagleson was, shall we say, cut from a different cloth. For
years, the hockey media cast him as a lovable rogue. But in my experience, there was nothing lovable about him. He was just a con artist.

Eagleson was the executive director of the National Hockey
League Players' Association (NHLPA), though that was merely one of
his many hats. He was also the sport's most prominent player agent;
he represented hundreds of players over the years, beginning with his
first client, Hall of Famer Bobby Orr. Working closely with the NHL,
he had also created the first of many international hockey tournaments, including the Soviet-Canadian series and the Canada Cup,
which later became World Cup Hockey. In Canada, they called him
"Mr. Hockey."

Mr. Hockey and I met when I defended his deposition in the *Robertson* case. At that time, he had hired our law firm to explore a potential
free agency antitrust lawsuit against the NHL, just like the one we had

filed against the NBA. After only a few weeks, however, he dropped the idea without explanation.

Then, in May 1989, only a few days after Larry had died, I got a call from Eagleson.

Eagleson was tall and wiry, with a quick sense of humor and a politician's flair for exaggeration and outright bullshit. Indeed, after graduating with a law degree from the University of Toronto and becoming a successful commercial lawyer in Toronto, he ran unsuccessfully for a seat in the Canadian House of Commons and then was elected to the Ontario Legislative Assembly, all before founding the modern NHLPA in 1967. He had friends everywhere; CEOs, prime ministers, bar owners—and journalists. For years he had been the darling of the Canadian media. Red Fisher, a Montreal sportswriter and the dean of Canadian hockey writers, wrote story after story praising "the Eagle's" negotiating skills and intellectual prowess.

Despite his outward charm, Eagleson was pugnacious, and he ruled the union with an iron fist. I saw firsthand that he could be mean and downright nasty to any player who dared to question his authority. A favorite putdown of his was "frog"; he would call players that in a room full of their peers.

By the summer of 1989, however, the Eagle was fighting for his life in hockey. A group of players, spurred on by two other agents, Rich Winter and Ron Salcer, had retained former NFLPA head Ed Garvey to topple Eagleson's regime. The Garvey group hired investigators and issued a scathing report that accused Eagleson of skimming money, submitting phony travel expenses, and making illicit loans of union money. The report also attacked Eagleson for his failure to fight hard for free agency in hockey, implying that he was too close to NHL management. The report caused a huge uproar, particularly in Canada; it ultimately led to a vote by the union player reps in which Eagleson narrowly beat back the opposition. This internecine fight didn't garner much coverage in the US, but those of us who followed other sports weren't surprised that there was trouble up North.

It was right after this vote that Eagleson called me. The NHL-PA's collective bargaining agreement would be expiring in a year or so, he said, and they needed to prepare for a new round of negotiations. Free agency was still nonexistent in the NHL. The league's old reserve clause had been struck down as illegal in the 1970s as part of litigation relating to the WHA. But the system that had been put in its place—with Eagleson's blessing—was equally effective at chilling competition for players.

The euphemism the NHL and Eagleson had come up with was "equalization": when a player signed with another team, his former team was due equal compensation, as determined by the league. Guess what? The awards were so high that clubs were discouraged from signing other clubs' free agents—hardly different at all from the reserve system.

In our telephone conversation, Eagleson noted that basketball seemed to be thriving under free agency. He said he was particularly interested in our recent threat to decertify the NBPA, which had led to a very favorable settlement the year before. He asked me to come to Toronto to meet with him and members of the union's leadership: Islanders center Bryan Trottier, Whalers forward Kevin Dineen, Capitals goalie Mike Liut, Rangers forward Mike Gartner, and Kings defenseman Marty McSorley. Through the course of the summer, I flew up to Toronto several times to do just that. The players were excited about the possibilities of free agency, and I was hired to advise them on antitrust and related labor issues. But there was an odd vibe to the whole thing. From the start, I had the feeling I was being used as a prop by Eagleson—having me onboard was his proof that he was "getting tough" with the owners. What Eagleson was really concerned with, however, was hanging on to his job.

Feeling pressure from the Garvey report and growing discontent within the ranks, Eagleson orchestrated a "unanimous" vote of confidence in fall 1989 from the 22 player reps, many of whom just happened to be his clients. Even they couldn't save him. The "unanimous" vote came with a price tag: Eagleson had to agree to retire in a year and form a search committee to find his successor. I was asked to work with the six-member committee and meet candidates.

Bob Goodenow, a Detroit lawyer and player agent who represented star forward Brett Hull, among others, quickly emerged as the consensus choice. Goodenow, a tough Irishman with a red face and a big smile, had captained the Harvard hockey team and played minor league hockey before going off to law school in Detroit. He was smart and tough-minded, with a sharp Gaelic wit. He was capable of sanctimony and sarcasm in the same sentence. I really liked the guy. Goodenow taking over from Eagleson seemed exactly like the clean break the players' union needed.

At the All-Star Game in Pittsburgh on January 21, 1990, Goodenow was introduced as the deputy executive director, effective immediately, with the plan being that he would succeed Eagleson the following year. Goodenow agreed to give up his agent business and devote himself full time to the union. Shortly after Goodenow moved into the NHLPA's Toronto headquarters, he asked me to come up from New York to brief him on what was happening in basketball and football. By then the NFLPA had decertified, and we were about to file the *McNeil* case.

When I arrived, I was ushered into the tiny, cramped office that Eagleson had assigned to Goodenow; Eagleson occupied a spacious office suite down the hall festooned with hockey memorabilia from around the world. Already the two were barely speaking. I looked at Bob. "What the hell is going on?" I asked. He looked up with a smile. "Don't worry, the son-of-a-bitch will be gone in a year," he said.

It had quickly been decided by the players that Goodenow, not Eagleson, would lead the negotiations for a new collective bargaining agreement. One of the first things that Goodenow did was to initiate complete salary disclosure so that all players would know what everybody else was making. Up to this point, the league, in cahoots with Eagleson, had fiercely opposed salary disclosure. Now the players and their agents would have access to the same information that owners and the general managers already had, making contract negotiations fairer and more transparent. Salaries throughout the league went up almost immediately. Securing real free agency was the obvious next step.

Eagleson, meanwhile, was getting his comeuppance. An investigative reporter named Russ Conway from an obscure, small-town paper, the *Eagle-Tribune* of Lawrence, Massachusetts, had been digging into allegations of Eagleson's wrongdoing, and in early 1991, he published a series of articles called "Cracked Ice," which eventually became an award-winning book entitled *Game Misconduct*. Another book, by David Cruise and Allison Griffiths, *Net Worth (Exploiting the Myths of Pro Hockey)*, also published in 1991, hurled many of the same accusations at Eagleson. They portrayed "the Eagle" not as a loveable rogue but as a full-scale criminal.

Eagleson's misconduct went much deeper than I'd ever suspected. It had seemed relatively obvious to anyone who was paying attention that Eagleson had run a compliant house union and made sweetheart deals with the owners. But Conway's exposé included details on his embezzling of union funds, skimming of profits from the Canada Cup series (which he had founded), and other fraudulent activities involving the union and international hockey events. He was like the union bosses from the 1950s, an old-fashioned gangster. The FBI and the Royal Canadian Mounted Police opened investigations.

By the time Eagleson formally stepped down as NHLPA executive director on December 31, 1991, he was in a great deal of trouble. A Boston grand jury had been empaneled, and many of his former clients gave devastating testimony, including Bobby Orr. Two years later, after an extensive investigation, Eagleson was indicted on charges of racketeering, embezzlement, and fraud. He would eventually receive a prison sentence of 18 months, though he only served 6 before being released. Shortly after that he was disbarred and expelled from the Hockey Hall of Fame, where he had once sat on the board.

The "Czar of Hockey" was no more.

• • • •

During the Eagleson years, no progress had been made on the free agency front. The hockey owners, like the owners in football, had adamantly refused to agree to change the equalization system, which applied throughout a hockey player's career regardless of age. Eagleson had sheepishly complied. He had become close friends and drinking buddies with NHL board chairman and Chicago Blackhawks owner Bill Wirtz, as well as NHL president John Ziegler.

His complacency had been temporarily hidden by the existence of the WHA. The WHA had been another brainchild of sports entrepreneur Gary Davidson, who had also helped found the ABA (basketball) and the WFL (football). Over its brief eight-year life (1971–79), the WHA featured some of the biggest names in hockey, including Gordie Howe, Bobby Hull, and Bernie Parent. For that short while, the rival WHA had given NHL players at least some bargaining leverage.

• • •

Hockey has never been as big a business as football, baseball, and basketball, but because its owners had done such a good job of holding down player salaries, big clubs like New York, Detroit, Chicago, Toronto, and Montreal raked it in. During the 1980s, the players' share of NHL revenues had dropped below 50 percent, a direct effect of no interleague competition with the WHA and the NHL's strict anti–free agency rules.

Gil Stein, the NHL's top lawyer and onetime interim league president, confirmed this view in his own book, *Power Play*, writing that, back then, "There were no poor owners in hockey." He also described what he called "staged" negotiations, in which Eagleson, Wirtz, and Ziegler would agree on issues in advance; then, when players were present, they would put on a show of supposedly "real" tough bargaining.

Goodenow was determined to change that. He immediately set out to meet with every player in the league. Most of them were Western Canadian farm boys and Europeans with green cards, a very strange mix. They didn't know an antitrust suit from a suit of clothes; they thought decertification was something that you did to milk to make it taste better. Goodenow convinced them that if they stuck together, they would have the leverage necessary to change the way the NHL treated its players, thereby dragging the league out of its dark ages.

By this time, a group of highly skilled player agents had sprung up in hockey. In addition to Winter and Salcer, there were Rick Curran, Don Meehan, and Mike Barrett (Wayne Gretzky's agent). Barrett also represented Marty McSorley, known as Gretzky's bodyguard on the ice—an "enforcer" of the highest caliber. Marty would soon become my bodyguard as well. Goodenow, as a former agent, knew how important it was to keep key agents aligned with the goals of the union. He quickly mastered the art of keeping the agent group in line as negotiations proceeded. Over the years, the more influential and better-informed agents played an important role in our many fights with the leagues by encouraging their players to stand with the union, particularly during the early free agency battles. They quickly recognized that what was good for their players was also good for their business.

The NHL collective bargaining agreement was due to expire in September 1991, just days before the start of the 1991–92 season. Formal negotiations for a new contract kicked off in the fall of 1990, and Goodenow asked me to participate in some of those meetings. By that time, the *McNeil* case against the NFL was in full swing—everybody with a financial stake in professional sports was fixated on the outcome of the *McNeil* case, and that included NHL owners. Their suppression of players' salaries was already coming apart. In 1988, Bruce McNall, owner of the Los Angeles Kings, had paid $15 million to Edmonton Oilers owner Peter Pocklington for Wayne Gretzky's contract, then had turned around and gave Gretzky a multiyear, multimillion-dollar contract. It was the first real big money since the crazy days of the WHA in the early 1970s.

Every league has had guys like McNall—reckless, unpredictable, and driven to win at all costs. Much as they are ridiculed and even vilified—and though they often crash and burn, just like McNall did—free markets actually depend on outliers like that. They force the hand of risk-averse grinches. In their own bizarre way, they move the league forward. Which is exactly what happened in hockey. After Gretzky got his millions, Mike Ilitch in Detroit and Jeremy Jacobs in Boston had to shell out huge contracts to satisfy their stars, Steve Yzerman and Ray Bourque. The NHL salary dike was beginning to crack.

We met periodically with the NHL owners over the fall and winter of 1990 and 1991, mostly in Toronto. The owners' team was led by NHL president Ziegler and his number two, general counsel Gil Stein. A number of NHL owners also participated, among them Ed Snider, the Philadelphia Flyers owner who headed the NFL labor committee; Barry Shenkarow, owner of the Winnipeg Jets; and Chicago's Bill Wirtz. From time to time, other owners attended, including Jacobs (Bruins), and Ilitch (Red Wings), and Marcel Aubut (Quebec Nordiques). Jacobs and Ilitch were both powerful owners whose other businesses had made them very wealthy: Jacobs ran Delaware North, one of the largest food-service companies in the US, while Ilitch had founded Little Caesar's Pizza and later acquired the Detroit Tigers.

Like the football owners, these hockey guys had had it good for a long time. Most teams, particularly in the larger markets, made money, their player systems were totally inflexible, and their players mostly compliant. It was clear from the outset they saw no reason to change a thing. If anything, they had a list of demands to make their system even worse.

I had first been introduced to Wirtz and Ziegler by Eagleson, and his very cozy relationship with the two men left me surprised and troubled. Ziegler, a lawyer from Detroit, had been a minority owner of the Red Wings and then had risen to the NHL presidency in the late 1970s, largely through Wirtz's influence. Ziegler was good looking, dapper, and a bit of a lightweight.

It was obvious to me from the beginning that Wirtz was the real man in charge. Ziegler deferred to Wirtz on all matters hockey. He owed his job to Wirtz, and he knew it. Wirtz was known to be stubborn and cheap, so cheap that the Blackhawks let their greatest player, Bobby Hull, leave the team for the WHA at the peak of Hull's career. Wirtz was a bull of a man with slicked-back gray hair. His family had made a fortune in the rough-and-tumble business of Chicago real estate, and Wirtz ran the Blackhawks as his personal plaything for more than 40 years. The man, in a word, was a prick. I remember looking at his rugged face and thinking that this was not going to be easy. But over those many months, Wirtz and I ended up having a perfectly pleasant relationship because we never said a word to each other.

Our side consisted of Goodenow, Ian Pulver (a young union labor lawyer), and me. A few months later, we were joined by Ted Saskin, the NHL's new head of business and marketing, who quickly became Goodenow's number two. At my suggestion, we also added a real labor lawyer to the team, my good friend George Cohen. He and Goodenow hit it off right away. A core group of players also attended: union president Bryan Trottier, Mike Gartner, Kevin Dineen, and Rangers goalie John Vanbiesbrouck. To a man, these guys were extremely likable: bright, dedicated, and eager to learn, although a bit naïve about the hard-knock business of hockey. They were all committed to doing their absolute best for their fellow hockey players. Other players attended meetings from time to time over the course of the next 18 months, including Detroit's star center Steve Yzerman, Calgary's star center Joe Nieuwendyk, and the Islanders' young forward Ken Baumgartner.

At Weil, I had initially asked Jeff Kessler to participate along with Bruce Meyer, but it soon became clear that Goodenow and Kessler were not a good match. While Goodenow appreciated Jeffrey's brilliance, he found him too brash. At one point Goodenow said to me, "Can't you ever get him to shut up?" Within months I maneuvered Jeffrey to focus primarily on football and basketball, leaving hockey to me and Meyer, who got along well with Goodenow.

As much experience as I'd had up to that point in sports labor issues, nothing was as wacky as labor negotiations in hockey in the early 1990s. In February 1991, we were meeting with a group of NHL owners at the Four Seasons Hotel in Toronto. Goodenow laid out a number of issues to be discussed, including the issue of free agency. He then asked me to review with the owners' group some of the antitrust issues that had been raised in other sports, along with a full history of the litigation that had ultimately led to free agency in baseball and basketball.

As I started to speak, one owner, the Flyers' Ed Snider, interrupted me. He pointed his finger at me, bellowing, "Who the fuck are you and what the fuck are you doing here?"

I calmly explained my role as outside counsel to the union. "I don't give a shit about the antitrust laws," Snider replied, glaring at me. "Let's you and I go outside in the hallway and figure out what's what, OK, buddy?" It was all rather fitting for the owner of the team known as the "Broad Street Bullies."

Sitting over my shoulder was Marty McSorley, Gretzky's on-ice bodyguard and now, I hoped, mine. He was the sweetest guy in the world but one tough son of a bitch on skates. I looked at Snider, then looked at Marty.

"I tell you what, Ed—that's your name, isn't it?" I asked. "How about you go outside with Marty back here?" Marty stood up, Snider sat down. The meeting progressed without further disruptions. A few minutes later, Goodenow asked George Cohen to describe for the NHL's owner the way free agency worked in baseball. As George began to speak, Mike Ilitch blurted out, "I'd rather shove an ice pick in my eye than agree to the baseball system." Two weeks later, Ilitch bought the Detroit Tigers. Strange guy.

As the negotiations wore on into the spring of 1991, we got into arguments about everything, right down to how to split trading card revenues. But free agency cast a shadow over everything. The owners followed the script—their first objection was that the small-market teams would suffer disproportionately. At nearly every meeting, Barry Shenkarow from Winnipeg and Marcel Aubut from Quebec—the two franchises that, along with Edmonton and Hartford, were the "Green

Bays" of the NHL—would break out the violins and play us their sad song about financial ruin.

Neither Shenkarow nor Aubut was particularly bright, but they sure liked the sound of their own whiny voices. Shenkarow in particular would ramble on about the perils of free agency for his little city of Winnipeg. Finally, at one meeting in early May, I simply couldn't take it anymore. "Barry, you understand that God never pronounced the need for a hockey team in Winnipeg," I said to Shenkarow. I then patiently explained that there were lots of options: "Why not get the rich owners in Boston, Chicago, New York, and elsewhere to agree to share revenues with you and the other supposedly 'poor' cousins and prop up small market teams? Or you could just move your franchise to a larger city that could support a major league hockey franchise. The fact that you want to keep your team in Winnipeg is not the players' problem, it's your problem."

That really pissed Shenkarow off. He looked at me with daggers in his eyes. "We don't need fancy New York lawyers telling us what to do," he fired back. As usual, those talks broke down with no real gains.

On June 14, 1991, in Toronto, Meyer and I presented a paper we had written called "Players Position on Free Agency Issues." In it, we raised the specter of an antitrust lawsuit against the league and the "treble damages" that teams would be subject to. Now there was a problem for Winnipeg and Hartford. The owners sat in stony silence as they read our position paper. Then, after a few choice words, they got up and walked out.

We realized later that we must have hurt their feelings. On August 20, 1991, the league sued the union (*NHL v. NHLPA*), claiming that the owners were entitled to court protection because we had threatened to bring an antitrust lawsuit.

They filed this bizarre lawsuit in Minneapolis, hoping to take advantage of the NFL's 1989 *Powell* ruling that prevented unionized players from bringing antitrust suits. The owners asserted that my mere presence at several of the bargaining meetings was proof that we were going to sue them. The whole thing would have been funny if it weren't so pathetic.

In a tongue-in-cheek opinion tossing the lawsuit out as a sham, Judge James M. Rosenbaum, the chief judge of the District of Minnesota, referred to the NHL's lawsuit as a "power play." He then proceeded to call "offsides" on the owners, blew his judicial whistle, and threw the case out. He noted that while the NHL cited my presence "as a clear and present antitrust danger," there was nothing wrong with the NHLPA hiring a lawyer to give them advice. He also noted that since the players had yet to threaten, much less to actually file a lawsuit, there was nothing that the league needed to be protected from. In what he called "the Zamboni," he ruled, "Based upon the files, records and proceedings herein and for the reasons set forth above, it is ordered that this matter is dismissed and let judgment be entered accordingly." The case was ridiculous.

Despite the lawsuit, meetings resumed shortly after Labor Day with some urgency, since the collective bargaining agreement was set to expire in mid-September. Although the negotiations had stalled, both sides agreed to continue discussions and to play the season without a formal collective bargaining agreement. This was not unprecedented; the basketball players had done it several times.

I knew that this had been Goodenow's strategy all along. He had no plans to bring an antitrust lawsuit, which he feared could take years to resolve. In that sense, I was also a cover for Goodenow's real agenda. If no agreement was reached over the winter, Goodenow planned to call for the first strike in the history of the NHL. And he would do it right before the playoffs were about to begin, in April 1992. Under the way the NHL operated at the time, the players were paid their full salaries by the end of the regular season. The owners, however, received a large portion of their revenues from the playoffs, so the players would be giving up little while the owners would be losing a lot. That is what we call leverage.

Frankly, I was a little skeptical of this approach given the recent failed strikes in football. But it was Goodenow's call, and I fully supported it.

The 1991–92 winter was a long, cold one for the NHL and its players.

Negotiations got nowhere, and the NHL owners' attempt to intimidate the players abjectly failed. On April 1, 1992, to the shock and bewilderment of the NHL owners, their players went on strike. The owners simply could not believe their ungrateful players would have the audacity to actually stand up for themselves like this. Seeing red but bleeding green, Wirtz, Ziegler, and the others quickly backed off all of their demands. They called for a new round of negotiations and began offering concessions.

On April 7, 1992, Judge Rosenbaum, in timely fashion, threw their silly antitrust case out of court, which was a huge psychological victory for the players. Three days later, on April 10, 1992, the players and owners announced an end to the strike. The playoffs would start immediately, only slightly behind schedule. The parties hastily entered into a short-term, two-year deal, and the players won significant concessions relating to licensing, trading cards, salary arbitration, and pension and other benefits. The deal was a frantic bit of patchwork—it retroactively covered the prior season and ran only through the next one. The NHL had bought itself a little time, not everlasting peace. The players had effectively put the league on notice. The 10-day strike, though brief, fundamentally altered the relationship between the NHLPA and the NHL. As Goodenow later told the *New York Times*, "It wasn't until the strike that the owners understood the players were serious."[66]

The NHL owners had gotten their first black eye, and they didn't like it. Needing someone to blame other than themselves, they fired John Ziegler shortly after the settlement. He was replaced on an interim basis by Gil Stein, his loyal acolyte. A Philadelphia lawyer who worked for the Flyers before becoming NHL general counsel in the late 1970s, Stein was among the most humorless and colorless people I have ever met. He made up for his lack of humor with a pomposity that rivaled the haughty likes of Bowie Kuhn.

Stein lasted barely a year as president; his only real accomplishment was getting himself inducted into the Hockey Hall of Fame. His admission was later rescinded, though, when it was discovered that he had rigged the voting. In December 1992, his reign officially concluded when the NHL owners voted to hire Gary Bettman, executive vice president and general counsel of the NBA, as their new leader. Bettman, as far as anyone could tell, knew nothing about hockey, but with Stern and Russ Granik firmly entrenched at the top of the NBA, the ambitious Bettman, just 41 years old, had no route to the top. He had established a reputation as Stern's mad-dog protégé, slavishly copying his mentor in both style and substance. Now he had his own league to play with.

When Goodenow asked me what I thought of Bettman, I replied, "Smart as a whip, arrogant as hell, with a patronizing demeanor to make sure everyone knows that he is the smartest person in the room." Bruce Meyer told Goodenow, "I predict you won't like him." This proved to be an understatement.

Bettman, barely 5'5", had a bit of a Napoleon complex. Goodenow was himself strong-willed and not given easily to compromise. "This is not going to be a marriage made in heaven," I thought to myself.

Bettman grew up in a Jewish family in Queens, studied labor relations at Cornell, got a law degree from NYU, and joined Proskauer, the NBA's law firm, in 1977. In 1981, he moved over to the NBA's legal department, where he became the monitor of the new salary cap—their capologist extraordinaire, charged with holding down player salaries at all costs. This naturally led to frequent skirmishes with the basketball union and its lawyers, which is why the NHL went after him. They wanted someone unafraid to drop the gloves. The prior NHL presidents had traditionally been weak figureheads controlled by a small group of powerful owners. Bettman had no interest in a job like that. Knowing he was negotiating from a position of strength, he had insisted that he become the first NHL commissioner, with powers commensurate with commissioners in the other three major sports. He got them. David Stern was not going to out-commission Gary Bettman.

In the early 1990s, before Bettman arrived, the economics of hockey had begun to change rapidly. Even without free agency, the onset of multimillion-dollar player contracts had driven the players' percentage of league revenues well above 50 percent. As a result, in 1991 Ziegler had announced an ambitious plan to more than double league-wide revenues of less than $500 million to a billion dollars or more by the end of the decade. This was to be accomplished by accelerated franchise expansion in the US—the Americanization of hockey—that would hopefully lead to lucrative US television network deals. The process began in 1992 with the addition of three new franchises: the San Jose Sharks, the Ottawa Senators, and the Tampa Bay Lightning. The NHL now seemed focused more on revenue growth than profitability—a dubious strategy, to say the least.

Bettman's mandate was threefold: US expansion, particularly in the South; a new national TV deal in the US; and labor peace on the owners' terms. NHL owners liked the idea of their own salary cap and were also prepared to push a luxury tax plan, whereby teams that spent over a certain limit would be forced to subsidize the other teams. This was also under hot discussion in baseball. Owners in both sports believed that a luxury tax would create discipline in their own ranks and keep small-market clubs in the black.

Goodenow was unalterably opposed to any form of salary cap. He was open to discussing some modest luxury tax as long as it had no serious effect on player salaries. As to the small markets, Goodenow believed that a real revenue-sharing plan, in which the big market teams subsidized the small market teams, was the answer to the problem. This was already being done in baseball and football and to a lesser degree in basketball. No such plan existed in hockey.

Bettman made swift progress in meeting his first two objectives. Within the first few years of his reign, the Quebec Nordiques became the Colorado Avalanche; the Winnipeg Jets became the Phoenix Coyotes; the Minnesota North Stars became the Dallas Stars; the Hartford Whalers became the Carolina Hurricanes; and new franchises popped up in Miami, Atlanta, Anaheim, and Nashville.

Bettman's "Southern Strategy" had mixed results. It was hard in many of these new, warm-weather markets to establish loyal fan bases. The Phoenix franchise was in and out of bankruptcy, and the Atlanta franchise eventually moved back to Winnipeg to become the "new" Winnipeg Jets. But filling out the blank patches in the American map got the attention of TV executives—the league scored national deals, first with Fox and later with ESPN.

It was on his third objective—labor peace—that Bettman had a much tougher time. Hockey became the fiercest labor battleground in all of sports and would stay that way for nearly two decades.

Just days after he took over as NHL commissioner, Jeff Kessler and I ran into Gary at the NHL All-Star Game in Montreal, in February 1993. He asked us if we had any suggestions for improving the game. We came up with at least two thoughts that I can recall. First, we told him to get rid of the old conference names (Adams, Norris, Patrick, and Smythe), as no one had a clue who any of those long-deceased people were. We noted that East, West, North, and South seemed to work well with other sports, why not hockey? Second, we told him that every team should be required to have two Zambonis (the machines that resurface the ice) to speed up the intermission between periods. Both suggestions were eventually implemented, for which Kessler and I will take credit until our dying days.

Unfortunately, when it came to economic freedom for players, Bettman didn't care much for our ideas.

Negotiations for a new labor deal began in the spring of 1993. This was to be Bettman's show, and he wanted everyone to know it. Bettman had brought on Jeff Pash, fresh from the *McNeil* trial, as his new general counsel, in what had been Gil Stein's role. Pash, a Harvard-trained lawyer, was forever youthful, always friendly, extremely bright, and never to be completely trusted. He also added a veteran management labor lawyer from the Proskauer firm, Bob Batterman, another NYU graduate. Batterman was short, wiry, bearded, highly intelligent, and very experienced. He was a clever management ideologue and made for a perfect hatchet man in those instances where Bettman sought to be a statesman. This was quite a formidable team.

The early meetings with the NHL were pleasant enough. There were statements of optimism and expressions of hope that we could reach an agreement well before the September 1993 labor contract expiration. But as the weeks and the months wore on into the summer, the same old issues, with their attendant resentments, quickly popped to the surface. Bettman and Batterman lectured us about the fragility of small market franchises and the NHL's need for absolute "cost certainty."

This was like a bad Broadway show, with Bettman, Batterman, and Pash playing the leads. Batterman would give us occasional lectures on the US labor laws, while Pash typically sat quietly, smiling and thinking of new ways to screw the players. Batterman was truly diabolical—soft-spoken and pleasant, but always conjuring up clever ways to control player salaries. For the most part, few NHL owners attended the sessions, so after a while we no longer saw the need to bring many players. We were getting nowhere fast. Occasionally, John McMullen, owner of the New Jersey Devils, and Bill Wirtz (both of whom were hardliners) showed up to scowl. McMullen was then also the owner of the Houston Astros and a leading hardliner among the baseball owners. In turn, Mike Gartner, who had replaced the retired Bryan Trottier as NHLPA president, attended several meetings for our side.

As time wore on, Bettman and Pash began to flex their diminutive muscles in an effort to harass the players into submission. First, during the summer of 1993, Bettman refused to recognize the status of two young Swedish players, Marcus Naslund and Peter Forsberg, as free agents, prompting litigation. Ultimately, both players signed lucrative contracts: Naslund with the Pittsburgh Penguins and Forsberg with the Quebec Nordiques as part of a trade that sent Eric Lindros to the Flyers.

Then in December 1993, the NHL filed another lawsuit against the NHLPA regarding the licensing of player jerseys, a right that the players had obtained in the prior collective bargaining agreement. According to the *New York Times*, "The lawsuit had been authorized by Jeff Pash, the new Senior Vice President and General Counsel for the League." Gartner told the *Times* on December 9, 1993, "I am most distressed to see the League trying to take away a right which was expressly recognized by everyone in the last collective bargaining agreement."[67] The case, which we defended, was eventually settled in the players' favor.

In addition, again in an effort to hold down salary escalation, Bettman invalidated offer sheets from the San Jose Sharks to several players including Edmonton's Greg Simpson and Washington's Kelly Miller. This time, we sued. We attacked Bettman for making decisions that should have been sent to an impartial arbitrator, asserting Bettman's obvious bias in seeking to hold down salaries. The court sided with the league based on an arcane provision of the expired collective bargaining agreement.

By late August, the odds were clearly against getting a deal done by the time the prior agreement expired in mid-September. As the deadline approached, the parties agreed to play the 1993–94 season without a formal collective bargaining agreement.

Fearing a repeat of the 1992 playoff strike, Bettman insisted that we enter into a no-strike, no-lockout agreement at least until the end of the 1993–94 season. In the hope of eventually getting a deal, we agreed.

During the fall and winter of 1993–94, we held sporadic bargaining sessions that typically devolved into lecturing back and forth, sniping at each other, and forced cheeriness. Even George Cohen, the ultimate optimist, was discouraged. During this period, the Bettman-Goodenow relationship began to disintegrate. From the start, there was little love lost between them, but as the weeks and months wore on, it turned from distaste to distrust to intense dislike. Goodenow began referring to Bettman as "that little dickhead" so frequently that my two younger daughters, rabid New York Rangers fans, picked it up. "Look, Daddy, the little dickhead is on television," they would say when we watched games together. It was sad and hilarious all at once.

Since we were getting nowhere, the parties decided to take a break from negotiations to attend the Winter Olympics in Lillehammer, Norway. At the time, there were ongoing negotiations with the International Olympic Committee about having NHL players participate in the next Olympics, set to take place in Japan in 1998. It was a controversial idea because it would mean that every four years, the NHL would have to suspend its season for two weeks. Bettman and Goodenow were involved in those negotiations. Goodenow invited George Cohen and me and our wives to attend the games with him and his wife, Wendy.

It was the coldest Olympics in history. The only way to keep warm was human contact, so we crowded into bars and walked shoulder to shoulder down the village streets.

Fortunately, the games were amazing. We had a hell of a time watching Olympic hockey, ski jumping, downhill skiing, and ice-skating. This was the year of the infamous Tonya Harding scandal, which kept us all captivated. The trip was a huge success in every way except for the reason we actually went—that it might lead to a thaw in our frozen negotiations. It did nothing of the kind. When we returned to the bargaining table, the NHL continued to stonewall us. We made modest proposals, like free agency after six years in the league or after the age of 27. Their response: "Never."

As the playoffs got under way in the spring of 1994, Bettman began threatening to impose a lockout if the players didn't agree to some form of salary limit. Then came the Stanley Cup Finals, which the New York Rangers won for the first time in 45 years. As a lifelong

Rangers fan, I made sure I was at the deciding game in June 1994 with Goodenow and Meyer; I had never seen anything like it, before or since. As the horn sounded, clinching the Rangers' 2–1 Game 7 victory over Vancouver, I looked over and saw a handwritten sign from a Rangers fan that read, "NOW I CAN DIE." People were literally weeping around us; the party went on in the streets of Manhattan until dawn.

Because it was New York, the media coverage was intense. Hockey was "in," and everyone was hopeful that this excitement would continue over to the next season. Bettman made sure that it didn't.

As talks remained stalled through the summer, I tried convincing Goodenow to decertify the union if Bettman went ahead with his lockout. Then we could bring an antitrust lawsuit. Goodenow was reluctant. By this time, our negotiating team had been joined by two of his old friends: John McCambridge, a Chicago lawyer and Goodenow's Harvard roommate, and Rob Reilly, a law school colleague from Detroit. McCambridge was a typical hardnosed litigator; Reilly was soft-spoken and more cerebral. Both were smart, dedicated, and good guys, though neither had a clue about collective bargaining in sports, much less in the NHL. They strongly advised Goodenow not to consider decertification because in their view it was too risky, notwithstanding our experiences in both football and basketball. They were concerned that if the case dragged on too long in the face of a lockout, the players' resolve might collapse. It was uncharted territory.

As the new season approached and the threat of a lockout loomed, I sensed that because of my prior involvement with salary caps, Goodenow was concerned about the optics of my continued involvement. He did not want to signal to the other side any willingness to compromise on a cap. Sensitive to this, and knowing that I had a trial scheduled for Westinghouse to start in the beginning of September in Pittsburgh, I stepped back from the negotiations, though I continued to strongly advise Goodenow to decertify the union. Clients don't always take your advice. This time, Goodenow may well have been right.

Late that summer, Bettman played his hand. He formalized his list of demands, a draconian package that included a salary cap and a luxury tax as well as the elimination of salary arbitration and guaranteed contracts. Oh, and he wanted to drastically cut pensions and benefits. It was as if he had never heard a word we'd said.

On October 1, 1994, with less than a week before the start of the season, Bettman announced, "with great regret," that the players were being locked out. This lockout was the first of its kind in sports. It was designed by Bettman and his henchmen Pash and Batterman to be the ultimate pressure tactic to force the players to surrender. Hockey fans were outraged, and the Rangers dynasty was short-lived, much to my daughters' dismay.

Though I was neck-deep in my case in Pittsburgh, I stayed in touch with Goodenow, who was absolutely convinced that the owners would blink first. His players weren't panicking. Some decided to play in Europe, others remained in North America to play in a number of charity event tournaments organized by the NHLPA. There was a "four-on-four challenge" tournament, and many NHL stars, including Patrick Roy, Luke Robitaille, Joe Sakic, Doug Gilmore, Rob Blake, and Mike Richter were involved. Meanwhile, Wayne Gretzky and a group of friends formed the so-called 99 All-Stars Tour and played a series of exhibition games in the US and in Europe. Not that it was all hunky-dory. Chris Chelios, the star defenseman for the Chicago Blackhawks, warned that Bettman needed to "watch out for his own well-being," which struck some as a threat. Others concluded that Chelios, a friendly Greek, was simply being protective.

By the end of December, Bettman was under enormous pressure from wealthier team owners in Detroit, Philadelphia, New York, and Toronto to end the lockout. They made it clear to him they did not want to be the first league in North American sports history to wipe out an entire season for the sake of keeping teams in Hartford and Quebec City. Bettman couldn't hold the fort. Though he and Goodenow had virtually no direct contact throughout the lockout, Bob remained steadfast, communicating with players, agents, reporters, and even a few owners, successfully undermining the owners' resolve.

On January 11, 1995, the parties announced a new six-year collective bargaining agreement. After 103 days of lockout, the owners came away with no salary cap, no luxury tax, and a few minor concessions on salary arbitration and rookies. Benefits were increased and guaranteed contracts remained in place. Most importantly, Goodenow had forced the owners to agree for the first time to unrestricted free agency for players at the age of 31, dropping down after two years to age 30 or after nine seasons. While this may have seemed insignificant at the time, it kicked the legs out from under the entire NHL salary structure. Since a fair number of top players were able to play well into their 30s, this new form of unrestricted free agency quickly boosted salaries. Now, for the first time, there was also a competitive marketplace for younger players seeking salary arbitration to use as a guide. The six-year deal was later extended four more years.

One result of the deal was hastening franchise movement. The following summer, the Quebec Nordiques moved to Denver, and in 1996, the Winnipeg Jets moved to Phoenix. Barry Shenkarow had apparently taken my earlier advice and sold his beloved Jets to new ownership in a larger market. The Hartford Whalers became the Carolina Hurricanes in 1997.

But free agency was actually good for the competitive balance of the league. In the decade following the 1995 agreement, several smaller market teams (namely, Colorado and Tampa) used free agency to win Stanley Cups. The league's rapid expansion strategy also led to an explosion in league revenues, which exceeded $2 billion by the end of the 10 year deal, a four-fold increase from 1990. Profitability, however, suffered. NHL owners just could not keep their checkbooks in check; competition for players led salaries to consume 70 percent or more of the league's revenues. The league limped along, losing its national TV contract along the way. Bettman's initial lockout strategy had backfired, and he seethed quietly as players' salaries continued to skyrocket. I ran into him from time to time, and he was always cordial, but I had the sense he was a man on a mission.

Over the next decade, Goodenow and I maintained our warm relationship over periodic drinks and steak dinners in New York and elsewhere. I marveled at his ability to keep this player bonanza going in the face of the terrible economics being reported by the league year after year. I warned him more than once that this couldn't last forever.

Despite this turmoil, Bettman managed to hang onto his job by promising his owners he would do better next time. He seemed to have matured as a leader, and his owners continued to have confidence in him. As the end of the deal approached in the fall of 2004, Bettman made it clear to the hockey world that this time he was going to get his salary cap. He had hired Arthur Levitt, formerly of the Securities and Exchange Commission, to prepare a financial report, which purportedly showed that player salaries and benefits absorbed more than 75 percent of the league's gross revenues and that the league had lost nearly $300 million the previous year. The numbers were certainly exaggerated, but the underlying truth was hard to deny. Like basketball in the early 1980s, hockey was in financial distress. Pittsburgh, Ottawa, and Buffalo had declared bankruptcy in the preceding years, and Edmonton had already announced that they would have to fold if there was not a lockout. Washington was also in trouble. The NHL had lost its major US television network contract and attendance was down in a number of cities.

Bettman looked at the players with their fat new contracts and thought, this is all their fault. Goodenow was willing to consider a luxury tax system, similar to the one already in place in baseball, but that was as far as he would go. A salary cap was out of the question. Bettman said if there was no cap, there was no season. He had seen that the NBA lockout strategy utilized by his former mentor David Stern in 1999 had forced the basketball players to cave and was convinced that the same tactic would work in hockey.

So when the old agreement expired at the stroke of midnight on September 15, 2004, the second lockout in NHL history commenced. Both sides dug in for a long one, and that's exactly what transpired. Christmas came and went without hockey.

As the lockout extended into 2005, I would call Bob and tell him what I'd told him for a decade: "If you're not going to agree to a cap, then decertify and sue." Don Fehr, who had become a mentor to Goodenow over the years, advised him to do the same. But Goodenow remained confident and stubborn. He was sure the NHL owners would collapse just as they had a decade earlier.

In early February, the parties got together for one last shot at salvaging a season. The NHL was represented by its chief legal officer, Bill Daley (who had once been a young associate working on the *McNeil* case for the NFL), and the ever-present Bob Batterman. The union was represented by then senior director Ted Saskin and John McCambridge. NHLPA president Trevor Linden, Vancouver's star center, who had always been a staunch Goodenow supporter, had apparently become frustrated and declined to participate. The parties met, as they had for many weeks, without the participation of the guys at the top, Bettman and Goodenow—never a good sign.

By this time, the players had already offered a 24 percent rollback of salaries across the board—an enormous concession—that the league soundly rejected. When I first heard this, I was shocked. If you are going to concede that much that soon, you should just agree to a salary cap and take advantage of the upside in revenue growth.

Final offers were exchanged in early February and once again came to nothing. Unless the lockout was resolved by mid-February, Bettman declared, the season was over. The union finally accepted a salary cap untethered to revenue growth. It was too little too late. On February 16, 2005, Bettman officially called off the season. The little dickhead seemed genuinely upset about it. I'll give him that.

By the time it was all over, it would be the longest labor outage in the history of North American sports. The longer it went, the greater the leverage for the owners—for the simple reason that time was more precious to the players. Losing a whole season had been a massive sacrifice. Losing two seasons was unthinkable. In July, the players, led by Trevor Linden, pushed Goodenow aside.

Over the next few weeks, with Saskin, Linden, and McCambridge leading the negotiations, a deal was cut that included a truly hard salary cap and a huge reduction in the players' share of revenues to 55 percent. It amounted to an unconditional surrender on the part of the players. The deal was finalized on July 22, and one week later, Goodenow resigned.

This was the worst disaster for sports unions ever. After a work stoppage of 10 months and 6 days, the players got nothing but grief and lost opportunities—not to mention lost wages. Unrestricted free agency was attained (at age 27 or after seven seasons in the league), but only at the exorbitant cost of a true hard cap, by far the most restrictive in the industry. The new executive director of the NHLPA, Ted Saskin, was rewarded with a $2 million contract, something that Marvin Miller, baseball's former union head, found outrageous, telling the press that "Saskin was being paid to surrender."[68]

I was entering into a new round of negotiations in football, and I wanted to be as far away from hockey as possible. We were about to demand an increase in our share of football revenue, and the last thing we needed were NFL owners sensing an edge after the victory of their brethren in the NHL. Don Fehr, still leading the MLBPA, had already avoided a salary cap in baseball by agreeing to a luxury tax system that had little impact on salaries. He too wanted to guard against a spillover effect from the hockey debacle.

The NHLPA descended into chaos for the next several years. Saskin was fired in 2007 after an investigation for, among other things, secretly accessing player email accounts. Apparently he'd feared a coup. The next guy was Paul Kelly—the same Paul Kelly who years earlier had investigated and successfully prosecuted Alan Eagleson. The union "lost confidence" in Kelly within two years, and he too was fired. His interim successor resigned after only a few months. It was total mayhem, an after-effect of Bettman's scorched-earth triumph.

Order was eventually restored by the appointment of Don Fehr, who had stepped down from the MLBPA at the end of 2009. Though he'd had informal contacts with the hockey players for years, he was reluctant to take the job, finally relenting after entreaties by dozens of hockey players past and present. Fehr's appointment would lead to my return to the NHL a few years later.

The hockey lockout presaged a new era of volatility throughout the sports world. The good news was that free agency was now an accepted feature of all four major leagues. The not-so-good news was that a new corporate mentality was emerging—the mom-and-pop days were ancient history. Franchise values were through the roof. Billions of dollars were at stake. Sophisticated new investors were on the scene, demanding more control and greater returns. We all knew who they thought was going to pay the price for that.

CHAPTER 17

A Union in Turmoil

LARRY FLEISHER WOULD HAVE BEEN A TOUGH ACT for anyone to follow, but Charlie Grantham was really out of his depth. He was smart enough, and he knew the issues pretty well. But a union leader in a high-profile industry like sports needs a lot more to succeed. The great ones (Miller, Upshaw, Fehr, and Fleisher) are willing to sweat the details, take decisive action, and always, always put their players' interests ahead of their own. Grantham had two principal flaws: he didn't like to get his hands dirty with the details, and he was always looking for an opportunity to take credit for the accomplishments of others. He sometimes claimed to have been intimately involved in the creation of the salary cap and the development of the NBA drug program. In fact, he had little to do with either. He also claimed to have been a principal negotiator of the four collective bargaining agreements between 1980 and 1995, which was also not true.

He attended a few of the key sessions, but when he was in the room, he was basically a backbencher. Taking over as NBPA executive director, he spent much of his time giving interviews and accepting awards for things he hadn't done. It was a good thing Fleisher was dead. Watching Grantham make a mess of his old job would have been hell for him.

The union in the post-Fleisher era had another serious handicap, and his name was Isiah Thomas, the man who succeeded Alex English as NBPA president. In my time with Larry, I can only ever remember him having differences with a handful of players. He rarely complained about anyone, except Isiah. He did not like Isiah Thomas at all. He considered him supremely selfish and untrustworthy. "He doesn't particularly like white people," Larry told me, "particularly if they happen to be Jewish."

With Charlie and Isiah at the helm, I began to let Kessler and Meyer take the lead in day-to-day union issues. I didn't have any personal connection to the new union leadership like I'd had with Fleisher and earlier NBPA presidents (Oscar, Silas, Lanier, and Junior Bridgeman). But Grantham did insist that I stay involved in all major disputes with the NBA. He had some sense of what he was up against.

Unlike Fleisher, Grantham was not a lawyer, so he had to hire a general counsel. There were a number of strong candidates, including Ted Wells, a prominent African American lawyer who would go on to become one of the nation's top trial lawyers and the author of the now infamous NFL "Deflategate" report. But Grantham made a bizarre choice, selecting Simon Gourdine, the former NBA deputy commissioner, who Stern had effectively forced out a decade earlier.

Gourdine, a graduate of Fordham Law and a former assistant US attorney, had joined the NBA in 1970. When he became deputy commissioner to Walter Kennedy in 1974, he was the highest-ranking black executive in sports. But after Kennedy was replaced by Larry O'Brien, Gourdine was eclipsed by Stern, who quickly became O'Brien's most trusted advisor. Gourdine left the NBA in 1981 and bounced around a number of New York City municipal positions. I had known him from the *Robertson* days and always considered him to be a nice man but a plodder. He was no match for David Stern.

I was appalled when I heard Grantham had hired Gourdine. The notion of hiring someone who had worked for the league to be the union's chief lawyer made no sense. Grantham hadn't consulted me, and by the time I became aware of his decision, it was too late.

Conflict with the new union leadership emerged almost immediately. A major part of the day-to-day running of the union was carefully overseeing the NBA's numbers to ensure that the players got their full share of the revenue-sharing system put in place back in

1983. There was so much money pouring into the league from so many different sources that the union had to be supervigilant in its oversight—any income that wasn't counted wouldn't get shared. No one at Weil had ever been charged with this task. It was the job of the NBPA staff.

Unfortunately, they weren't actually doing it. After the 1990–91 season, Jeff Kessler told me he suspected that the NBA was not including all basketball-related income in the salary cap calculation as per our agreement. Obviously, the more revenue included in the calculation, the higher the salary cap and the more money that would be available for players.

From a quick review, it appeared that the NBA and its teams were either underreporting, or not reporting at all, revenue from luxury suites, arena signage, and certain TV rights sales. Kessler thought that these "oversights" could amount to tens of millions of dollars or more over the last three seasons. Knowing the NBA, I wasn't particularly surprised, but I was angry.

We immediately raised this with Grantham and Gourdine, who seemed embarrassed that they had somehow missed this. They directed us to investigate, and on closer inspection we determined that more than $90 million had not been reported properly. We confronted league officials who, as usual, feigned innocence and claimed that these amounts did not need to be included, which we thought was ridiculous. We filed a proceeding before the new Special Master, Ted Clark, former president of the Bar Association of the City of New York.

At this point, Weil had been working with the NBPA for a quarter of a century. We knew the NBA free agency and salary system cold; after all, we had been intimately involved in their creation. We had had a close working relationship with the players, their agents, and the union for more than two decades, which made getting things done a lot easier. We also knew the enemy better than anyone.

After we filed the proceeding with the Special Master in the fall of 1991, we met with Isiah and other members of the NBPA's executive committee at the NBPA office on Broadway. Bruce Meyer and I attended along with Grantham and Gourdine and other committee members, including Dallas guard Rolando Blackman, Los Angeles Clippers guard Norm Nixon, and Portland forward Buck Williams.

We outlined the situation to the committee and told them our plans. Out of nowhere, Isiah began accusing Bruce and me of having "fucked this thing up." He said he couldn't understand why we, the lawyers, had missed this. I told him calmly that we had never been asked to review the salary cap calculations and that we'd assumed it was being handled by the Players Association.

It was only because we were doing minimal due diligence that we, and not the NBPA staff, had uncovered the shortfall. Thomas kept insisting that it was our fault. He stood up and started yelling; I stood up and started yelling back. Blackman and Nixon pulled us apart. I quickly calmed down and outlined our strategy as Isiah sat staring menacingly at me. I thought to myself, "Now I understand what Fleisher was talking about." Meyer sat there flabbergasted. Neither of us could understand why Grantham and Gourdine didn't come to our defense. They knew the truth but didn't say a word throughout the meeting. As Bruce and I walked back to the office, I said to him, "I'm not sure we can trust these guys anymore."

I never spoke to Isiah Thomas again. He stepped down as president the following year. Buck Williams, a decent and reasonable man, replaced him.

We presented our evidence to the Special Master, who made it clear during the hearings that he wasn't buying the league's "my dog ate my homework"–type arguments. They had no credible way of explaining how, say, a luxury suite was not directly related to basketball. Everything was about basketball. But the adversarial relationship we had with the NBA was not conducive to quick resolutions. The thing dragged on.

Finally, at the All-Star Game in Orlando in February 1992, the parties announced a settlement. Grantham wanted to avoid lengthy appeals and lock in significant benefits for the players immediately. The NBA agreed to increase the salary cap by $62 million over the next two years while refusing to admit guilt. These revenue streams were eventually included in the next collective bargaining agreement. The NBA had shown us its true colors. We had caught them hiding money. The "partnership" with the players that David Stern had been so bubbly about was obviously a crock.

For our firm and me personally, working with the NBPA had, for the first time, become strained and uncomfortable. It wasn't just the crazy outburst by Isiah. My relationship with Gourdine and Grantham had become more and more distant. I knew we were heading for a showdown.

The seven-year deal that we had negotiated with the NBA in 1988 in the wake of the *Bridgeman* lawsuit was due to expire in June 1994, and a lot had happened in the sports world during those intervening seven years. The football players had won free agency with the *McNeil* case, the hockey players had staged a successful strike, and the baseball players had won hundreds of millions of dollars from their owners in the collusion cases.

As the deal's end approached, the NBA looked healthy enough on the surface. The Bird-Magic rivalry, Detroit's "Bad Boys," Michael Jordan, and the 1992 Olympic Dream Team were driving the game's popularity to new heights—and along with it, revenues from attendance and TV. But player salaries had continued to skyrocket too, accounting for nearly 60 percent of league revenues, and Stern was grumbling that he, like his former acolyte Bettman in hockey, needed "cost certainty." Stern claimed that many teams were losing money and talked incessantly about preventing the further escalation of player salaries. Then he raised the specter of a lockout, the first ever in the history of the NBA.

After the *White* settlement in football in mid-1993, Kessler and I met with Grantham and Gourdine on several occasions to discuss strategy. As we had in hockey, we urged the union leadership to consider decertification in the face of a possible lockout because we believed that under those circumstances, a lockout would be illegal. They demurred. I suspected that both Grantham and Gourdine were worried about their jobs, something that had never bothered Fleisher or Upshaw.

Late in the fall of 1993, I was summoned to the NBPA office for a one-on-one meeting with Gourdine, where I was informed that Weil was being replaced as their outside law firm. At first, he gave no reason. I wasn't particularly surprised, but I sure wasn't happy. I pressed him for a reason, and he said simply that we had philosophical differences over how to approach the next bargaining session. That just told me that they didn't have the guts to decertify. I walked out without shaking his hand. I didn't even see Grantham that day. He didn't have the balls to face me.

Leaving the office, I thought about all that our firm had done for the NBPA for nearly a quarter of a century, often on shoestring budgets or without being paid at all. Not even a thank you. I had mixed emotions about it all. I was angry we had been fired despite our knowledge and expertise, relieved I didn't have to deal with people I didn't respect, and concerned that we were leaving the union in the hands of these clowns. I didn't give a damn about losing the business; it never paid well anyway. I still had plenty to do in football and in hockey, and by now, I was knee-deep in my trial practice. I decided it was time to move on.

I learned soon after that Gourdine had hired Cravath, Swaine & Moore to represent the union in the upcoming negotiations. The head lawyer for Cravath was Frederick A. O. Schwarz Jr., a former New York City corporate counsel. He and Gourdine had worked together when Gourdine was on the municipal payroll, and they were good friends. I knew Cravath to be a terrific firm, but they knew absolutely nothing about collective bargaining in sports. Moreover, they had no experience with the labor defense and how it would play out in the context of the negotiations.

It wouldn't be long before David Stern put the NBPA's new counsel to the test. A few months later, on June 17, 1994, the very day that the *Bridgeman* agreement expired, the NBA seized the initiative and filed a lawsuit in federal court in New York, seeking a ruling that the NBA and its owners were still protected by the labor defense from antitrust lawsuits even after the collective bargaining agreement ended. You might not recall much coverage of this in the media because it happened to be the same day that Game 5 of the NBA Finals was interrupted by O. J. Simpson's infamous low-speed car chase in his white Bronco. But make no mistake—what Stern and the NBA did was a major development. They had jumped the gun on the union, catching the NBPA and its new lawyers flat-footed. In complex litigation like this, the first to file has distinct advantages: the choice of where to sue to try to find a friendly court and the ability to frame the issues in a way most favorable to your side. This was exactly the maneuver we had warned Gourdine about before he fired us.

The case, *NBA v. Buck Williams* (Williams was NBPA president), was assigned to Judge Kevin Duffy, a former prosecutor and an old-line conservative—a good judge but a very bad choice for the players. The NBA also brought in a new set of lawyers: Frank Rothman and his *McNeil* sidekick, Shep Goldfein, to supplement Howie Ganz and Jeff Mishkin, the old Proskauer hands. The case went poorly for the players from the start. Judge Duffy pummeled both sides with glee, making it clear that while he didn't appreciate Rothman's bombast, he didn't like the union's legal position at all. Ultimately, Duffy sided with the NBA, citing former Yale professor Ralph Winter's article "Superstars in Peonage." So long as there was a union in existence, Duffy ruled, the NBA owners were immune from being sued by the players under the antitrust laws. It was now painfully obvious that the NBPA should have decertified.

Shell-shocked, the NBPA was forced to take an immediate appeal to the Second Circuit Court of Appeals. As the appeal process dragged on into the fall of 1994, both sides agreed to start the season without a labor agreement. Stern insisted on a no-strike, no-lockout clause to guard against the players striking at playoff time, as had happened in hockey in 1992. Meanwhile, negotiations for a new collective bargaining agreement proceeded at a snail's pace while the parties awaited the outcome of the appeal. Once again, Stern wanted to make the players responsible for saving the NBA owners from spending themselves into bankruptcy. Stern was now insisting on a new luxury tax system on top of a revised salary cap with no exceptions, a double whammy for the players. Even Grantham and Gourdine knew enough at this point to resist Stern's outrageous demands.

The *Williams* appeal was argued in the New York appeals court on September 22, 1994. Rothman argued for the NBA; Fred Schwarz for the players. The players never had a chance. The three-judge panel was presided over by former professor, now federal appeals judge, Ralph Winter, who made it clear from his questions that the players were going to lose. On January 24, 1995, the panel denied the players' appeal in an opinion written by Judge Winter. Winter followed his old law review article to the letter, and he affirmed Judge Duffy's ruling in all respects. He also relied on the earlier *Powell* decision in football, which had ruled that, absent decertification, the labor exemption would protect team owners from antitrust lawsuits. The *Powell* ruling was what had led us to decertify the NFLPA back in 1989. The final word on the issue would come two years later from the United States Supreme Court, but it was clear by now that in order for the NBA players to maintain their powerful antitrust rights, they would have to disclaim collective bargaining in favor of litigation. But the Grantham-Gourdine team stubbornly declined to do so.

When negotiations resumed a few weeks later in March 1995, Judge Winter's decision placed the players at a distinct disadvantage. Then in mid-April, the players suffered another setback. Grantham abruptly resigned over "irreconcilable differences" and was replaced by Gourdine.

Nobody was buying Grantham's story. Players and agents demanded an explanation for why he had resigned so abruptly without their knowledge. They suspected the union leadership was engaged in some sort of cover-up.

Though the reasons for Grantham's resignation have never been fully disclosed, I was told later by a number of players that there had been irregularities in Grantham's travel expenses amounting to tens of thousands of dollars over several years. Whatever the truth, the union was now in disarray, with a management lawyer in charge of the negotiations for the union. Gourdine had apparently been the one who forced Grantham's resignation. Some said Gourdine had stabbed Charlie in the back—*Et tu*, Simon? Gourdine would now have his chance to go head-to-head with his former rival, David Stern. I didn't like Gourdine's chances from the outset, I'll tell you that much.

Watching all this from the sidelines was driving me nuts. I was afraid that Gourdine and his new lawyers would give away everything we had fought so hard to achieve—free agency with a soft cap, a highly competitive marketplace, and the majority share of basketball-related income.

I had been getting calls throughout the spring from a number of agents, including Marc Fleisher (Larry's son) and superagent David Falk, asking me what was going on at the NBPA. I had known Marc for many years and had recently officiated at his wedding in Acapulco. Falk was then the number one agent in basketball; his clients included Michael Jordan, Patrick Ewing, Alonzo Mourning, and Reggie Miller, among others.

Marc Fleisher and Falk were appalled at what was going on in the Players Association—the confusion, the chaos, the lack of leadership. They had no faith in Simon Gourdine as the lead negotiator. He was a management lawyer at heart, some said; others worried that he was just incompetent. Either way, the consensus was that David Stern was going to eat Gourdine alive at the bargaining table.

On Saturday of Memorial Day weekend as I was at our house in Cape Cod preparing for another Westinghouse trial, Marc Fleisher called and asked if I could jump on a conference call right then and there. He had David Falk, Arn Tellem, Bill Strickland, and several other agents standing by.

I asked Marc what was going on.

"Just wait—you won't believe it," he responded. I sat on the floor of our master bedroom, where the only working phone was located, and proceeded to get an earful. They told me that Gourdine was about to sign a disastrous deal that included a new luxury tax, a gutting of the major salary cap exceptions, and a rookie wage scale. Gourdine had apparently been spooked by Stern's tough talk about a lockout.

I told them the only thing they could do was to try to decertify the union as quickly as possible, fire Gourdine, and take over the negotiations. I also told them that I was about to go to trial down in Texas in a week and would be out of action for months, but that I would ask Jeff Kessler to get involved because he knew the decertification issues better than anybody. I called Kessler right away and told him the situation. We set up another conference call for the next day to review our options.

This was to be Jeff Kessler's first real test under fire. He was no longer the junior partner; he was now about to be the guy in charge. Not yet 40 years old, Kessler had a combination of brilliance and enthusiasm second to none. He was the ultimate optimist and would march through walls for the players. There wasn't a lot of time, but the agent group pledged their cooperation. Working with Kessler, they began to mobilize the opposition. The group had to act quickly to block Gourdine from signing off on any deal. This was to be the summer of the players' discontent.

On June 22, 1995, after a late night of negotiations, the NBA and Gourdine announced the deal we all feared. Stern finally had his hard cap, at least for the time being.

At virtually the same moment, a group of 17 players, led by Michael Jordan and Patrick Ewing, filed a petition before the NLRB to seek to decertify the union. An election, supervised by the NLRB, would have to be held. A majority of players—200 or more—would have to vote to decertify. Stern immediately went on the attack, calling Kessler "a disgruntled lawyer whose firm [Weil] was terminated by the Players Association."[69] He also attacked the agents and particularly Marc Fleisher, who he called "the self-proclaimed spokesman for the group who seems only interested in ousting the union leadership that replaced his father."[70] Stern never did pull his punches.

Politics does indeed make for strange bedfellows. In this case, the NBA and Gourdine joined forces against a large portion of the union membership. The decertification election was set for the end of August, and a summer of basketball politicking ensued. Stern and Gourdine predicted chaos: If the union were to be decertified, what system would the NBA operate under for the 1995–96 season? If the so-called dissidents were successful in blowing up the union, antitrust lawsuits were sure to follow, as they had in the NFL. "There is an absolute groundswell of dissatisfaction of players who believe it's no longer in their interest to have a union represent them," Kessler told the media. "They prefer to assert their legal rights [in court] against the league without being encumbered by the union."[71]

Gourdine tried to push through an immediate approval of the deal; the agents and their players balked. They claimed they needed more time to review the specifics of the deal, and they wanted to await the outcome of the decertification vote. Meetings were held throughout the summer in DC, Chicago, and elsewhere. Kessler even recruited Gene Upshaw to speak at one of the opposition meetings. Upshaw emphasized the negotiating leverage that decertification gave the NFL players and how it led to us winning the *McNeil* case.

Throughout the long summer, Kessler was working tirelessly with Jordan, Ewing, and the key agent group; they met with literally hundreds of players. But the league and union's leadership—with Gourdine using president Buck Williams and first vice president Charles Smith, the Knicks forward, as his proxies—worked just as tirelessly to undermine the decertification vote.

The NBA held its own meetings with players and used scare tactics and misinformation to try to pummel the players into submission. Stern threatened to cancel the season—he scheduled a lockout for July 1, 1995—and the NBA even offered to pay certain players' airfare to voting venues. The "dissidents" were a bunch of spoiled superstars, the NBA claimed, and were merely puppets of their evil agents. The league's attempt to separate the superstars from the rank and file was counterproductive. Superstars like Oscar Robertson in basketball and Reggie White in football led those fights in the past precisely because they were respected as leaders by their peers. The reality is that a competitive marketplace benefits all players, superstars and journeymen alike.

In fact, many of the rank-and-file players rejected the league's superstar argument. As reported by Phil Sheraton in the *Philadelphia Inquirer* on August 17, 1995, "The players tried to downplay the role of the superstars. Journeymen like Washington's Jim McIlvaine and Indiana's LaSalle Thompson and Miami's Matt Geiger added their support for decertification. 'The reason you see people like Patrick Ewing and Michael Jordan in the headlines is that people listen to them,' McIlvaine said. 'But this affects a middle-of-the-road player like myself more than it does the All-Stars. These guys deserve credit for sticking their necks out for us.'"

As the threat of decertification became a realistic possibility, Stern realized he had overstepped and joined with the union to sweeten the pot. First, Gourdine, described in the press as "the union's beleaguered executive director,"[72] announced at the end of July, "We now have a clear mandate from the players to eliminate the tax."[73] Then the NBA dropped its attempt to gut the Bird exception; suddenly Stern's cap went soft again. Already, the decertification threat was having a positive effect.

As the deal improved, the NBA and the union began to emphasize to the players that they could lose tens of millions of dollars in salaries if the lockout continued into the season. They also harped on the chaos of life without a union and the loss of many more millions in pension and other benefits. Finally, they tried to get the players all stressed out about protracted antitrust lawsuits, pointing out that the *Williams* case had already gone badly for the players. Their propaganda was relentless and effective.

Fearing that a mail ballot might give agents undue influence, Gourdine insisted on a secret, in-person ballot. The NLRB agreed, and the voting was set to take place at regional NLRB offices. But even as the league softened the terms of the deal, they continued their intimidation tactics. "At stake in the election, besides the fate of the union, is the fate of the 1995–96 season,"[74] Russ Granik warned.

The NBA then offered to fly players to polling places as needed, but only those players who they expected to vote against decertification.

The voting was held on August 30 and 31, and the results were announced two weeks later. The NBA's threat to shut down the league had its desired effect: the union membership voted against decertification by a margin of 226–134, with 85 percent of eligible voters casting ballots. Within a week, the NBA owners and the union leadership tentatively approved the revised deal, and training camps opened a few days later. The NBA's first-ever lockout had lasted 73 days, though not a single paycheck or game had been lost. "A lot of players got intimidated by the threat of the owners that the season was going to end," Kessler said. "The strategy the NBA carried out was effective."[75]

The final deal included a rookie wage scale and the tightening of some of the salary cap exceptions, but there was no luxury tax, and the Bird exception was left intact. The opposition players had turned a terrible deal into something less terrible. The mere threat of decertification had worked. The revenue sources that had been the font of the prior dispute (luxury suites, signage, etc.) were now expressly included, increasing the salary cap going forward. And because the actual details of Gourdine's deal had not been finalized, there was some room left for further negotiation.

Meanwhile, Buck Williams and the union leadership tried to paper over the rift exposed by the decertification battle. "Michael, Patrick, and Alonzo are fine gentlemen," Williams said. "We just disagreed on how union business should be conducted."[76] I had known Buck for a number of years and respected him as a good man and a good leader. Unfortunately, he allowed himself to be the tool of someone else's agenda. That fall, Gourdine negotiated for himself a new multiyear contract, signed by Buck and rubber-stamped by the executive committee.

I returned from my trial in Texas a few months later to discover that although the vote had been held, the revolt was not over. Kessler and the agents were busy getting many of the so-called dissident players elected as player reps for their respective teams. By December, players who had voted in favor of decertification were representing more than 20 teams. Gourdine, absorbed in getting his own new contract, seemed oblivious to this development. Under the union bylaws, it was the board of player reps—not the union president or executive committee—who had the authority to hire or fire the executive director.

When these new player reps learned that Gourdine had manipulated Buck Williams into agreeing to a new contract, they were outraged. In mid-January 1996, several of the new player reps, led by Patrick Ewing, called for a meeting of all player reps to review the situation with Gourdine's contract. A conference call was convened, and Kessler and I were asked to participate. Ewing then asked for a vote on the renewal of Gourdine's contract. The vote was 22–5 to reject the contract and fire Gourdine. I had the pleasure of telling Simon, who was also on the phone, that he was terminated. A little revenge goes a long way.

In the months that followed, the negotiations to finalize the four-year deal that had been tentatively approved back in September resumed. Cravath, Swaine & Moore was gone, and Kessler and I were back at the table on behalf of Weil, along with Buck Williams, Patrick Ewing, Jim McIlvaine, and Alex English, among others. English had stepped in as interim executive director while we searched for Gourdine's replacement. Patrick Ewing replaced Buck Williams as president of the NBPA later that year.

Negotiations dragged on, and by June 1996, we still had not reached final agreement on licensing, the pension fund, salary cap details, and a few other matters. The *New York Times* reported that Stern was fed up and was once again threatening a lockout.

By that time, the key issue of when the labor defense ends had finally made it to the United States Supreme Court in the *Brown v. NFL* case in football. That was the case (a holdover from our earlier battles with the NFL) involving the NFL's fixing of taxi squad salaries at a flat thousand dollars a week.

Upshaw had decided to bring in a professional Supreme Court advocate, Ken Starr, the former US solicitor general. Starr had sided with us some years earlier when we unsuccessfully sought Supreme Court review of the earlier *Powell* decision. Starr had not yet been appointed special prosecutor in the Clinton-gate scandals, so he had time for us. He was clearly brilliant although totally lacking in charisma. Kessler and I spent hours with Starr trying to get him ready to argue the complex antitrust and labor concepts that both Kessler and I knew far better than he ever would. It wasn't his fault. Starr hadn't lived with these issues for decades like we had, and his responses to our moot court-type prep questions were never quite right. We were both worried.

The case was finally argued in the majestic Supreme Court building on March 27, 1996. Greg Levy, a Covington lawyer who had played a minor role in the *McNeil* trial, was now the NFL's lead outside lawyer. He knew the issues cold. I sat at the counsel table with Starr, crossing my fingers and holding my breath when he got up to argue. It was clear from the start that we were screwed. I remember Justices Scalia and Breyer bombarding Starr with questions, and he couldn't muster an adequate response. It was all I could do not to jump in and scream the answers—the most frustrating experience of my legal life. Nothing else comes close.

Levy, on the other hand, was brilliant, easily handling the few tough questions he got while laying out clearly why the NFL owners were entitled to a labor defense as long as there was a collective bargaining relationship with the union.

Several months later, on June 20, 1996, in an 8–1 decision, the Supreme Court ruled for the NFL. The only good news for our side was the statement, echoing Judge Doty in *McNeil* and the appeals court in *Powell*, that "the [labor defense] lasts [only] until the collapse of the collective bargaining relationship as evidenced by decertification of the union."

That was our backdoor victory. It was now finally clear that if the union decertified, the players could sue under the antitrust laws. The tactic was fully weaponized.

Days after the *Brown* decision came down in late June, as we still were trying to finalize the prior year's deal, Stern and I fell into a philosophical discussion over the same legal issues we had clashed over for more than two decades. As we bantered back and forth, Stern was bubbling over about the *Brown* decision and needling me about our "loss." Then he looked at me and said, "You know, Tagliabue made a big mistake in letting the *McNeil* case go to trial. I would have locked you out and never would have given you a chance to get to trial."

That fucking Stern. He was right, I thought to myself. Tagliabue allowing us to play while we were suing the league is what gave us the ability to get to a jury and ultimately win free agency for the football players. But I wasn't about to say that out loud. "You know, Stern, we thought you guys were right from the start," I said in reference to the *Brown* case. "What the hell took you so long to finally win? We got 20 years of benefits, and the Supreme Court said we were wrong all along?" Then I started to laugh.

Stern looked at me again, this time with a bit of a twinkle in his eye, and said, "Fuck you, Quinn." And then he laughed too. A few days later, we signed off on the deal, which would run through June 1998.

Two months later—August 1996—the NBPA player reps met in the blistering heat of Las Vegas to choose Gourdine's replacement. There were seven finalists, including former NBPA president Alex English, my old pal Paul Silas, and another old pal, Dick Berthelsen from the NFLPA, the only non–African American candidate. There was one wild card: Billy Hunter, a lawyer from San Francisco whom the search firm had put forward at the urging of his Syracuse classmate, Hall of Famer Dave Bing. I felt pretty good about the field except for Hunter, who I knew nothing about.

The night before the vote, I had dinner at a Vegas steakhouse with Kessler, Berthelsen, and our old colleague George Cohen. We discussed the field and agreed that Dick was a long shot. He had already been told by some of the player reps that "you're probably the most qualified, but you won't get it because you're white"—hardly surprising for an organization that is nearly 80 percent black.

Each of the candidates made a presentation to the player reps, and we heard that Hunter instantly stood out. His background was certainly impressive. He had been the captain of the football team at Syracuse and had drunk a cup of coffee in the NFL before going to law school at the University of California, Berkeley. At the age of 33, he became the country's youngest US attorney in history, appointed by President Jimmy Carter. Billy knew how to "talk the talk." All the other candidates seemed more qualified, but when Billy made his presentation, he was spellbinding. According to several players in attendance, Hunter argued like he was in front of a jury about how he would unite the players and fight for their interests.

Given what the players had just been through a year earlier, this message resonated. When the votes were in, Hunter won and was hired on the spot.

Later that day, Kessler and I reflected on all the upheaval in the union over the last few years: the botched search for Fleisher's successor, leading to Grantham's chaotic reign; Weil's firing; Gourdine's duplicity; and the internecine decertification fight. Now there was to be a new unknown leader whose seeming sagacity and soaring rhetoric about unity and toughness had apparently made him a reassuring figure in the eyes of the players. We just shook our heads and hoped for the best. It would prove to be a very bumpy ride.

CHAPTER 18

"Litigator to the Rescue"

AFTER THE BASKETBALL DEAL WAS BELATEDLY
signed in June 1996, I immersed myself in other work representing
major corporate clients. It was about this time that I really hit my
stride as a big-time trial lawyer. Because of the publicity from the
sports cases, I had acquired a bunch of new clients including Exxon,
Disney, CBS, and ESPN. I was trying jury cases all the time, and it
was fun, not to mention very lucrative. I had a $5 billion libel suit by
boxing promoter Don King against ESPN thrown out because we
were able to prove that King was libel-proof. When Dan Rather sued
CBS after he was ousted from his anchor chair, I had the case tossed by
showing that he had no legal right to be America's mouthpiece forever.
I convinced a Delaware jury to award half a billion dollars to Exxon
by showing that the Saudi government had defrauded Exxon. It was
all pretty heady stuff and a lot different from the sports cases that, with
the exception of the *McNeil* case, hardly ever go to trial.

Meanwhile, my close friend and partner Jeffrey Kessler took the
lead in dealing with the NBPA.

I never stopped following the NBA, of course. These were very
good years for my Knicks, and I knew better than to take my eye
off David Stern for long. As Bird and Magic gave way to Michael
Jordan, Stern cashed in with huge TV deals and a new emphasis on
international growth. Much more than the other leagues, the NBA
had turned into a legitimately global product. The revenue potential
seemed practically limitless, and the price tag for franchises reflected

this—it had gone from $100 million to half a billion in the blink of an eye. Rich guys wanted to own teams not just in Los Angeles and New York but in Cleveland and Milwaukee. The rising tide of the NBA was lifting all boats. Stern wanted to make sure that as much revenue as possible went into the owners' pockets rather than the players', and he wasn't too happy with how that was working out under the terms of the 1996 deal. The players' share had ballooned once again to almost 60 percent. With the collective bargaining agreement expiring in June 1998, King David was back to gunning for rollbacks and givebacks.

At the outset, it seemed that this time he would face a stronger opponent in the person of the new NBPA executive director, Billy Hunter. In my early dealings with Hunter, I found him to be pleasant enough, but like Grantham, he didn't get his hands dirty with the details, and he was also secretive and not particularly receptive to criticism. The players, however, had confidence in Hunter's ability to stand toe-to-toe with Stern.

By the end of June 1998, both sides were poised for a fight; Stern was now demanding a cap on individual player salaries, as well as the luxury tax that he hadn't gotten back in 1995; he also once again wanted to eliminate exceptions to the salary cap. He threatened another lockout. It was, as Yogi Berra famously said, "déjà vu all over again."

Stern was particularly focused on getting a maximum individual player salary as well as a luxury tax; he also added a new escrow concept, whereby the NBA owners would hold back up to 10 percent of players' salaries in any given year. This was supposedly to ensure that the NBA owners would not overpay in the event revenues remained flat or went down. In addition, for the first time, there was a focus on reducing the players' percentage of revenue to below 57 percent, which was the salary cap formula as originally negotiated. These weren't so much negotiating points as decrees. If the players didn't acquiesce, Stern was going to take his ball and go home, which is exactly what he did. On July 1, 1998, the owners locked out the players, which didn't mean much until September, when training camps failed to open.

Then in October, the regular season failed to start. On Thanksgiving, there was no pro basketball to be thankful for, and on Christmas, fans got nothing but coal in their stockings.

Through much of the fall, NBPA executive director Hunter and president Patrick Ewing did a solid job of holding the players together. They held a rally in Las Vegas at the end of October. "Players want to play," Charles Barkley told *Sports Illustrated*, "but we're not going to accept a crappy proposal just to get back on the floor or appease the fans. The owners have given us three proposals, but they've just been the same crap in different packages."[77]

Michael Jordan, Karl Malone, Michael Curry, Shaquille O'Neal, and David Robinson all stood shoulder to shoulder at the press conference after the meeting. There were, however, some dissenters. Danny Schayes, a member of the union's executive committee, raised questions about the union's refusal to compromise, and Utah guard John Stockton asked at one point if the players shouldn't at least consider accepting a smaller percentage of revenues. Things were beginning to fray.

Stern kept the pressure up relentlessly; he repeatedly threatened to cancel the entire season, much as Bettman had threatened to do in hockey back in 1994. During this time, I sounded my familiar refrain and urged Hunter to decertify the union. Kessler had also raised this with him several times over the course of the multimonth lockout. But Hunter was adamant that his players would stick together and that there was no need to take what he considered such drastic action. I could see this thing was heading in the wrong direction.

I was nervous; the players were losing big paychecks every week. I was afraid they would crack with the threat of losing the entire season—shades of the summer of 1995. I was stuck in another Exxon trial, but I talked to Kessler every few days. Not surprisingly, Jeff, ever the lead dog, was more optimistic, believing that the players' resolve remained strong.

Stern continued to make noises about ending the Bird exception, extending the rookie wage scale from three to six years and getting a hard cap and a luxury tax all at once. He also repeated the usual claptrap about the need to protect the small markets. The players responded that that was the owners' problem and that they needed to share revenues in much the same way as was being done in the NFL.

Hunter faced several serious problems, not the least of which was the perception of his union members as overpaid and overpampered. Hunter himself was perceived by some as anti-agent, and his close-to-the-vest style kept many of his players and their agents in the dark as to what was really going on. Unlike other successful union leaders, Hunter made little effort to keep the agents in line with his strategy, if he had one. He just seemed to be winging it. Worse, the old days of player solidarity and a willingness to fight to the death were long gone. Hunter did not have a tight rein on his constituents.

At the start of the season, former Fordham Law dean John Feerick was brought in to arbitrate whether the league had to pay players who had guaranteed contracts; in November, he ruled against the union. It was indicative of the general drift of things. The owners were winning the war of public opinion, due in part to some unfortunate comments from players about needing to feed their families on multimillion-dollar salaries. Celtics point guard Kenny Anderson unwisely said if the lockout continued, he might have to sell one of his eight sports cars in order to pay child support for his several children born out of wedlock.

In mid-December, Stern announced that the NBA was about to make its last and final offer before canceling the season. Right before Christmas, I got a call from Hunter asking me to get involved behind the scenes. He asked me to reach out to Russ Granik, with whom he knew I had a good relationship, to see if there was some way to bridge the gap. Over the next 10 days, including what was meant to be my vacation, Granik and I had a series of conversations and meetings. I remember one dinner in a Midtown Italian restaurant where I kept getting calls from my London office about some crisis or another. I told them, with a smile on my face and Granik looking over from the other side of the table, "Stop bothering me, I'm trying to save basketball."

At first, we talked about family and golf and how we were both missing vacation time. When we got down to business, we began by talking philosophy: How could the players and owners work together to make the league more popular, more profitable, and so on? We broached the current divide haltingly. What do the owners really want? What do the players have to have? It was all very touchy-feely.

Three days after Christmas, Stern issued another of his proclamations. The NBA had made their final offer, and he insisted that Hunter call a meeting of the players to vote on it by January or we could kiss the season good-bye. Stern also hinted at using replacement players.

When Don Fehr was asked about this, he said, "The whole notion of replacement players strikes me as positively bizarre. The market is there to watch NBA quality players, not a group of guys who couldn't play if the others were there."[78]

Under mounting pressure, Hunter agreed to hold a vote on the NBA's proposal on January 7, the very day that Stern had set as the deadline for canceling the season. There wasn't much else he could do. Player support was beginning to fracture. More than $400 million in salaries had been forfeited. The situation was dire.

Meanwhile, Granik and I had continued our back-channel discussions, which came to a head on January 6. Granik had just returned from a short Florida vacation. He and I met for a drink that afternoon and then walked over to the NBA offices on Fifth Avenue around seven o'clock that evening and sat down at a conference table, just the two of us.

We got down to specifics. Granik made it clear they had to have more cost certainty, maybe some kind of individual player cap within the overall per-team cap. I responded that our side absolutely had to preserve a strong free agency market with the current exceptions and the soft cap. I began to see the possibility of some kind of grand bargain here. But I was out on a limb; I had no authority to actually cut a deal without client approval.

After several hours alone, Granik and I finally called in Stern and the others, including Hunter, Kessler, and NBA general counsel

Joel Litvin. We were all crowded into a tiny, windowless conference room filled with pizza boxes. I was convinced that this was all part of Stern's plot to torture us into submission. It almost worked. In an ironic twist, Bob Lanier, former NBPA president who had signed off on the first salary cap back in 1983, was in the NBA offices that night. He did community outreach for the league. Lanier and I had several off-the-record conversations that night. Naturally he was urging that we get a deal done but, as he winked at me, "only if the players don't get screwed."

I became the catalyst; I was determined to move both sides toward a deal. Stern had staked out the individual player maximum as critical. He somehow saw this new concept as the key to his much-heralded need for cost certainty. Hunter had refused to agree. Sometime around midnight, in a sidebar discussion, I convinced Billy that salary cap exceptions like the Bird exception would keep driving up salaries. This is something we had learned way back in 1983. The Bird exception gave owners and general managers a way to subvert their own cap. We absolutely couldn't give that back.

I then echoed Bob Lanier's words about Moses Malone from years earlier, with a slight edit to take into account NBA salary inflation. I told Billy, "The max players should be able to survive on $15 million a year." It was worth doing to keep Bird and the other salary cap exceptions.

We continued to negotiate through the night, trading concessions until six in the morning. We finally gave in on the maximum player salary provision, which had been the stickler. The luxury tax and 10 percent escrow had already been conceded, but we saved the Bird and other salary cap exceptions. There was to be no hard cap in the NBA—not then, not ever.

As dawn broke, we ended our session and took the elevator down to the lobby of the NBA offices in the Olympic Tower. It was freezing cold, and the three of us didn't have a car. Hunter, Kessler, and I walked up Fifth Avenue together, knowing at least that we had likely saved the season. I went to my New York apartment to shower and get ready for a meeting in New Jersey with Exxon, which had long been set for that morning at nine o'clock. I called home to tell my wife and daughter Kerrin about the deal, then drove out to New Jersey at eight. When I got to my meeting, Exxon's assistant general counsel John O'Hern looked at me and asked, "What the hell happened to you?"

"I just saved basketball," I replied, "so don't give me any shit."

I drove back to the city shortly after noon, deposited my car in the parking garage on 58th Street, and walked up the street to the General Motors Building. When I got to the corner of 58th and 5th Avenue, I saw that the building was surrounded by satellite trucks and teeming with reporters. I realized that they were there for the player vote, the outcome of which was still up in the air. That morning, nearly 200 NBA players had come streaming into the General Motors Building. The final tally on a new seven-year deal was 179–5, in favor.

As I walked into the building, I thought about how much had changed in my 25-plus years in sports. Once upon a time, we had hammered out labor deals in dingy hotel rooms and woke up the next day to read maybe a paragraph about it buried in the newspaper. Now the minutiae of professional sports had turned into a 24/7 media spectacle. Average fans became conversant in salary caps and luxury taxes. It was a whole new ballgame.

I made my way to the large conference room in Weil's 25th-floor conference center, where the voting was taking place. I saw union president Patrick Ewing sitting by himself, head in hands. As I walked over, Patrick looked up and asked, "Quinn, did I mess this thing up?"

I bent down and responded in a whisper, "No way; you fought a good fight against tough, well-financed opponents. It will turn out fine." And it did.

On the face of it, the deal appeared to be a clear win for Stern. He pushed the players' share of revenue down to 55 percent, plus he got his luxury tax, his escrow, and the max salary. But the biggest thing for the players was that we maintained the softness of the cap,

278 DON'T BE AFRAID TO WIN

which meant that salaries would continue to go largely unchecked. Ironically, the individual player maximum had the perverse effect of having more players insisting on max salaries.

Over the seven years of the deal, the players enjoyed an 80 percent increase in salaries and benefits; when it expired in 2005, the average salary in the NBA was well over $4.5 million. Free agency, as a principle, was set in stone. The fight now was about the revenue split—how the enormous and ever-growing revenue pie was to be shared by owners and players. Times had changed.

And for a few brief, shining moments, I was hailed as a hero. In a column entitled "A Litigator to the Rescue," Murray Chass of the *New York Times* wrote,

> Jim Quinn, whose entry into the stalled National Basketball Association labor dispute marked the beginning of the end of the six-month impasse, is the most prolific litigator of sports antitrust cases in the quarter-century history of those high-powered court battles.
>
> But he is usually often behind the scenes, as he was Tuesday night, when his hour-long meeting with Russ Granik, the N.B.A.'s chief negotiator, laid the groundwork for the agreement.
>
> When the basketball agreement had been achieved, Quinn said he remarked to David Stern, the commissioner, "Now I can go back to obscurity."[79]

It was mostly bullshit, but I loved it. Several weeks later, *USA Today* added a few details to my personal legend:

> All anyone wants to talk about is the evening two weeks ago when he strolled a few blocks to initiate all-night talks to end the NBA lockout by dawn.
>
> But a call home prompted pragmatism. His teen-age daughter, Kerrin, went to school to make about $75 in bets that the lockout was over. Quinn laughs, with perhaps some pride: "I told her

if she keeps it up, she may hear from the Securities and Exchange Commission someday."

This week, Quinn returns to obscurity as the NBA returns to business.[80]

I returned to my trial practice and continued to try cases for many Fortune 100 clients. Little did I know that I would be called out of that relative obscurity to play the "savior" role once again a decade later.

CHAPTER 19

Death and Treachery

THE 1993 *WHITE* SETTLEMENT IN FOOTBALL HAD ushered in a period of untold riches for the NFL and its 32 owners. Over the next 12 years, league revenues nearly doubled to $6 billion. By 2005, according to *Forbes* magazine, the average NFL franchise was worth over $800 million. Three franchises (the Redskins, the Cowboys, and the Patriots) were now each valued at over a billion dollars; even the lowest-valued franchise, the Minnesota Vikings, came in at nearly $700 million. The total value of all 32 franchises was more than $25 billion. This was big business—really big business. New revenue sources like DirecTV's Sunday Ticket, Sunday Night Football, and the technology-driven explosion of computer games like Madden NFL and fantasy football had the league and its owners swimming in money.

Player salaries also went up significantly, more than doubling in the first 8 years of the deal. But we no longer believed that the players were getting their fair share of this bonanza; not a penny of the appreciation in team values went into their pockets. Moreover, under the originally agreed-on salary cap formula, certain categories of revenue, particularly licensing and local team revenue, were excluded from the totals used to determine the salary cap. As a result, the players' percentage of the overall revenue stream had steadily decreased from 62 percent in 1994 to less than 57 percent 10 years later. Needless to say, this was not a trajectory we liked. Something had to give, and we were determined it would be the NFL owners.

The *White* deal had been extended several times without any significant changes to the salary cap revenue-sharing formula, but the agreement was set to terminate at the end of the 2006 NFL season. Unless it was extended again, that season would be an uncapped year, as set forth in the original 1993 deal. The prior extensions had always been negotiated a year in advance to prevent the uncapped year from coming into play. The owners' collective fear of an uncapped year, we knew from experience, gave us enormous leverage. The last time there had been an uncapped year, back in 1993, players' salaries went up by 30 percent in a single season. The NFL owners were terrified that it could happen again.

In back-channel discussions with Commissioner Tagliabue, Upshaw and I made it clear that we wanted our original revenue percentage restored and that any split going forward would have to include the revenues that had been excluded from the original deal. Players, we demanded, were going to get a 60/40 split of the league's expanded revenues.

Tagliabue was careful not to concede anything. Instead, he frankly told us that in order for the union to get such a split, he needed to look out for teams that had less revenue, a point he made without the usual tear-jerking about small markets. We replied that we were prepared to support an enhanced revenue-sharing plan.

In spring 2005, Tagliabue invited Upshaw and me to a private dinner at the 21 Club in Manhattan with members of the newly constituted NFL Management Council (now known, for some reason, as the CEC, or Council Executive Committee). Present were four new members: Robert Kraft (New England), Jerry Jones (Dallas), Jim Irsay (Indianapolis), and the new committee chairman, Jerry Richardson, the owner of the Carolina Panthers. Holdovers Pat Bowlen, Dan Rooney, Wellington Mara, and John Shaw (president of the St. Louis Rams) attended as well.

This was the first time I had met Kraft and Jones, both of whom would play critical roles in negotiations. It was also the first time I met Richardson, a former Baltimore Colts end who had made a fortune in the fast-food business. Richardson was a plainspoken southerner who lacked any trace of Southern charm. He and Upshaw, as ex-players, got along fine, but I had the sense that Richardson took an immediate dislike to me because I was a lawyer and could be a bit of a wiseass. He never forgot, or forgave, my crack after the *White* settlement back in 1993, when I referred to the owners as "our junior partners."

We started the evening with cocktails in an upstairs private room followed by a sumptuous 21 Club dinner. It was all pleasant enough until Upshaw offhandedly remarked that the players were prepared to go to the uncapped year unless we got 60 percent of expanded revenues. Richardson reacted immediately and said that was never going to happen because small market teams could not afford it. The rest of the owners looked glum. Tagliabue quickly changed the subject.

When dinner was over, Upshaw and I went down to the 21 Club lounge to ponder the meeting over drinks. After one or two single malts too many, we vowed to stick to our 60 percent target. The die was cast.

Formal negotiations began a few weeks later and stretched out over the summer. From our side there were the usual suspects: Upshaw, Berthelsen, Allen, Kessler, and me. By this time, Kessler had left Weil and joined another prominent New York law firm, Dewey Ballantine. He later would become cochair of another powerful firm, Winston and Strawn. Jeffrey and I remained close friends and colleagues, and we continued to jointly represent the NFLPA.

In the early negotiations, Harold Henderson took the lead for the NFL along with his colleague, Peter Ruocco, who I had first met back in the old USFL days. Peter was the NFL's less-crazed version of a capologist, deeply steeped in financial data. Peter often talked about the interest of his college-age son, Ryan, in broadcasting; Ryan is now doing play-by-play for the Yankees.

Tagliabue was also at every meeting, carefully monitoring any progress along with a smattering of owners. Over the course of the summer, there was much discussion about local revenues, stadium debt, cost sharing, and franchise values, but very little progress. The sticking point remained our 60 percent number.

During the meetings, newcomers Kraft and Jones were particularly vocal. Kraft, always calm and businesslike, would explain in his recognizable Boston accent why our demands were unrealistic, arguing that the smaller markets couldn't afford the large salary increases that would inevitably flow from an increase in our share. I disagreed, obviously, but appreciated the civil tone. Jones, on the other hand, was highly annoying. He lectured us nonstop in his Texas drawl about the "good of the game," the need for us to be "reasonable," his "enormous investment" in his new Dallas stadium, and so on and so forth. On and on it went. At one point, after one of Jones's long harangues, I said nicely, "Jerry, you know you really are full of shit." He smiled and nodded and said, "Yeah, I know, I can go on sometimes."

It was kind of funny listening to Kraft and Jones, whose teams had loads of money, express such earnest regard for their small-market counterparts. But they weren't being magnanimous—just the opposite. They knew that if they couldn't get the players to sacrifice on behalf of the Green Bays and Jacksonvilles, it was going to have to come out of their pockets.

In September 2005, at a hotel near the Detroit airport, Tagliabue brought the full complement of his labor committee to a meeting with us. Upshaw asked me to review a PowerPoint presentation that focused on the enormous success of the NFL, making our customary and irrefutable point that NFL's great product was its players and that without their excellence, what kind of league would there be?

When Jim Irsay started singing the weepy ballad of the small markets, Upshaw responded, "Damn it! Then share more of your revenues." Richardson and others then chimed in that revenue-sharing among the owners was really none of the players' business. Upshaw quickly disagreed. "We don't want to hear that small markets can't pay the freight," he said. "If the big markets don't want to share with the little markets, so be it, but that's not going to change our demands."

As we were walking out, Dan Rooney pulled me aside and said, "You guys are just asking for too much. I don't think even Michael Collins could get this done," referring to the Irish patriot that Dan had introduced me to a decade earlier.

In the fall, Tagliabue took over the lead in the negotiations. During the latter part of the negotiations, the league's chief operating officer, Roger Goodell, began to participate in our meetings for the first time. While Goodell did not play a prominent role, Tagliabue was clearly grooming him.

Over the next few months, the parties inched closer together. We agreed to share some of the increased debt load from the construction of new stadiums by having more of this come out of the players' percentage of revenue. Otherwise, we gave no ground. The clock was ticking toward the March 1, 2006, deadline.

By late February, we were having round-the-clock negotiations, but after several short deadline extensions, no deal was in sight.

On March 6, 2006, after a second three-day extension had expired with no agreement, we left the NFL's Park Avenue offices all ready for the uncapped year to begin. As I hopped on a plane late that afternoon to Los Angeles for another case, panic struck the ranks of NFL owners. They were now prepared to agree to the players' last offer and give us our 60 percent. Within days, NFL owners voted 30–2 to approve a new deal, under which the cap jumped to almost $110 million per team—more than three times the size of the original, set back in 1994. At the time, this felt like sweet victory, but it would prove to be the start of our fiercest, most prolonged battle yet.

The new agreement, intended to run from 2007 through 2013, included a provision that allowed either side to terminate the deal two years early. Shortly after the deal was approved, Tagliabue announced that he would step down as commissioner before the start of the next season. Negotiating the labor deal as well as a new TV contract and a contentious revenue-sharing plan had taken a toll on him. Tagliabue was often criticized for being too friendly with Upshaw, just as Upshaw was criticized publicly for supposedly being in "Tagliabue's pocket." It was sheer nonsense. In fact, they had worked together for 15 years to ensure labor peace and prosperity for all. And they had succeeded.

When I heard about it, I was saddened. While Tagliabue was always a tough adversary, he was also a truly decent man with a wry sense of humor and a genuine worldview. His actions in canceling the games after 9/11 and his enormous efforts in helping New Orleans rebuild after Katrina were a testament to that broad vision. A few days after I heard the news, I wrote him a note to the effect that "no good deed goes unpunished." Some weeks later, I got a handwritten note back from Paul expressing his appreciation. We have remained friends.

Within months of the signing of the 2006 deal, we heard reports that some owners were upset and were pointing fingers at Tagliabue for having gone soft on the players. This was ominous.

In August 2006, the NFL owners elected Roger Goodell as the new commissioner on the fifth ballot: Goodell barely won, by a vote of 17–14. His chief rival was Greg Levy, the NFL's longtime counsel from the Covington law firm. Tagliabue officially stepped down on September 1, 2006. Goodell and Upshaw had a cordial relationship, but there was no history of dealings or trust between them.

Over the next year, the NFL owners' unhappiness with the 2006 deal became more and more evident. Richardson and others were quoted as saying it was too one-sided. They claimed they weren't sure they could afford to build new stadiums in half a dozen cities, including Dallas, New York, and the San Francisco Bay area, among others. A new guard among the NFL owners was beginning to assert itself. Wellington Mara had passed away in the fall of 2005, and Dan Rooney was about to be named ambassador to Ireland by President Obama. This new group included a number of staunch antiunionists, including Arthur Blank of Atlanta, Bob McNair of Houston, and Stan Kroenke, then of St. Louis (now Los Angeles). The real reason for all this discontent would soon become clear: with all the new revenue sources and massive increases in network and other television revenues, the owners believed that the players were getting too big a piece of the expanding pie. They were determined to take back as much as they could. These were some of the richest men in America, and they were consumed by the desire to get richer.

In the post-Tagliabue era, differences started to become more personal. It was around this time that I attended a charity dinner in Houston honoring a close friend by the name of Ron Krist, one of the most prominent lawyers in Texas. Krist was boisterous and funny and was friendly with all the Texas bigwigs. After dinner, Krist insisted that he take me over to chat with his buddy Bob McNair, the Houston Texans owner. McNair had made a fortune in the energy business before launching the Texans as an expansion franchise in 2001. I told Krist that I didn't think it was such a good idea, but he insisted. As we approached his table, McNair looked up and scowled. Just as Krist was introducing me as "Jim Quinn, the lawyer for—" McNair interrupted him and said coldly, "Ron, I know who he is, and we really have nothing to talk about." He didn't even bother to get up. Based on what I had heard about him as a labor hardliner, I wasn't a bit surprised. As we walked away, I said to Krist, "I told you he was an asshole."

Our suspicions that the owners planned to opt out early were confirmed when Goodell brought in a new team of labor negotiators. Harold Henderson was gently pushed aside, replaced by Bob Batterman from Proskauer, who had been involved behind the scenes during the NBA lockouts in the 1990s. He earned his spurs as a management lawyer working on the team that had led the yearlong lockout in hockey a few years earlier. Jeff Pash, who had left the NHL and become the NFL's general counsel in the late 1990s, now took a prominent role as the spokesperson on labor issues.

Upshaw prepared for war. At the NFLPA annual meeting in Hawaii in March 2008, Upshaw asked Kessler and me to outline potential strategies for the anticipated new round of negotiations, including the possibility of decertifying the union again. Barely two months later, in May 2008, the NFL owners voted unanimously to trigger the early termination of the 2006 deal. They were not required to give us notice until November 2008. Clearly, they were sending us a message.

For nearly eight years, Trace Armstrong, a five-time All-Pro defensive end, had been president of the NFLPA; he had worked closely with Upshaw on collective bargaining and other matters. In 2004, Armstrong retired and was replaced by All-Pro Philadelphia Eagles cornerback Troy Vincent, who served until 2008, when he too retired. Kevin Mawae, the veteran Tennessee Titans center and former Jet, was elected president at the March meeting to replace Troy Vincent. Mawae had no idea what he had just gotten himself into.

A few weeks after the NFL notified us that they were opting out, Goodell arranged for a small dinner at the Capital Grill in DC. We dined in a private room, presumably to set the stage for the new round of negotiations. He brought Dan Rooney and Jerry Richardson while Gene, Dick, and I attended for the players. During the lively discussion, the owners emphasized the enormous cost of the new stadiums and why the players had to contribute more to the multibillion-dollar investments needed to sustain the league's growth. Richardson was particularly peeved that he had to pay for his new multimillion-dollar stadium scoreboard all by himself and insisted that the players chip in. Upshaw made plain his disagreement, which riled Richardson. Nobody said anything about a lockout or the uncapped year, which was still two years away. As we left, we had an uneasy feeling that they were up to something; we just didn't know what.

As Upshaw was preparing for this next showdown with the NFL, he also faced dissension within his own ranks. Now 63, Upshaw had been head of the union for more than 25 years, and his contract was due to expire at the end of 2010. From time to time over the years, he and I had discussed possible successors. Gene had two in mind: the former NFLPA president Trace Armstrong, now an agent, and the current NFLPA president, Troy Vincent.

Upshaw had taken Vincent under his wing in 2007, giving him an office at the NFLPA's headquarters in DC so he could see how the union functioned. Vincent also spent time at the NFL headquarters in New York, supposedly getting a better handle on league operations. Armstrong was already well-tutored in union and league functions, having been NFLPA president for eight years. Of the two, Vincent was way more ambitious; he kept pushing Upshaw to anoint him as his chosen successor. Since Vincent was about to step down as union president, he wanted this to happen at the March 2008 NFLPA annual meeting in Hawaii. Gene told him that it was premature to designate anyone, particularly with the looming fight with the NFL. At the meeting, he vowed instead to stay on until the next deal was completed, however long that might take.

Vincent wasn't prepared to wait; he began maneuvering behind the scenes, among both the union staff and members of the NFLPA executive committee. In April 2008, Matt Stover, the Baltimore Ravens veteran kicker who had been involved in union business for many years, emailed a letter to the executive committee that was leaked to the press. "I feel that the Board must begin to prepare for a change in leadership immediately," Stover wrote. "I believe we have the proper environment with our teammates and leadership within the Board to execute the process of this selection."

Upshaw was outraged. "I would never leave until this deal is done," Upshaw told ESPN. "Matt Stover has no clue. Whoever is pulling his chain is doing a disservice to the union. I could understand the idea that they need to get rid of me if I wasn't doing a good job but, shoot, the owners are mad because they think I've done too good a job."[81]

Most players rallied to Upshaw's defense. "Matt Stover's letter does not reflect the view of the entire Executive Committee or the Board of Player Representatives," Kevin Mawae, the new NFLPA president, told ESPN. "The Board is in the process of preparing for the possibility of a work stoppage and understands the importance of having Gene, with his experience and history, lead the direction of the NFLPA."[82]

But Vincent had a number of supporters on the executive committee too, and although he denied that he was the political force behind the movement, Upshaw knew better.

Upshaw was also in the midst of another battle, this one with a handful of retired players. Led by Joe DeLamielleure, former Hall of Fame offensive lineman for the Buffalo Bills; Bernie Parrish, former Cleveland Browns cornerback; and Herb Adderly, former Green Bay cornerback, they viciously attacked Upshaw as a "traitor" and an "ingrate," claiming he had done nothing to improve their pensions and disability insurance. The claims were demonstrably false. Even though it was not legally required, Upshaw had insisted that current players contribute to retired player benefits out of their share of revenues, which averaged $182,000 annually from each player in the league. In one year alone, $147 million of the $571 million that went to player benefits was paid to retired players for pension and health care.

Upshaw had a short fuse. When the ex-players continued their personal attacks, Upshaw fumed. "The bottom line is I don't work for retired players," he told the press, which was literally true, since only current players are members of the bargaining unit. As for DeLamielleure, Upshaw said, "I'm going to break his goddamn neck."[83] Several retired players, including Parrish and Adderly, then filed a class action against the NFLPA over licensing money they claimed was owed to them.

In mid-July, a month after the DC dinner with the owners, Kessler, Upshaw, Berthelsen, and I had one of our periodic dinners in New York to discuss our bargaining strategy and the upcoming retired players trial, which was a few months away. Kessler was set to handle that trial, since I had another case to try that fall. We ate at the Post House on East 63rd Street, a high-end steak place that we had known and enjoyed for years. I had not seen Gene for several weeks; he looked a little drawn and seemed to have lost some weight. It didn't strike me as particularly unusual because Upshaw was always on some kind of crazy diet. After several bottles of wine, we all vowed to fight with no givebacks. We laughed and joked, reminisced, and made fun of each other as we always did when we were together. It was the last time I ever saw Gene.

On August 21, 2008, I awoke early and checked my BlackBerry. There was an email from Jeff Klein, with the subject, "Gene Upshaw: Assume that you have heard—he passed away this morning. Very very sad."

I was shocked. Thoughts of Fleisher's unexpected death flashed through my head. I turned on ESPN; it was headline news. Upshaw had collapsed, checked into a hospital near his vacation home in Lake Tahoe that past Sunday night, and died of pancreatic cancer three days later. The pain he had endured must have been excruciating. He was one tough son of a bitch.

My heart ached for his family, for his friends—and for myself. I loved the guy. Over the years, we had become close friends and golfing buddies, having played all over the country, from Hawaii to Florida, from California to Cape Cod, and dozens of places in between. But it was more than that. We came from far different backgrounds but were the exact same age and had graduated college the same year. Over drinks or on the golf course, we talked about everything—politics, religion, philosophy, and occasionally even sports. We had remarkably similar views on most things. I remembered sitting in a rickety outdoor bar on the Big Island of Hawaii a few years earlier, talking about how we grew up, what we believed in, who we were, and who we still wanted to be. And now that was gone forever.

The reaction to Upshaw's death was swift and enormous, from friend and foe alike. At a memorial service held a few days later in DC, there were many laughs, many tears, and lots of "Gene stories." The hall was packed with hundreds of people: players, coaches, owners, and friends from all walks of life. His wife, Terri, and his three sons sat quietly as a dozen or so speakers eulogized Upshaw with memories and heartfelt love for the man. But two speakers stood out: Tagliabue spoke with more emotion than I had ever seen from him, praising Upshaw not merely as a worthy adversary but as a wonderful leader of men. And finally, there was Art Shell, Hall of Fame Oakland left tackle who fought in the trenches side by side with Upshaw for more than a decade. Their love for each other as men, as brothers, and as players was never more evident. Art's stories and tears bore a hole in each one of our hearts.

We knew we had to carry on this fight for Upshaw. The executive committee immediately appointed Berthelsen as interim executive director; Berthelsen made it clear from the outset that he would not run for the position because he was nearing retirement.

Berthelsen hired Bob Reilly of Reilly Partners, a Chicago-based search firm, to lead the hunt for a new director. Reilly Partners had earlier been involved in the search for a new executive director for the NHLPA, which eventually led to the hiring of Paul Kelly. Reilly, a rough-and-tumble Irishman and a Notre Dame grad, was the right fit. He was a no-nonsense guy who would run a transparent and fair search process. I liked him right away.

The leading candidates were Armstrong and Vincent, both former NFLPA presidents and Upshaw protégées, though Vincent was reviled by some for having betrayed Upshaw. The process got pretty ugly. Kessler and I watched it unfold with great discomfort. Vincent reminded me of Isiah Thomas—a self-promoter and backstabber extraordinaire. Armstrong, in my view, had the upper hand in experience, maturity, and presence, but he was white and it seemed doubtful that the NFLPA, a largely black organization, would replace its highly respected black leader with a white guy.

One other candidate emerged during the interviews: DeMaurice Smith, a trial lawyer, former prosecutor, and a partner at Patton Boggs, the powerhouse DC law firm. Smith was self-deprecating, well-connected, and a great communicator. He was also very, very funny.

As the wrangling in the executive committee continued, the youngest member, Baltimore Ravens defensive back Domonique Foxworth, spoke up: "Listen guys, we need to come together here to find the best candidate regardless of our own personal feelings. We have a job to do and we have to put our own interests aside." Everyone knew what he was talking about. The ice was broken and the committee finally came together as a unit. (Three years later, Foxworth would unanimously be elected NFLPA president.) In late February 2009, the executive committee recommended three candidates for the vote in Hawaii: Armstrong, Vincent, and DeMaurice Smith.

At the NFLPA annual meeting in Hawaii, Smith carried the day, winning on the first ballot. Vincent lobbied him for a job as his deputy, and when he didn't get that, he went to work for the league. Many players still regard him as a traitor. The night of the vote, Kessler, Berthelsen, and I went out together to get drunk and celebrate the fact that our long personal nightmare in finding Gene's successor was finally over. We had no idea what was yet to come, but we were relieved that we had a solid candidate whose only interest was to put the best interests of the players ahead of all else. Late that night we ran into Smith at the bar of the hotel. He shook our hands and said, "We've got a lot of work to do, and I am going to need your help." That turned out to be a major understatement.

Following his election in March 2009, the peripatetic DeMaurice (a.k.a. "De") Smith jumped into the job with relish. A high-energy person who moved in several directions at once, Smith was an intellectual whirling dervish. Upon election, he resigned from his law firm and moved into his new office at the NFLPA virtually overnight. He met with everyone on the NFLPA staff from top to bottom, spending hours with them. He then systematically widened his circle of communication to include the NFLPA executive committee members, player reps, and the player membership at large. He wanted to get an in-depth understanding of the players' concerns and their views on which issues would be critical to them in the upcoming collective bargaining negotiations.

Within a few days, Smith had a meet and greet with Roger Goodell and then flew to North Carolina to meet with Jerry Richardson at his home; Richardson kept him waiting for over an hour, presumably just to show Smith "who was boss." Richardson was that kind of an asshole.

At the same time, Smith began putting together his own team to help him run the NFLPA going forward. He brought over Ira Fishman, managing partner of his old Patton Boggs law firm, to take on the new job of chief operating officer. He also hired George Atallah as the NFLPA's new director of communications. In addition, since Berthelsen had earlier announced his retirement, Smith appointed Tom DePaso, a longtime NFLPA lawyer dating back to the pre-*McNeil* days, as the NFLPA's new general counsel. DePaso and I had been good friends for years. He was smart and funny, and he knew the ins and outs of dealing with the NFL league office better than anybody alive.

The new hires each had their unique strengths. Fishman, a one-time Clinton White House lawyer, was highly intelligent and both acerbic and amusing in his own offbeat Chicago kind of way. As a former law firm managing partner, he brought real management skills coupled with a hatchet man mentality. Over the next few years, we reluctantly developed a real mutual respect and friendship. Underneath the gruff exterior, he was a guy with common sense and a heart of gold, which he hid well.

Atallah, the DC type, was an expert in new technology; he was quick, with a wonderful, wiseass sense of humor. He would soon become the "Twitter King" of football. And because players seldom used email, I soon learned to tweet and text.

Within the first few weeks, Kessler and I briefed Smith and his new team on the negotiations. All agreed from the outset that if the owners continued to insist on massive givebacks, this was going to be a tough fight. Every weapon would have to be on the table, including disclaiming union status and launching another round of full-blown antitrust litigation.

By the spring of 2009, the NFL owners had announced that if they did not achieve their economic goals through bargaining, they intended to lock the players out. The NFL had seen how successful the lockout had been in hockey in 2005. This was an entirely new situation. The last time we decertified the union there was no lockout. We were able to play and fight in court at the same time. The key legal issue was now going to be whether a decertified, nonunion NFLPA could successfully enjoin a lockout as an unlawful group boycott under the antitrust laws. We believed that the law was on our side. But there are no sure things in litigation, and this had never been done before. Any legal showdown was probably two years away; there was still time for collective bargaining to succeed.

Goodell reshuffled the NFL's team of negotiators, but it didn't make much of a difference. We had grown accustomed over the years to dealing with grumpy, disrespectful hardliners, and we got more of the same. Bob Kraft and Jerry Jones were still in the mix, though Richardson, fortunately, was not. He had moved upstairs as chairman of the NFL Board of Governors.

By 2009, the financial crisis had cratered the economy, which gave the NFL owners—32 of the richest men in America—an excuse to cry poverty and warn of the imminent collapse of their business. Since we had access to the league's actual revenues through the salary cap process, we knew it was pure bullshit, but the specter of the recession and the huge bank bailouts did give them a little extra ammo.

The NFL said they wanted to lay out for us their long-term financial plans. Goodell had hired a former Goldman Sachs managing director, Anthony Noto, to take the lead in this presentation. Our first big meeting was held at the NFL's Park Avenue headquarters in the summer of 2009. Noto, a ramrod-stiff West Point graduate and former Army Ranger, told us that the league's goal was to triple their revenue and cross the $25 billion threshold in revenue by the year 2025. That required billions in investments in state-of-the-art stadiums and new technologies, Noto said, and the owners expected the players to invest along with them, presumably on a dollar-for-dollar basis. At that point, Bob Kraft helpfully explained that the players' "investment" would take the form of a significant reduction in their share of revenue.

We listened patiently then said, "Thanks but no thanks." If owners wanted to build great coliseums, God bless. But since players did not share in the appreciation of their franchise values, the idea of them investing along with the owners was preposterous. We made clear that unless they were willing to share the $25 billion on the same basis that we were currently sharing revenues, we would get nowhere fast. They presented a chart that purported to show that under the 2006 deal, the players were getting a higher percentage of whatever new revenue was being generated by the NFL. We said, "Yeah, so what? That's what the deal was."

It was an inauspicious beginning, and it went downhill from there as Noto and Smith developed a deep enmity for one another. Given the NFL's repeated references to the faltering US economy, we asked them if the NFL owners were claiming some kind of financial hardship. If so, we were entitled by law to see their individual team financials, just as we had in the *McNeil* case. They demurred. The NFL had become the most profitable sports league in the country, maybe the world, but they liked to pretend they were just barely keeping their heads above water.

When a second meeting with Noto broke up, we were further apart than ever. All this talk of big-picture economics was getting us nowhere, so we suggested that we exchange formal collective bargaining proposals as soon as possible.

In the months following Gene's death, I'd had a number of back-channel discussions with Goodell and Pash about how to bring our sides closer together. After the debacle of the 2009 summer meetings, these discussions resumed. The first thing I told them was to get rid of Noto; he and Smith were not a match made in heaven. In fact, nobody on our side could tolerate him. And to Goodell's credit, we never saw Noto again. Some months later, he left the NFL and returned to Goldman Sachs. Much later he became the CFO of Twitter.

After months of delay, the parties finally exchanged detailed collective bargaining proposals in mid-November 2009. Our proposals were relatively modest. We focused primarily on player health and safety concerns, increasing player benefits (particularly for retired players), and player discipline issues—namely, the commissioner's unlimited power to punish players for alleged misdeeds off the field.

We were prepared to live with the economics of the 2006 deal except for one thing: for the first time, we wanted NFL owners to contribute out of their own pockets to retiree pension and health benefits.

Since the *White* settlement, it had been the current players who were funding these increased benefits for the retired players. This reduced the amount of revenue available for players' salaries. We told the owners that it was a matter of fairness that they take on at least part of this increasing burden going forward. The current players should not be funding the retired player benefits alone, we said. In exchange, we made it clear that we would agree to increase the players' contribution to the building of new stadiums. This concept had been part of earlier deals and was a direct investment by the players in the future of the game. From the players' perspective, this investment was worthwhile because new stadiums generated significant increases in revenues, which we shared as part of the overall salary cap system.

The owners' proposals were both detailed and draconian. In literally dozens and dozens of pages, they represented a mind-boggling effort to turn back the clock to the 1980s, or maybe earlier. They wanted a rookie wage scale that cut starting salaries by more than half, as well as absurd restrictions on free agency. They even wanted to reduce the player benefits they didn't pay for. On top of all that, the 32 billionaires proposed a massive, 20 percent reduction in the players' revenue shares, which would go directly into their already bulging pockets.

After the exchange of proposals, both sides knew we were miles apart on virtually every issue. The holidays passed quietly. Shortly after New Year's, the league asked us to meet with them on the Saturday before Super Bowl XLIV. The Saints and the Colts were set to square off the next day in Miami. The NFL brought its entire 10-person labor committee, plus a dozen or so league officials such as Goodell, Pash, Batterman, and a bunch of lesser souls. It was a standoff. We again asked to see their financials; they again told us they were paying the players too much money.

I'd never seen anything quite like it before. Thus far, Goodell had barely spoken in the meetings; the hardliners were firmly in control. Goodell seemed out of his element. Even the Giants' mild-mannered John Mara, now chairman of the CEC, was solidly aligned with the hardline group. They had something up their collective, monogrammed sleeves, but what?

It was now only a matter of weeks before the new free agency signing period was scheduled to begin on March 1, 2010. The "Uncapped Year" was fast approaching. As part of the mutually assured destruction provision we had agreed to in the original *White* settlement, free agency would also move from four to six years, which meant hundreds of players would have to wait an extra two years for free agency.

In the past, the fear of the uncapped year had inevitably led to a settlement. Why were owners no longer fearful of this potential for skyrocketing salaries? It would take us several years to uncover the answer.

The next big meeting took place during the NFL combine in Indianapolis in March, after the free agency period was under way. This time, the owners' spokesperson was Mike Murphy, a former player who ran the Green Bay Packers. Murphy had once been a player rep in the NFLPA and was now regarded as a turncoat by most of the current players. Several other owners, including Richardson, Mara, and Cincinnati's Mike Brown, showed up for the NFL, in addition to the commissioner, Pash, and Batterman.

Brown, the hardest of the hardliners, had been involved in the labor issues since the *McNeil* days. He seldom talked, but when he did, he showed nothing but contempt for the players. Murphy, whose role was justifying the league's overreaching economic proposals, was a slightly less obnoxious version of Noto.

At one point during the meeting, they said, OK, if you won't reduce your share of revenues, here's a laundry list of stuff you have to pay for. It included everything but actual laundry, though come to think of it, maybe that was on there too. They seriously wanted the players to pay for things like transportation, overhead, and interest expense, effectively subtracting nearly 20 percent of revenue from players, amounting to more than $5 billion over the next five years. It was a joke. Instead of growing smaller, our list of differences kept expanding.

It was shortly after this most recent debacle in Indianapolis that we heard rumors that over the past year or so, the NFL had renegotiated its television deals to ensure they'd be paid even if the owners locked out the players and shut down the 2011 season. Without this provision, the owners would not have been able to drive such a hard bargain with us because they needed TV money to service their multibillion-dollar debt obligations.

The whole thing seemed crazy. We understood why the owners wanted this, but why would the networks agree unless they got a discount? And if that were true, it would be a direct violation of the *White* settlement agreement, which required the owners to "act in good faith and use best efforts to maximize total revenues for the players."

On June 9, 2010, the NFLPA filed a Special Master proceeding charging the NFL with just such a violation. Since I regularly did legal work for several of the TV networks that would be key witnesses, I couldn't have direct involvement in the case. Kessler led the team for the players, though I obviously remained very interested in the outcome.

Discovery in that proceeding confirmed our suspicions. Internal NFL documents revealed that the league had carefully planned their lockout strategy from the moment they exercised the early opt-out in May 2008. The renegotiation of TV deals was a key element of that plan. Little did we know that this was just one part of the NFL's outrageous scheme to bludgeon the players into giving them billions of dollars. It would take many months before the full scope of the NFL's deception came to light.

Meanwhile, our side was meeting to develop a strategy. We knew well that the brevity of NFL careers makes any work stoppage almost unbearable, and lengthy antitrust litigation in the face of a lockout wasn't too appealing either. We began to discuss internally how to structure a compromise—players would receive the same percentage of existing revenue sources while accepting a smaller share of revenue from new sources. This was a significant concession on our part, but it avoided a fight that could cost both side hundreds of millions, if not billions, of dollars.

Starting soon after the television case was filed, and continuing throughout the summer of 2010, Kessler, Fishman, and I began testing potential new revenue-sharing formulas. At the same time, De asked me to reach out to Jeff Pash, who I had known for more than two decades, to set up some back-channel meetings among the principals.

Over the course of that summer, we held a series of secret meetings involving just the four of us: Pash, Goodell, Smith, and me. We met under assumed names at various hotels in New York and DC, though the Essex House in New York and the Ritz-Carlton in DC were among our favorites. We spent hours together hashing out the issues, with a particular focus on rookies, health and safety, and the revenue split.

I had spent some time with Roger Goodell over the past year and a half, with the occasional lunch or dinner and some phone conversations. We had a pleasant if somewhat guarded relationship. But it was during these small, informal sessions that I came to know the true Roger Goodell, and I didn't like what I saw. Goodell had spent his entire career at the NFL, beginning as an intern in 1982 and holding a variety of business jobs over the next 25 years until his selection as commissioner in 2006. He had an aura of undeserved self-importance. World peace is not at stake here, I kept wanting to tell him, so take it fucking easy.

We covered a wide range of issues in these meetings. Pash was much more engaged in debating the finer points of the split and the salary cap. Goodell was aloof and taciturn even when Smith peppered him with questions. I was struck by just how inflexible and uncompromising Goodell was. I couldn't figure it out. Was he insecure, just not very bright, or maybe both?

Whenever there was any discussion about the commissioner's authority to discipline players, Goodell would get red in the face.

This was clearly "The Man Who Would Be King." Pash had a way of talking a lot without saying much. Goodell just said nothing. After these meetings, Smith and I would typically have a drink and talk about what happened, always working our way to the same conclusion: "Goodell just doesn't get it."

As discussions continued through the summer of 2010, literally hundreds of players were on the open market without any salary restrictions, but the offers were suspiciously low. In 2009, free agent contracts went up by an average of 10 percent. In 2010, with no cap, it was flat. We smelled a rat, but what could we do? We had no proof of collusion, no basis to assert another claim under the *White* settlement.

Meanwhile, even as the NFL revealed its bad faith in practically every encounter, we tried to be constructive and unveil our concept for a compromise on the revenue split. Early in September, after working the numbers, revising, honing, and rerevising, we proposed our formula: on all new incremental revenue, up to $2 billion above a base of $8 billion, the owners would get a 55/45 percent split in their favor, while we would retain the current split on the base $8 billion revenue of approximately 55/45 percent in our favor. We estimated this concession to be worth nearly a half-billion dollars over four years, but with rising revenues, we thought it was still a good deal for the players. *That's what compromise is all about.*

Smith and I presented this to Goodell and Pash at the Essex House on Central Park South on September 10, 2010. We gave them the formula and told the NFL that to avoid an industry shutdown, we were willing to do this even without inspecting the clubs' financials. We naïvely believed this would get the ball rolling. They listened carefully, but they were suspiciously noncommittal.

We waited for a prompt response. It didn't come. Finally, after more than a month, we set up a meeting in early October with the NFL near O'Hare airport in Chicago. Smith had been flying all over the country to meet with players, updating them on the negotiations and outlining potential strategies in the event of a lockout. We were scheduled to meet with the Bears as part of the Chicago trip. As I watched Smith do his work, I was struck by what an extraordinary educator and communicator he was. The players listened carefully, asked good questions, and appreciated the openness and candor that Smith brought to these meetings. His style was a lot different than Gene's but just as effective. Where Gene had been blunt and direct, Smith was more like a Baptist preacher.

The meeting with the NFL was small. Smith, DePaso, and I attended for the players. The other side consisted of John Mara, Jerry Richardson, and Mike Murphy, along with Goodell, Pash, and Batterman. This time Mara spoke for the NFL. While soft spoken, he lacked the friendly Irish charm of his father. He told us that our proposal was completely unacceptable and that we had not been listening to their needs. He then handed us a one-page sheet with one figure on it: 42 percent.

That was their proposal for how much the players' share should be going forward. It would cut the cap for each team from the current level of $120 million to barely $100 million. Teams would have to cut scores of players, mostly veterans, and renegotiate downward the contracts of hundreds of others. It was essentially the same 20 percent shift they had talked about earlier in the year in Indianapolis but repackaged in an equally unacceptable box.

Gordon Gekko would have been proud.

We said no way, this was never happening. Further, we said that if the NFL owners were unwilling to share their financials with us, there was no point in continuing these discussions. Everyone left in a huff. We had been bargaining now for nearly two years without making an inch of progress.

Over the next couple of months, nothing of substance happened. Smith continued his face-to-face player meetings to prepare and educate the membership on what was shaping up to be a total shitshow. It was obvious that the NFL had no serious interest in compromise. They were dead set on locking us out on March 1, 2011. Smith told the players that if that happened, we would have no choice but to decertify the union again and bring antitrust claims charging the NFL with an illegal group boycott. Smith had also done something truly unprecedented: with the approval of the NFLPA's Player Executive Committee, he had secretly obtained a $500 million insurance policy, payable to the players in the event of a lockout. If the owners could create a lockout fund, we could create a lockout insurance policy—a true standoff.

But the real key to our strategy was our ability to enjoin the lockout. A principal part of the lockout would be an agreement among the NFL owners to refuse to sign free agents and other players not under contract, including rookies. Such a collective agreement would almost certainly violate the antitrust laws. If we were successful, the NFL's principal leverage—the threat of no season—would collapse. The potential for billions in antitrust treble damages would force the NFL owners to withdraw their outrageous financial demands and then, just maybe, we could get a reasonable deal.

There was one fly in this ointment, though: the Norris-LaGuardia Act, which prohibits the filing of injunctions in the context of a labor dispute. It was an artifact of the 1930s, originally enacted to protect employees who wanted to form a union from being sued by their employer. But after the *McNeil* verdict, when we sued the NFL in *Jackson* to enjoin its Plan B free agency, they tried to flip Norris-LaGuardia and argued that it also protected employers from being sued by their employees in a labor dispute. Judge Doty, thankfully, wasn't impressed and threw it right in the trash. But that didn't mean that another judge might not look more kindly on it.

We continued the back-channel discussions. After a number of phone calls, Pash and I set up a meeting at a hotel near Dulles Airport; we both had our full contingents. The meeting broke into subgroups, and Kessler and I met separately with Pash and Batterman to go over the split numbers. We reviewed the details and then recounted the various proposals. Amazingly, Pash and Batterman claimed that they had really never understood our proposals and that in fact we were now even further apart than we thought. Kessler and I were pissed. There was no way they didn't understand our proposals, and we sure as hell understood theirs. If the Chicago meeting was a disaster, this was—I don't know—an apocalypse? Both sides walked out in silence. No handshakes were exchanged. The stench of their bad faith was in the air.

Meanwhile, throughout the fall, the TV lockout fund case hearings were taking place before a Special Master. I was technically walled off from the proceeding, but Kessler reported that he thought it had been going well. Unexpectedly, shortly before Christmas, the Special Master ruled against the players. The NFLPA took an immediate appeal to Judge Doty. This was yet another big issue hanging over our heads.

After the aborted January meeting in DC, Berthelsen once again set out to find potential plaintiffs for our seemingly inevitable antitrust lawsuit. Smith got personally involved; he felt strongly that we needed to have a number of superstars among our plaintiff group. We would also need several prominent free agents and at least one high rookie draft pick to ensure we had standing. This process would take several weeks.

In yet one more last-ditch effort, the NFL owners invited us to meet with them the day before the Packers and the Steelers played Super Bowl XLV in Dallas. We met at a hotel in downtown Dallas. If we did not reach an agreement within the next three weeks, they were going to lock us out, at which point we were going to decertify and sue. Both sides knew exactly where the other stood.

The atmosphere was tense. The NFL once again had its entire labor committee in attendance, along with Richardson, Goodell, and the ever-present Pash and Batterman. We brought a dozen or so players, many from the executive committee, as well as several superstars, including Peyton Manning and Drew Brees.

The meeting turned bizarre right away. Jerry Richardson insisted on making an opening statement. NFL officials later told me they had begged him not to do it, but Richardson would not be denied. He launched into a lengthy, often incomprehensible diatribe attacking the players as ingrates for refusing to make billion-dollar investments in the game. He railed against the old 2006 deal as unworkable, though he had been the chairman of the labor committee that approved it. He then raised the issue of his $50 million scoreboard, which set my eyes rolling to the back of my head. This guy was incredible.

At one point, he said that he had always thought he and Gene were on the same page, but then, referring to Upshaw, he said, "He got uppity with me." Brian Waters, Tony Richardson, and the other black players bristled while the rest of the room cringed. Kraft kept tugging at Richardson's arm to make him stop. Before we could respond, the NFL asked to take a break. During the break, several players spoke up, saying, "Can you believe what he said about Upshaw?" It was surreal.

After a few minutes, the NFL representatives returned, with Kraft now as their spokesman, trying to calm the waters. But the players were pissed. We reminded the owners of our willingness to substantially increase our contributions to the construction of new stadiums, but we repeated that the players would not roll back our share of revenue to the pre-*McNeil* days.

We again made clear that we were not prepared to make any further financial concessions unless the owners opened their financial books to us. They refused.

At one point, Peyton Manning spoke up and explained why he thought our position was reasonable and fair to the owners. In response, Richardson accused Manning of being a financial neophyte who did not understand accounting and who "couldn't tell a debit from a credit." Manning just sat there calmly and smiled, comfortable with the fact that he was among the most financially savvy athletes in America.

Later, both Kraft and Goodell reached out to Smith and apologized for Richardson's behavior. That was good of them. But although Richardson's coarse language made even his fellow owners uncomfortable, the truth was they were all in perfect alignment on the substance of the matter. They were trying to stiff the players who made the game of football great—and who made their businesses so damn profitable.

CHAPTER 20
The Brady Bunch

A FEW DAYS BEFORE THE DALLAS MEETING, THE director of the Federal Mediation and Conciliation Service (FMCS) contacted both sides to offer to mediate the dispute in an effort to avoid a lockout and an industry shutdown. This was typical in high-profile labor disputes.

Coincidentally, the head of the FMCS was none other than George Cohen. I had known George for over 30 years as a colleague and as a friend, and we had worked closely together on both basketball and hockey. We had kept in close touch over the years. George had been appointed by President Obama to lead the FMCS two years earlier. I thought that mediation at this stage was likely to be a waste of time, since I was convinced the NFL wanted the lockout to test the players' resolve. Nonetheless, we talked it over and agreed to give it a shot, thinking that George would at least be understanding and sympathetic to the players' position.

Thus began two of the most frustrating weeks of my life. The mediation got under way a few days after the Super Bowl at the headquarters of the FMCS, which was then located at 2100 K Street in DC, only a short walk from the NFLPA offices. Every day for the next 10 days, we dutifully walked the few blocks from the NFLPA offices to the FMCS headquarters. Over the course of the mediation, we brought literally dozens of players—executive committee members, player reps, and players at large—so they could see for themselves just how intransigent the NFL and its representatives were. This was not just bad faith—it was no faith at all.

I missed a planned vacation with my kids and grandkids at our house in Arizona. Fishman and Smith had the good sense to send my wife flowers and an expensive bottle of wine, apologizing for holding her husband hostage at the FMCS headquarters.

A few players initially expressed concerns and a willingness to compromise. We then explained that the owners' demands would effectively cause the salary cap to go down by $10 to $15 million per club. The cap had never gone down before; it had only gone up. The effect of this would be "blood in the locker rooms," as scores of players would have to be cut or have their salaries vastly reduced to allow their teams to stay within the cap. At that point, Jeff Saturday, the Pro Bowl center for the Indianapolis Colts, said, "No fucking way." He personally told Goodell it was never happening.

On February 14, 2011, in the middle of the FMCS mediation, acting with its usual bad faith, the NFL filed an unfair labor practice against the NFLPA, claiming ironically that *we* were somehow not bargaining in good faith. This effort was led by Bob Batterman, not someone who was known for his subtlety. In one of George Atallah's more amusing tweets, referring to the fact that the NFL had filed their charge on Valentine's Day, he tweeted, "Hey, Batterman: You could have just sent me flowers and chocolate." The Twitter war was on.

With the March 1 deadline looming, Cohen called both sides back to the mediation table. We were ready to decertify; they were ready to lock out. But Cohen somehow still held a false hope that he could get the parties to settle. The players knew well that because their careers were so short, any gains they might make were more for future generations than for their own personal enrichment. This gave owners a huge amount of leverage. For players who were about to start losing paychecks, the notion of the unselfish greater good argument was not always easy to swallow. That was precisely the reason it was so important to our strategy to be able to enjoin any attempted lockout from the start.

Moreover, getting the TV networks to guarantee their multibillion-dollar payments to the NFL for the 2011 season regardless of whether there were any games to actually show on television was a diabolical masterstroke, like something out of Darth Vader's playbook. But there was no way it could stand up in a court of law, we felt sure about that. We turned out to be right.

On March 1, 2011, only days before the lockout was to begin, Judge Doty overturned the Special Master's ruling and blocked the NFL from receiving $4 billion in broadcast fees. "The record shows that the NFL undertook contract renegotiations to advance its own interest and harm the interest of the players," Doty wrote. Though there was no immediate effect on the NFL's negotiating position, we were elated. Down the road, we knew we would be able to use this to our advantage.

The players' relationship with the owners was at a low ebb. Even relatively minor stuff became complicated and charged. At one point, Smith and I went to talk to a small NFL group about the commissioner's authority to discipline players for off-the-field behavior. We had a simple objective—we wanted the commissioner's decisions to be subject to third-party review, as they were in the other three major leagues. "You simply don't need the aggravation," I said to Goodell. "Why subject yourself to claims of being biased?" He sat there stone-faced.

"We think he can be fair," John Mara replied weakly. As we persisted, Goodell's head looked like it might actually explode. The meeting broke up in silence. If the NFL had listened to us, we could have saved Goodell an awful lot of grief in the years to come. But they didn't believe a word we said.

The mediation dragged on for another week, with the NFL clearly just playing for time. As the revised deadline of 11:59 p.m., March 11, 2001, approached, we met for one final time with mediator Cohen present. The NFL, in what appeared to be a show of force or solidarity or something, brought in its entire labor committee. Nothing at that point could possibly have surprised us, but I must admit that I did not expect the NFL to *lower* their offer. That, however, is exactly what they did. With Pash acting now as their lead negotiator and spokesman, they actually increased their demand for givebacks, specifically targeting the revenue-sharing formula. They were also demanding to eliminate the few things we thought had tentatively been resolved, including their funding of retiree pension and health benefits.

After huddling for a few minutes, we rejected their offer, calling it out as a publicity stunt. We thanked Cohen and his staff and left the mediator offices to prepare to decertify the union and file our antitrust lawsuit seeking to enjoin the lockout. The owners went straight to the media. In a television interview, Pash accused us of having reneged on prior points of agreement and walking out on them. Incensed, Smith asked me to go downstairs and rebut these outrageous claims in front of the TV crews that had assembled outside the NFLPA, which I promptly did. It was carried live on many channels, though the NFL Network pulled the plug halfway through my statement. (So much for the NFL's view of the First Amendment. The NFL owners were never known as constitutional scholars.)

The fight now moved from the bargaining table to the courtroom. Our antitrust lawsuit was all ready to go, and we filed it in federal court in Minnesota minutes later. Berthelsen and Smith had done a terrific job rounding up plaintiffs. We had New England quarterback Tom Brady, New Orleans quarterback Drew Brees, Indianapolis quarterback Peyton Manning, San Diego wide receiver Vincent Jackson, Minnesota linebacker Ben Leber, New England guard Logan Mankins, Minnesota defensive end Brian Robison, New York defensive end Osi Umenyiora, Kansas City linebacker Mike Vrabel, and a rookie, the soon-to-be-drafted All-American linebacker from Texas A&M, Von Miller. Stars, free agents, and a top rookie—the perfect roster for our litigation! There had been some dispute over who would be the first named plaintiff, so we listed them in alphabetical order on the complaint. Hence Tom Brady came first, and the case became *Brady v. NFL*. We called our group "The Brady Bunch."

"The NFL brought this fight to us—they want $1 billion back, we just want financial information to back up that request," Brees tweeted the next day. "They refuse to give that information to us. They think we should just trust them. Would you?"

The next day, the AFL-CIO issued a strong statement of support: "Unfortunately, the NFL and its 32 team owners, who have enjoyed the fruits of a $9 billion dollar industry in a devastating economy for working families, would not reach a fair deal with the men who risk their health and safety to play professional football. In light of this unfortunate situation, the players have decided to renounce the NFLPA's status as their exclusive bargaining unit. Working people stand shoulder to shoulder with the players, and they are right to protect themselves and their families through antitrust laws that prohibit illegal and greedy corporate behavior."

We sought to have the case assigned to Judge Doty, but Barbara Berens, his former law clerk and now our counsel in Minnesota, told us Doty was in Tucson, Arizona, as a temporary replacement for a federal judge who had recently died. The case bounced around the St. Paul courthouse for several days until it was finally assigned to Judge Susan Nelson, the newest judge on the federal bench there. Berens assured us this was a good pick. Nelson was a former plaintiffs' lawyer and a personal friend of Judge Doty. We crossed our fingers and hoped she was right. The future of pro football hung in the balance.

The NFL had plenty of legal firepower at their disposal. They added celebrity litigator David Boies and nationally recognized appellate advocate Paul Clement, a former US solicitor general, to their legal team. Along with Kessler, I continued to lead our team, pursuing the ground war in district court before Judge Nelson. Knowing that the losing side would definitely appeal, we too added an appellate specialist to our team: Ted Olsen, who had preceded Clement as US solicitor general, the government's top appellate lawyer. (Olsen and Boies were actually cocounsel at the time, fighting to legalize gay marriage.)

Shortly after the case was assigned to Judge Nelson, we filed a motion for a preliminary injunction, seeking to bar the NFL owners from continuing their illegal lockout. Our argument was simple:

we're no longer a union, so the labor laws don't apply. We were now in the antitrust arena, a place the NFL owners clearly did not want to be. Meanwhile, the NFL continued to pursue its unfair labor practice charge, claiming before the NLRB that our decertification was a sham—the exact argument that they promised repeatedly in writing never to make. The NFL and its lawyers were shameless.

The hearing before Judge Nelson was set for April 6 in St. Paul. In a huge ceremonial courtroom packed with fans, reporters, and a bunch of stuck-up rich guys who owned football teams, it was going to be me arguing against the great David Boies. I had known David for over 20 years; he is an extraordinary advocate, brilliant and likeable and capable of a razor-sharp focus. His great strength is the ability to clear away the underbrush and hone in on what really matters. David has only one weakness—he is so damn busy, he doesn't always have time to properly prepare. I wasn't particularly concerned; we had argued against each other in the past, and I had come out on top more often than not. I also had one big advantage: I had lived these issues for nearly 40 years; Boies had not.

Boies cut right to the chase—our decertification was a sham, he argued, and this case didn't even belong in federal court. It was a matter for the NLRB. Seeing he was getting no traction from the judge on either argument, he quickly shifted to their main argument: the Norris-LaGuardia Act prevented injunctions of any kind to be issued in the context of a labor dispute, he said, and that's what this was. Boies conceded, as he had to, that the act was passed to protect employees, but he argued that the plain language of the statute was broad enough to protect employers as well. So even if the lockout constituted an illegal boycott under antitrust laws, Norris-LaGuardia tied the players' hands. The NFL could keep the lockout in place until the trial on its legality was completed.

Judge Nelson listened carefully to both sides, asked a number of penetrating questions, and noted, much to Boies's displeasure, that the players "appeared to have a strong case" and that it was clear that the lockout, which was causing them "irreparable harm," should be ended immediately. This was not a ruling, but it gave us a very strong indication of how she was going to come down. We walked out of the courtroom feeling good.

While Judge Nelson pondered our injunction request, she ordered the parties to another round of mediation, this time under federal court supervision. Judge Nelson appointed US magistrate judge Arthur J. Boylan to act as the mediator. He was a nice man, but he was completely overwhelmed by the whole process. He was basically a "chucklehead" who believed that the players made more than enough money, so why were we making such a fuss? To the extent he even tried to understand the economics of football, he bought the owners' poppycock about how the players should contribute to the construction of new stadiums and all that.

This point of view is exhausting to me. I've had to fight against it my entire career—the idea that money in sports is somehow a problem when it goes into athletes' pockets, but not when it goes into owners' pockets. It's bad enough when you hear this on sports radio. But when it comes from an officer of the court, you just want to tear your hair out. One thing I knew for sure: mediators were not going to be much help in settling this case.

Two weeks later, Judge Nelson granted our request for an injunction and ordered the NFL owners to lift the lockout. The NFL sought an immediate stay of Judge Nelson's order, and the Eighth Circuit Court of Appeals granted it, effectively keeping the lockout in place. The appeals court also made an ominous reference to the Norris-LaGuardia Act, indicating that the NFL's interpretation of it might have legs after all.

Over the next month, the two sides met mostly in secret up and down the East Coast and occasionally back in Minneapolis.

As the weeks went by, the parties moved closer on the core economic issues. We began to sense that without their lockout kitty from the networks (which Judge Doty had deprived them of), the owners were no longer so confident about outlasting us. While Jerry Jones went on with his hectoring, the moderate, more reasonable voices of

Clark Hunt and Art Rooney, both sons of NFL family icons, began to cut through the din. By mid-May, they had abandoned their demand for a nearly 20 percent rollback and were now pushing an even split on revenue. In the absence of financial proof—which they continued to withhold—this was still a huge and unacceptable concession for the players, representing a giveback of about $250 million a year from the current levels. We were willing to consider something in the neighborhood of half that.

As time passed, our own camp was fraying a little. Of our four key player negotiators, Jeff Saturday, Kevin Mawae, and Mike Vrabel were on the verge of retirement and would lose their last year if the upcoming season was canceled. Kessler and I were the hardliners, not wanting to give up any more ground. But these guys had their own futures to think about. It was highly unlikely they'd ever make this kind of money again in their lives. Of course it affected their willingness to compromise.

Our fourth player at the bargaining table, Domonique Foxworth, was younger and much less concerned about losing a year. He was all for gutting it out. But on economic issues, De Smith was inclined to follow the lead of his veterans.

In late May, at an old resort on the eastern shore of Maryland, there was a breakthrough. It came in a small meeting that neither Kessler nor I attended. De Smith and Jeff Saturday had gotten together with Bob Kraft and John Mara and reached an agreement on a new 50/50 formula involving an expanded pool of revenue. The deal was contingent on the NFL's agreement to a much higher minimum guaranteed spend by each team. This would ensure that there would continue to be sufficient cash-over-cap spending, a key aspect of the deal from the players' perspective. Cash over cap, you will recall, occurred largely because of how signing bonuses were allocated over the years of the player contract, allowing sometimes large amounts of cash to be spent over the cap in any given year. By guaranteeing higher team minimums, it would force more teams to spend over the cap each year.

Any way you did the math, however, it transferred several billion dollars from the players to the owners over the next decade. The players were willing to live with that as long as they got significant gains on all the other major issues, including health and safety, player benefits (particularly for retired players), and other economic guarantees, like the expanded revenue pool. The bottom line for players was that the cap would continue to rise and there would be no "blood in the locker rooms."

For me, this was a low point. I thought it was far too early to make such a concession. We were still waiting for the appeals court to rule on the legality of the lockout. Furthermore, I had real doubts that the owners were truly prepared to shut down the entire season. It wasn't just all that debt they needed to service. These teams were fabulously profitable; I never saw the financial statements, so I can't say for certain, but my educated guess is that the average profit per team is in the tens of millions of dollars and that it averages in the hundreds of millions league-wide. Ultimately, if we'd held out, I feel certain the players would've gotten a greater cut. In my view, we blinked too soon.

On June 3, 2011, we took a break from the negotiations, and both sides headed for St. Louis to hear the argument on the NFL's appeal of Judge Nelson's ruling. Her ruling had remained stayed, pending a final decision by the Eighth Circuit Court of Appeals. It was a beautiful, warm, sunny morning in St. Louis as the two former US solicitor generals, Paul Clement for the NFL and Ted Olsen for us, got ready to square off against each other. On my scorecard, Clement and Olsen fought to a draw, but the three-judge panel, which included a pair of staunch conservatives appointed by Bush 43, demonstrated an obvious preference for the NFL in their questions.

On July 8, 2011, the appeals panel reversed Judge Nelson's decision solely on the issue of the Norris-LaGuardia Act, though there was a ray of hope in the majority opinion. The judges held that since free agents and rookies had no contractual relationship with any NFL team, they were still free, if they so chose, to seek a separate injunction.

Kessler and I felt strongly that we should pursue this aggressively, as a means to regain some leverage at the bargaining table. You seize every possible advantage. But I was sensing that the train had left the station—and I wasn't on it. The parties had moved closer on both economic and other issues, and nobody was listening much to me anymore. On the proposed 10-year length of the new agreement, I made a final stand, arguing that tying ourselves up for that many years could be a huge mistake. Who knew how the business of football would evolve—or what dirty new tricks the owners might dream up. Once again, though, mine was a voice in the wilderness.

Luckily I didn't have to stick around for the rest of the negotiations. I had a long-scheduled case in London in the middle of July. A week after I got there, the owners and players announced a new deal. Ten years. The lockout was over, and not a game was missed nor a paycheck lost. There were many benefits for the players, including huge improvements on health and safety issues. For the first time, the owners agreed to devote an additional $600 million of their own money to significantly increase pensions for retired players. In the past, that money had come solely from pockets of the active players. There were hugs and handshakes all around between some of the players and owners, particularly Bob Kraft, whose wife had died just days before. He had stuck it out through the negotiations despite the personal tragedy.

The players would also get unrestricted free agency after four years and, perhaps most importantly, each NFL team would be required to spend at least 90 percent of its salary cap each year. If they didn't, the shortfall would be paid directly to the players.

It wasn't the worst deal ever made. But all the same, I was glad that I was in London when it was announced so I didn't have to witness our side waving the white flag. It wasn't what Upshaw would've done, I can tell you that.

• • •

A few months later, we would learn the true depth of the NFL owners' double-dealing. In March 2012, the NFL revealed its intention
to punish the Dallas Cowboys and Washington Redskins for having
"violated" a secret salary cap agreed to by the owners during the 2010
season—the year when there was to supposed to have been no cap.
Now we knew why the owners had been so blasé about the uncapped
year: they had illegally colluded. And not only that, they no longer
cared about keeping it a secret. John Mara told the press that Dallas
and Washington were "in violation of the spirit of the salary cap."
Goodell was quoted as saying, "The rules were quite clear and they
were to be followed."[84]

The NFL owners had secretly come up with an audacious two-
pronged strategy: first, require the TV networks to supply them with
a "lockout fund" so they would be at no risk in the event that the
2011 season had to be canceled, although that part of their strategy
had been squelched by Judge Doty. Second, but far worse, they had
colluded among themselves in the same way that baseball owners
had years ago in refusing to sign free agents. The NFL's scheme was
so blatant that it was almost not to be believed, yet they had the audacity to announce it publicly. One owner even told Smith in writing that
they had enforced the secret salary cap at $123 million per team.

We immediately filed a lawsuit charging the league with fraud.
The courts ultimately determined that the suit was filed too late and
that somehow these unknown claims were released as part of the
July 2011 settlement. It was an outrageous and unfair outcome. The
players had lived up to their part of the bargain—during the supposedly "uncapped" year, they had to have six years of service, rather
than four, to qualify for free agency. Some players no doubt sacrificed
tens of millions of dollars. The owners had shamelessly violated their
part of the bargain, and now they were even boasting about it.

To me, this all came down to a lack of leadership from the
commissioner. A scheme like this would never have happened during Tagliabue's tenure—maybe under Rozelle, but definitely not

Tagliabue. The Goodell regime was something else entirely. It would take the silliness of "Deflategate," the reversal of the "Bountygate" punishment of several New Orleans players, and the Adrian Peterson blunder and Ray Rice fiasco—both domestic violence cases—to throw the abject dishonesty and incompetence of Goodell and his 32 bosses into full public view. The height of their folly came to light in the wake of the suspension of Dallas Cowboys star running back Ezekiel Elliot, when it was revealed that the NFL had sought to silence one of its own investigators because she had concluded that there was no basis for the suspension. In the immortal words of Jimmy Breslin, this was "The Gang That Couldn't Shoot Straight."

As one writer put it, referring to Goodell, "The NFL is presided over by a guy who couldn't pour juice out of his loafers if the instructions were written on the heel."[85] The players would come to loathe Goodell, but by that time, he was fully entrenched and all but untouchable.

CHAPTER 21

Into the Breach Once Again

AFTER FINISHING THE ARBITRATION IN LONDON and taking a brief vacation in Rome with my wife and two of my granddaughters, I returned to a life without sports. By the fall of 2011, I was already heavily enmeshed in litigating over who owned the rights to many of our most iconic comic book characters, including Spider-Man, the Hulk, Iron Man, the X-Men, and dozens more. My clients, Disney and Marvel Comics, were locked in a bitter dispute with the family of Jack Kirby, the world's most famous comic book artist, who had drawn these characters under Marvel's direction. The movies had made these characters worth billions. It would take several years before an appeals court would uphold our rights. I was also preparing to defend Exxon for allegedly having contaminated the underground water supply for the entire state of New Hampshire. That would turn out to be an uphill battle with a predictable outcome; most people don't like chemicals in their drinking water. Yet I was more than ready to get on with my challenging trial lawyer life.

And after my rescue mission back in 1999, I thought I was done with basketball. In fact, when Jeffrey Kessler left Weil in 2003, I told him it was fine with me if he took the NBPA with him as a client. Since the late 1990s, Jeffrey had become the firm's principal contact with Billy Hunter and the union. I had never developed a particularly warm relationship with Hunter, and to be honest, I didn't much like busting my ass for clients who had a habit of ignoring my bills. In 2005, Kessler had taken the lead on a new six-year deal that was set to expire at the end of June 2011, which happened to be when the madness with the NFL was wrapping up.

While I'd been away, the NBA had hardly suffered. Revenues continued to climb skyward. But not all NBA clubs were sharing in the good times. The escalation of salaries had left a few teams in financial trouble, and by 2010, Stern was making the same noises he had made back in the 1990s: NBA owners were losing money, the small market teams could no longer compete because of skyrocketing salaries, the 55 percent player split was no longer fair or equitable, and so on.

Like their counterparts in the NFL, the NBA owners envied the brass-knuckles success of the NHL lockout. They were also very carefully monitoring how the NFL was successfully putting the screws to its players. But the NBA's strategy was different, in large part because their business wasn't nearly as strong as the NFL's. Stern offered to share their internal team financial information with the union, which showed many of the NBA clubs deep in the red—in some cases, losing tens of millions of dollars per year. The NBPA recognized early on that givebacks were inevitable; it was only a question of how much.

During the long football fight, I had been watching the basketball negotiations from afar. Kessler always kept me updated on what he and Hunter were doing. There had been several meetings before the June 30, 2011, expiration date, but no progress. There was no plan to decertify. It looked like 1999 all over again—not good for players.

What the NBA wanted most of all was the 50/50 split the NFL owners had just achieved. On top of that, Stern sought to eliminate or curtail all the various salary cap exceptions, excluding the famous Bird exception. These other loopholes, of course, were just as sacrosanct to the players—they helped ensure a healthy market for unsigned players and kept upward pressure on salaries.

Michael Jordan, who had been one of the leaders of the 1995 player revolt, was now sitting on the other side of the table. He owned the Charlotte Bobcats and did not like the fact that he had to compete for players against the likes of Los Angeles, New York, and Chicago. No, he did not like that at all, and he was now applying his superhuman competitiveness to the cause of reining in player salaries. You could see how this might get ugly.

Facing deadlock, Stern broke out the *L* word—lockout! In the same way that decertification had become the go-to strategy for our side, lockouts were the not-so-secret weapon for owners. He announced that the NBA would shut down operations on July 1, 2011.

As he later told me, Kessler had urged Hunter to prepare the players for possible decertification or disclaimer of interest, which would enable the union to bring antitrust claims and attack the threatened lockout, much as we had done in football. Hunter adopted a different strategy. He went to the NLRB, charging the league with unfair labor practices, and he did so with his daughter's law firm, Steptoe & Johnson, representing the union. In other words, Hunter was forswearing the antitrust laws, the only weapon that had ever proved successful in tempering owner demands, and embracing the antediluvian labor laws that were responsible for this mess in the first place. It was completely backward.

When I heard this, I rolled my eyes. The NLRB was notoriously slow. Even in the unlikely event that the NBPA was successful before the NLRB, it would take many months, if not years, to resolve—a delay that the players could ill afford if they wanted to save the upcoming season.

The NBA was acting just as ass-backward, filing a bizarre lawsuit in federal court in New York asking the court to declare any attempt by the NBPA to disclaim union status to be a sham, even though no such effort had as yet even been made. The NBA wanted to keep their labor defense intact while at the same time threatening to declare all the current NBA player contracts void in the event the union was in fact dissolved. I saw this as an empty threat, since I doubted many NBA owners would risk having their superstar players declared free agents.

As the dispute stretched into the fall, NBPA president Derek Fisher and the rest of the NBPA executive committee stood firmly behind Hunter. But as weeks passed without progress, key agents began undercutting him. On September 13, 2011, ESPN reported, "Arn Tellem, Bill Duffy, Mark Bartelstein, Jeff Schwartz and Dan Fagan—who collectively represent nearly one-third of the league's players—spoke Monday about the process of decertifying the union. . . . The agents' view is that the owners currently have most, if not all, of the leverage in these talks and that something needs to be done to turn the tide. They believe decertification will do the trick, creating uncertainty and wresting control away from the owners."[86]

In the middle of October, Stern canceled the first two weeks of the NBA season. This unleashed a flood of angry and aggrieved tweets, including this one from LeBron James: "I wanna sincerely say sorry to all the fans . . . it's a sad day for all of us, especially you guys. There's no us without you & love you guys."

As time wore on, things began to get ugly. By that time, FMCS mediator George Cohen was on the scene. Much as he had in the NFL talks earlier that year, he attempted to bring the parties together. Once again, he was unsuccessful. Kessler told me later that it was déjà vu all over again at the FMCS. This was particularly frustrating for the players, since by that time, they had indicated a willingness to compromise on the split, although they were not yet willing to surrender to the 50/50 position the NBA owners insisted on.

A few days later, in late October, much to my surprise, Billy Hunter called me and asked if he could come over to meet with me alone. An hour or so later, he was in my office. He was nervous and upset—not the overly confident Hunter I had known from past encounters. He proceeded to tell me that he was concerned that NBPA president Derek Fisher might be having secret meetings with people on the NBA side. Derek was approaching the end of his career, and Hunter suspected that somebody on the NBA side had offered Fisher a future job. I told him flat out that if he really believed that to be the case, he should bring it to his executive committee immediately and force Fisher to resign. Hunter listened carefully, nodded, and we parted ways. Then nothing happened.

By the first week of November, the players were signaling that they would agree to a 50/50 split on revenues if the league kept the major cap exceptions. Stern, with his usual bluster, set a five o'clock deadline for Wednesday, November 9 for the players to accept the league's last proposal: "Take it or leave it." Without an agreement, he added, the entire 2011 season was in jeopardy. The players rejected Stern's ultimatum, and harsh words began to fly. Kessler accused the NBA of treating the players "like plantation workers." Stern called Kessler "the single most divisive force in the negotiations."[87]

Later that same day, I got another call from Hunter, who again asked to come see me. The next morning, we met in my office at Weil, and he briefed me on the stalemate. He said the NBA was holding firm on restricting free agency, and that the players simply would not agree. I asked him whether decertification (or "disclaimer") was now an option, and he indicated without specifics that it was under active consideration. He then asked me to reach out to Stern, whom I had known for so many years, to see whether I could somehow broker a deal. I agreed.

That afternoon, I called Stern. After some of our usual banter, I said, "Stern, what the fuck is wrong with you? Don't you know if you tell the players to take it or leave it they are going to leave it?" He was silent for a moment and then he said in a half chuckle, "Yeah, maybe I fucked up." We both laughed. He said he would welcome my involvement, and he asked me to get in touch with Adam Silver, his deputy and eventual successor as commissioner. I knew Adam's father, Ed Silver, from years ago when he negotiated deals with Fleisher, but Adam and I had never met.

When I got him on the phone, I was surprised by his openness and friendly demeanor—the polar opposite of his mentor, "King David." He suggested I come over to the NBA offices to meet with him and some of his colleagues, so they could brief me on how they saw the status of negotiations. We set up a meeting for the following day, and I asked Bruce Meyer to come along. Before the meeting, Bruce and I met with Billy Hunter and Ron Klempner, a former Weil associate and now a lawyer with the NBPA, to brief us on the issues remaining in dispute. Klempner's expertise in the arcane provisions of the NBA system was impressive, so we brought him along to our meeting at NBA headquarters that afternoon. Meyer, Klempner, and I met with Adam Silver and two of the NBA's top lawyers, general counsel Rick Buchanan and his deputy Dan Rube. I hadn't seen Rick in many years, and he reminded me that he had worked on the *McNeil* case for the NFL when he was a young lawyer at Covington & Burling in DC. It seemed that everyone in the industry had somehow been involved with *McNeil*.

We reviewed many of the open issues. They explained their positions with regard to such items as escrow amounts, the luxury tax, the midlevel exception, sign-and-trade rules, qualified offers, and the rookie salary scale, as well as several other items. After the meeting, Meyer and I had a much better sense of what was keeping the parties apart, and none of them seemed to be real showstoppers.

We soon began brainstorming with Ron Klempner on how to bridge the gaps. Over the course of the next two weeks, we held a series of meetings and back-channel telephone calls, particularly between me and Adam, where we explored ways to resolve the various systems issues. We went back and forth over a number of possible compromises. I found Adam to be candid, forthright, and fair, but no pushover.

It was slow going, but I kept Hunter in the loop. Meanwhile, without bothering to inform me or Bruce, he decided to move forward on a parallel course. Hunter and Derek Fisher informed the NBA of their intention to dissolve the union and pursue an antitrust lawsuit against the NBA. David Boies was brought on board to help Kessler file it in Minnesota. Stern's response was to attack Kessler. "Obviously Mr. Kessler got his way, and we are about to go into the nuclear winter of the NBA." He added, "It is a real tragedy,"[88] in his best Shakespearean voice.

The choice of Boies was surreal. Only months before, Boies had been arguing on behalf of the NFL owners that any union disclaimer was a sham and that these disputes belong before the NLRB and not in federal court. But I didn't doubt his ability to change positions on a dime. Boies called me later that same day to joke about working on the right side for a change. I told him I was now "Mr. Inside," and he was now "Mr. Outside," echoing the famous West Point football duo of the 1940s.

If Hunter had asked me, I would have told him that disclaiming union status this late in the game was not much of a threat unless the players were willing to forego the rest of the season, which I knew they weren't. Even on the most optimistic timetable, the season would be over by the time you got a decision enjoining the lockout. You would have to disclaim months in advance, as we had done in football.

In late November, we held an eight-hour-long secret meeting at Weil to push the two sides closer together. This time Stern was there, along with Spurs owner and chairman of the NBA labor committee Peter Holt as well as Silver and his legal team. I found Holt to be a genuinely decent guy who really wanted to reach a compromise. Meyer and I, along with Billy Hunter and Ron Klempner, attended for the players. In a conference room overlooking Central Park, we went back and forth for hours on each issue, inching closer together as time ticked by and the Thanksgiving holiday loomed. As the hours dragged on, I sensed we were on the right track. King David was on his best behavior—no bluster, no bullshit. He let Adam take the lead as we methodically went through the half-dozen or so open issues. It was clear Stern wanted a deal. Barely a year from announcing his retirement, he didn't want his considerable legacy to be tarnished by a lost season.

I was scheduled to leave with my wife for a short vacation the next day. We were celebrating our 45th wedding anniversary and had scheduled a Thanksgiving weekend getaway at Little Palm Island in the Florida Keys. As the night wore on well past midnight, I announced to all assembled that my life depended on getting on that plane the next day. As the hours went by, we munched on the usual sandwiches and pizza as each side caucused and recaucused. Compromises on most issues began to surface. For the first time, I had real hope that we might be able to save the season.

As the hour got later and later, Stern and I started to reminisce about the old days and, in particular, the *Robertson* lawsuit, where we had both cut our sports law teeth 40 years earlier. We told the story of the infamous Connie Hawkins deposition and his "oral" contract, much to the delight of all in attendance. Throughout the evening, Stern was at his charming best. For once, he actually sounded a little mellow.

At one point, I took Stern aside and said, "David, you got the split you wanted; the rest of this stuff does not mean that much. Let's just compromise and get this done." He looked at me with the usual twinkle in his eye, and I had a sense that we were going to get there. We broke up around two o'clock in the morning, still without a deal but knowing that we had made real progress. It was agreed that the parties would meet the Friday after Thanksgiving and that I would stay available by phone if needed.

As it turned out, I wasn't needed. After another 13-hour bargaining session, both sides reached a consensus, with Bruce Meyer playing the role of substitute mediator. The items resolved included the amount of the escrow, the midlevel exceptions, sign-and-trades, restricted free agency, and some luxury tax issues such as penalties for "repeat offenders." Early on Saturday morning, the weary parties announced a settlement, and the shortened season was saved. Neither side was happy with the deal. The players surrendered a significant percent of their share but the owners weren't able to eviscerate free agency. Salaries would continue to rise.

A month later, on December 24, 2011, Oscar Robertson wrote an op-ed for the *New York Times*:

NBA SHOULD HONOR ITS HISTORY
AND LEARN FROM IT

After a long and avoidable delay, the NBA finally opens its 2011–12 season Sunday. The new season brings two anniversaries worth noting. One you will probably hear quite a lot about: the 50th anniversary of the 1961–62 season. The other, the 35th anniversary of the Oscar Robertson Rule, maybe not so much. The second anniversary has a direct connection to this season in the person of Jim Quinn, a lawyer who should receive much of the credit for there being a season at all. He has a long history with the National Basketball Players Association, including previous successful negotiations with NBA Commissioner David Stern. Had the union included him in this year's bargaining from the beginning, the season might have opened on time. Three weeks after the games would have begun, when the talks had stalled for what seemed like the last time, Quinn stepped forward and brought the parties together. After a five-month stalemate, he needed about five days to lay the groundwork for an agreement. Forty-one years ago, Quinn was an outside counsel when the union's class-action antitrust lawsuit against the league carried my name as the union's president. A settlement he helped negotiate in 1976, known as the Oscar Robertson Rule, helped NBA players become the first professional athletes to achieve free agency.

When I read his piece the next morning, December 25, 2011, I thought to myself, "Thanks, Oscar, I couldn't have hoped for a better Christmas present."

CHAPTER 22

The "Lockout King" Redux

WHEN DON FEHR TOOK OVER THE NHLPA IN FALL 2010, he found a union still shattered by its crushing defeat at the hands of Commissioner Bettman in 2005. It was in total disarray. Fehr would be the fourth executive director in five years. He knew he needed to focus on recreating the same kind of unity that had existed during his many years at the baseball players' union. The current NHL collective bargaining agreement was not scheduled to expire until September 15, 2012, although the players had the option of a one-year early termination. Fehr quickly determined that, given the state of the NHLPA, early opt-out was not an option. But he knew trouble was on the horizon. Bettman was already making his usual noises about the need for more cost certainty.

This time around, Bettman was eyeing the players' share of revenue. Though drastically reduced from the pre-2005 days, their cut still hovered around 57 percent. Fights between players and owners were no longer about salary caps or free agency; those were now accepted parts of the industry. Instead, it was just about money—greedy owners and their now well-heeled employees had entered a new era: Who gets how much? Once again, another big fight was about to commence.

Throughout the eventful year of 2011, with brutal battles being fought in both football and basketball, Fehr and I kept in close contact, as you would expect from a 35-year friendship. The hockey owners had obviously watched with interest what had gone on in the NFL and the NBA—the lockouts, the litigation, and most importantly, the outcome, specifically as it related to the revenue split.

Emboldened by the gains of owners in football and basketball in 2011—the revenue split in both leagues was now about 50/50—Bettman set his sights on driving his players down into the 40s. In light of this, Fehr asked Meyer and me for advice in connection with a possible disclaimer of union status and potential antitrust options.

By that time, Bettman had already locked out his players twice: in 1994, with little success, and again in 2005, with enormous success. He set a new lockout date for September 15, 2012, unless the players agreed to his demands for not only a significant reduction in the revenue split but onerous new restrictions on free agency and the elimination of salary arbitration. These were battles he had lost in 1994, and he wanted to refight them.

Bettman agreed to open the teams' books, which revealed a significant number of poorly performing franchises. Bettman's "Southern Strategy" had continued to drain profits from the league. Phoenix had gone bankrupt in 2010, and Atlanta was forced to relocate to Winnipeg in 2011. A dozen or so other franchises were living on the edge.

Knowing that the league's shaky finances meant givebacks were likely, Fehr had done a superb job over the last year preparing his members for a fight. The reality was that even after all the prior concessions—the imposition of a salary cap, the endless relocation of franchises, and the round robin of new owners—the NHL still had too many franchises in bad markets. During the '90s, the NHL owners, greedy for expansion fees, let the league grow past the point of sustainability; now that greed was coming home to roost.

Throughout the summer of 2012, Fehr worked closely with his brother Steve, who had also been involved in baseball over the years, and the NHLPA's 31-player Negotiating Committee. They held a series of meetings with Bettman and his labor committee. While Don made it clear that any player was welcome to participate, a core group became key spokesmen for the players, including, among others, Kevin

Westgarth (Los Angeles forward), Chris Campoli (Montreal defenseman), Shane Doan (Phoenix forward), Manny Malhotra (Vancouver center), and George Parros (Anaheim forward).

By this time, Bill Daly, Bettman's deputy commissioner, was playing a leading role in the negotiations. He and Steve Fehr held many back-channel meetings throughout the summer and early fall of 2012 in a mostly fruitless effort to reach a compromise. Steve and Don Fehr were a study in contrasts. While Don was intellectually brilliant, he was a theorist and at times a bit spacey. It wouldn't be unusual for him to be watching C-Span while thumbing through the latest Stephen Hawking treatise. Steve, on the other hand, was smart, down-to-earth, and the detail man who knew how to get things done.

Bettman continued to insist on not only a 50/50 split but related provisions that would effectively gut free agency in the NHL. Both sides stood firm, and on September 15, Bettman announced his lockout. He threatened once again to cancel the season unless the players met the owners' demands. Sound familiar?

Negotiations started and stopped over the next two months with virtually no progress. Although the players moved closer to Bettman's 50/50 split, this was conditional upon the size of a "make-whole provision" to ensure that existing player contracts would be honored even if the salary cap was frozen or reduced as a result of the shift in the split of revenues. The players wanted nearly $600 million; the owners offered barely $200 million. This was a huge issue for the players—without this provision, veterans with big contracts would be vulnerable, and there would be blood all over hockey's locker rooms.

During the fall and into the early winter, many European players returned home to play in the pro leagues there. Others organized various tournaments and charity events supported by the NHLPA, as they had done in the 1990s. This drove Bettman and his owners up the wall.

In November, the FMCS got involved and failed, as it had in football and basketball, to bring about a resolution. The hockey owners were simply intransigent. As time went by, Bettman announced the cancellation of preseason games and then, like he was slicing cold cuts, regular-season games in two-week increments. By the middle of December, it looked like an entire season might be lost again.

While this was going on, Bruce Meyer and I spent hours with the hockey players in meetings and teleconferences, educating them on their options. We explained the benefits and the risks of decertification, and we reviewed with them in detail what had happened in football the prior year, including potential concerns over the Norris-LaGuardia Act. We still believed that the appeals court ruling gave players enough leverage regarding free agents and rookies that the lawsuit option remained viable. However, we also made clear that if the union were to disclaim interest and become decertified this late in the game, in all likelihood the season would be lost. The players to a man seemed prepared to take that chance.

By late November, it became known that the NHLPA planned to disclaim interest and file an antitrust lawsuit attacking the legality of the lockout and the other restrictions on player free agency.

The players held strong. They had been well tutored by Don and Steve Fehr and were willing to fight to ensure a strong free agency market and a viable salary arbitration option. Their position on these issues remained unshaken. At many of the meetings and conference calls in which Bruce and I participated in that fall, "Fuck Bettman" was a constant refrain among the players.

On December 17, the players voted unanimously to dissolve the union and become a trade association by early January 2013. We hurriedly prepared all the necessary papers and began drafting a new lawsuit.

The NHL, following the usual owner playbook, then filed an unfair labor practice charge with the NLRB, asserting that the NHL players were not bargaining in good faith and were threatening a sham decertification. They also filed a lawsuit in New York federal court against the NHL players, seeking to preempt any lawsuit we might file by choosing New York as a friendlier forum. As in the NBA's lawsuit filed a year earlier, the NHL also threatened to void all NHL player contracts in the event that the players successfully disbanded their union. We were convinced that this threat was an empty one. As in the NBA, owners would never go through with such a drastic step because it would make superstars free agents, and other owners would fall all over themselves trying to sign them. Nonetheless, this was Bettman's way of "upping the ante."

Shortly before Christmas, Don asked me to reach out to Bettman, since I had known him for 30-plus years, to see if there was a way to bridge the remaining gaps. Fehr's strategy was twofold: first, there was an outside possibility that, as in basketball, we could actually get something done. And second, by having Meyer and me show up, it would make it clear to Bettman and his owners that the hockey players were prepared to abandon union status and go the lawsuit route, even if it meant giving up the entire season.

With nothing to lose, I called Bettman, who pretended to welcome my involvement. Bruce Meyer and I met briefly the following day with him, Daly, and their outside counsel, Shep Goldfein. With the exception of Bettman, the four of us were all refugees from the *McNeil* case. There were a few pleasantries, Bettman left, and we spent the next few hours reviewing open issues with Daly and Goldfein. We didn't get anywhere, but Meyer and I now had a much better understanding of what the key issues actually were. These included the length of the deal (as well as limits on individual player contract lengths), the impact of the split reduction on the salary cap, and some pension- and benefit-related issues. By this time, the league had backed off on eliminating salary arbitration and most of their proposals for tightening free agency.

On December 29, 2012, the Saturday after Christmas, just three days before we were prepared to trigger the disclaimer and launch our antitrust option, we met at the Skadden Arps office of Shep Goldfein, who had been Frank Rothman's acolyte in the *McNeil* trial back in the day. Bill Daly had been a young associate at Skadden who did research for Frank during the trial. Steve Fehr joined the group as well. We spent the day going back and forth on the key open issues, with occasional telephone caucuses with Don Fehr. This time we made real progress. There were just a few days before the players would abandon union status, which they were ready to do. Bettman by then had canceled games through January 13, after which, he said, the season was over.

Exactly a week later, beginning at 1:15 p.m. on Saturday, January 5, the parties started a 16-hour marathon bargaining session. At 5:30 a.m. on January 6, 2013, the parties announced a settlement. Both sides had made concessions on revenue sharing and the make-whole provisions, as well as the lengths of both the deal and limits on individual player contracts.

It's hard to know for sure whether the threat of disclaimer or of losing another full season forced the parties to reach an agreement. But at least a repeat of the 2004–05 disaster had been averted. The lockout had lasted 113 days. In a particularly insightful comment, Shane Doan of the Phoenix Coyotes said, "It was concessionary bargaining right from the beginning. We understood that, as much as we didn't want that. We understood that the nature of professional sports has changed in the last couple of CBAs in football, basketball and now obviously hockey. That's the way it has been going for the last ten years."[89] His words aptly summarized the titanic shift in bargaining in the owners' direction in all three sports.

The season was shortened to 48 games, but at least there was a season. As the *New York Times* pointed out that day, "The lockout was the third since Bettman became commissioner in 1993. The three lockouts together have led to the cancellation of about 2,400 regular-season games, about 10 percent of the games scheduled. That percentage is more than three times as high as any other major league in the same 20-year period."[90]

That statistic certainly made Bettman the "Lockout King" of professional sports. It is hard not to see the irony in all this. Gary Bettman has overseen the business of hockey as its CEO for more than a quarter of a century. This is an industry that has, at least according to Bettman, lost hundreds of millions of dollars—perhaps as much as a billion—during that period. Yet he still has a job, largely because of the draconian salary cap and revenue split he was able to achieve at the expense of the players.

In any normal business, if a CEO were actually losing hundreds of millions of dollars for his company, he would be fired. Not so in big-time sports. Bettman's been at it for 25 years, and he's still getting paid $10 million a year. Go figure.

CHAPTER 23

From the Depths to the Heights

IN THE MONTHS FOLLOWING THE 2011 NBA LOCK-
out, turmoil roiled the leadership of the NBPA. The players had lost
nearly $400 million in salaries during the lockout, and the hefty reduc-
tion in their share of the revenue split would likely cost them another
$3 billion over the next decade. Recriminations and accusations flew
back and forth, particularly between Billy Hunter and NBPA president Derek Fisher. Fisher, as well as several leading agents, believed
Hunter had caved to the owners and made a terrible deal. Hunter
claimed that Fisher had sold out the players in secret negotiations
with the league.

Over the years, Hunter had turned the union into his personal fief-
dom and intimidated many players from asking too many questions.
Fisher, a wily veteran who had spent 18 years as an NBA player and
been president of the union since 2006, was not easily intimidated. He
was soft-spoken but tough-minded.

In April 2012, Yahoo! Sports ran a long story detailing the sordid
state of affairs inside the NBPA, including the huge salaries Hunter
bestowed on himself and family members and the millions more in
payments he authorized to law firms and other advisors affiliated with
his children. At Fisher's urging, the NBPA executive committee hired
the New York law firm of Paul, Weiss and its well-known litigator Ted
Wells to conduct a full-blown investigation. The US Attorney's Office
for the Southern District of New York, working with the Department

of Labor, announced that it was opening its own investigation. In a bit of irony, Wells, who was once considered as a candidate for the NBPA executive director's job, would later become a virtual household name, conducting various investigations for the NFL including the notorious Deflategate investigation.

Eight months later, on January 17, 2013, after conducting dozens of interviews and reviewing thousands of internal union documents, Wells and Paul, Weiss issued their report on Hunter's management of the NBPA. Running over 400 pages and fortified with exhibits and appendices, it was a scathing indictment of Hunter's leadership. CBS Sports called the report a "magnum opus of malfeasance." While stopping just short of accusing Hunter of criminal activity, the report found numerous actual and potential conflicts of interest and breaches of Hunter's fiduciary duties. Among other things, the report concluded that Hunter had hired his best friend of nearly 30 years, Gary Hall, as general counsel. According to the report, Hall in turn manipulated members of the NBPA executive committee into giving Hunter a five-year extension of his contract, worth as much as $18 million, without getting the approval of the NBPA player reps as required by NBPA bylaws. That provision had specifically been added to avoid what had happened 16 years earlier, back in 1995, when Simon Gourdine similarly manipulated an extension of his contract.

Not three weeks later, on February 16, 2013, during the union meetings at the All-Star Game in Houston, Hunter was fired. The 29 player reps in attendance and the eight members of the elected executive committee voted to a man to kick him out. Ron Klempner, my former Weil associate, was named acting director.

Up to this point, I had been a spectator to the chaos. But I would soon be drawn in.

In April 2013, I got a call from Klempner asking if I would meet with the NBPA executive committee to brief them on issues relating to the search process. I had been through this a few times now. I explained that Reilly Partners, and specifically Bob Reilly, had worked with the NFLPA's executive committee on the search that led to De Smith's selection after Gene Upshaw's death. Reilly met with several members of the NBPA executive committee and was hired at the NBPA annual meeting in Las Vegas that summer.

Throughout the process, I kept in close contact with Reilly, who was personally conducting the initial interviews. At one point, in the fall of 2013, Reilly called me and asked me if I knew a lawyer from DC by the name of Michele Roberts. I said I knew her only by reputation—we had once been chosen by the magazine *American Lawyer* as the top trial lawyers in the country in successive years. I asked, "Why?"

Reilly said, "I just interviewed her for the NBPA executive director job, and I thought she was terrific."

"Are you fucking crazy?" I remember saying to Reilly. "Do you think that a woman could be the head of the basketball players' union? How do you think she would do in the locker room?" I obviously had trouble seeing how a 57-year-old female DC trial lawyer would relate to mostly 20-something kids with headphones and multimillion-dollar contracts.

Reilly calmly responded, "Just meet her and you decide for yourself." The following week, I flew to Chicago, and we interviewed a number of candidates, including Roberts. I was blown away. She was absolutely terrific!

A basketball nut from childhood, she knew the NBA well. Born in the South Bronx in the 1950s, Roberts had been dragged to Madison Square Garden by her two older brothers and witnessed the best and worst of my beloved Knicks. She was a brilliant student and received academic scholarships to an elite prep school and then to college, finally graduating from Boalt Hall School of Law at the University of California, Berkeley, near the top of her class. She started her legal career as a public defender before eventually becoming Skadden's top trial lawyer. At the February 2014 All-Star Weekend meeting in New Orleans, Chris Paul was elected as the new NBPA president, replacing

Fisher. Paul and the two NBPA vice presidents, Roger Mason and James Jones, began to closely monitor the search process.

Ultimately, three candidates were invited to the NBPA annual player rep meeting for the vote in late July 2014 in Las Vegas: Terdema Ussery, CEO of the Dallas Mavericks; Dean Garfield, a Washington lobbyist; and Michele Roberts.

On Sunday, July 28, Reilly, Klempner, and I met with the executive committee members to review the process. The election would be by a secret ballot, with player reps plus the executive committee members all entitled to vote. A candidate needed two-thirds of the 36 votes to be selected. Literally hundreds of players were scheduled to attend; this was a huge event. The players really cared this time.

Reilly and I were nervous. We secretly hoped that Roberts would get the nod, but we had no idea where she stood with the players. There was a lot of tension even at the executive committee level. Later that Sunday, I received calls from some of the more prominent NBA agents. I spoke to Arn Tellem a half-dozen times. Jeff Schwartz also called. That night Arn asked me whether I would get on the phone with other agents the next day and brief them before the vote. I had known Arn for nearly 40 years; we had always been on the same side, and we trusted each other.

The meetings began promptly at eight o'clock the next morning in a packed auditorium at the Avia Hotel in Las Vegas. There were at least 150 players in the room. Outside the room was a huge, swarming pack of media. The three candidates—Roberts, Ussery, and Garfield—made their presentations. All were strong; Roberts was spectacular. She was the ultimate trial lawyer, persuasively delivering her closing argument with grace and grit and a sense of humor.

Over the next couple of hours, I got almost constant phone calls from Tellem and the agents. At one point I left the meeting and got on a conference call with Tellem, Jeff Schwartz, Bill Duffy, Mark Bartelstein, and Dan Fagan. They asked me about the candidates and particularly about Roberts. I told them how impressed I was with her.

Not only was she one of the finest trial lawyers in the country, but she seemed tough and savvy and clearly dedicated to the players' best interests. More than half of the voting players were represented by this group of agents. I knew I had to choose my words carefully. I truly believed that Roberts was the best candidate, but I didn't want to oversell her to this group.

Minutes before the vote was to take place by secret ballot, I got one last call from Tellem. I walked outside the meeting, and Tellem asked me point-blank, "Can you vouch for Michele Roberts? Is she the right one?" I thought for a second—I had only known the woman a few months—but I was sure she was the right choice.

"I absolutely will vouch for her," I responded. I walked back into the room just as the voting was beginning. The players went one by one, by team, as they were called to vote. The process took another hour or so. An independent accounting firm tallied the votes. The vote was 32–2 for Roberts with 2 abstentions. We then made the vote unanimous. Reilly and I were ecstatic, as were the members of the executive committee. There were lots of hugs and lots of high-fives. It was historic indeed. CBS's headline read,

NBPA MAKES HISTORY WITH ELECTION OF MICHELE ROBERTS AS EXECUTIVE DIRECTOR

I could not help thinking about Fleisher that day—the socialist with all his whacked-out, far-left views—and how pleased he would be that after all these years his union was now headed by an African American woman of such poise and talent. I knew that he would be "kvelling"; bursting with pride.

This time we got it right. Over the next two years, Roberts and her new team, including Roger Mason as one of her key deputies, got ready for the next round of collective bargaining. She jumped into the task with a relish similar to that of De Smith in football, but with a decidedly more laid-back style. Both Chris Paul and James Jones remained intimately involved.

In the fall of 2016, I attended several collective bargaining meetings between the players, the league officials, and the NBA owners. My role by then was more symbolic than substantive. We met in a gigantic conference room at the Four Seasons Hotel in New York City. The discussions were kept secret; the media had no idea what was going on until an agreement was later announced. In one of the meetings, I ran into Michael Jordan, owner of the Charlotte Hornets (formerly the Bobcats). "Michael, you turned on us," I said. "You are a traitor. How can you sit on that side of the table?" We then just laughed and hugged.

I was struck by a number of differences from the old days. First, the meetings were enormously civil; Adam Silver was a stark contrast to his predecessor. Silver had already distinguished himself two years earlier in the way he had dispatched the noxious Donald Sterling. He was clearly the man in charge, but he didn't lord it over anyone. He didn't seem to aspire to being the "Lockout King," "King David," or even "The Man Who Would Be King." He was calm and straightforward, a tough negotiator but fair and reasonable. The meetings were very businesslike—none of the screaming or table-banging of years past.

I was also struck by how truly engaged the players were, particularly Chris Paul, James Jones, and NBPA executive Roger Mason. It was apparent that the players would all make a lot of money, but it was different now. It was more about controlling their own future and giving back to the sport and their communities. These players were prepared to take stands on social issues; more NBA players than ever now had their own charitable foundations. A lot had changed since 1970.

Finally, in December 2016, the NBA and its players' union agreed on yet another historic collective bargaining agreement. The revenue split remained at 50/50, but the billions in new television money made the economics of the deal much simpler and eased tensions. The players obtained additional revenue as part of the split as well as many other concessions, including substantial increases in retiree pensions and health benefits. The average salary in the NBA would soon reach

$10 million a year. We had come a long way since the *Robertson* lawsuit, and men like Fleisher, Robertson, Silas, Lanier, and Bridgeman had planted the seeds. Now, with new union leadership, the National Basketball Players Association would once again be at the forefront, the missteps of the past long gone. I was glad that I was able to help bring about this exciting new beginning.

Epilogue

OVER THE PAST HALF-CENTURY, PRO SPORTS FANS
have seen extraordinary changes in the games they love. I was lucky
enough to have a first-row seat to many of the changes chronicled in
these pages.

We have seen the rise of powerful sports unions, the enormous
impact of free agency, the explosion of media coverage, and the advent
of new technology, with television morphing from local to network
broadcasts to blanket cable coverage to the streaming of games over
the Internet. Fans have gone from reading about their teams in the
newspapers of the 1950s and 1960s to watching the games from wherever they want on their iPhones and iPads, live and in color.

Both fans and the media have become as conversant with salary
caps, luxury taxes, and other CBA provisions as they are with individual players stats.

Moreover, the globalization of US professional team sports has
revolutionized how the games are played and how they're consumed
by fans. The games are broadcast (often live) worldwide; nearly a
third of those watching the Super Bowl every year are doing so on
a television located outside the United States. American team logos
are sold around the globe; there are Lakers fans everywhere from
Beijing to Bangkok; from Madrid to Morocco. Millions of people from
Japan cheer for the Yankees, Mariners, and Red Sox, or wherever one
of their countrymen is playing. It was only a few years ago that the
NBA's Yao Ming was one of the most revered people in all China.

Today, NBA and NHL players regularly participate in the Olympics, and teams from both leagues barnstorm the world promoting the

NBA and NHL brands. Baseball too has become internationalized, with ties to the Japanese leagues and what is, in effect, a Caribbean "farm system" feeding the major leagues with scores of Latino players from a half-dozen different countries. Even football now schedules regular-season games in London and on occasion in Mexico.

But more important, the teams themselves have become globalized. Baseball has been inundated with players from Japan, Korea, and now Taiwan. Nearly a third of big-league rosters are composed of Latino players. At baseball's annual All-Star Game, as many as half of those elite players are from foreign soils. NBA rosters are a mini–United Nations of players from Spain, Italy, Latvia, Serbia, and many other places. Many of the NHL's top stars hail from Sweden, Russia, Finland, and the Czech Republic. Only the NFL has remained uniquely American, with an occasional Canadian sneaking across the border. Now when we refer to the World Series, it actually means something.

Along the way, a lot of sports myths have been debunked. How often were we told that small markets could never survive in the era of free agency? Nonsense. In 2016, the Cleveland Cavaliers won the NBA championship, the Kansas City Royals won the World Series, the Pittsburgh Penguins won the Stanley Cup, and the Denver Broncos won the Super Bowl—all small-market teams.

Another myth: the overexposure of television will ruin gate receipts. No one will go to games; fans will stay home and watch on television. Wrong. Attendance in all four major sports has continued to rise over the last 25 years despite the fact that every single game in every major sport is now on television somewhere.

Another myth: guaranteed player contracts will ruin professional sports; players simply won't play hard if they get paid regardless of performance. More nonsense.

Today, virtually every contract in basketball, hockey, and baseball is fully guaranteed and more than half of the contracts in football are as well. As far as I can tell, the competitive spirit is alive and well in those leagues. These and other archaic shibboleths from the 1950s and 1960s have disappeared from today's sports lexicon.

More than ever today, societal issues play themselves out in the context of professional sports, be they domestic violence, substance abuse, racial issues, and even income inequality. Players are more willing than ever to speak out on these issues and to play an active role in their communities. Today's players are role models, whether they like it or not. All this was the inevitable result of free agency, which gave players not just economic security but also the self-confidence to utilize their celebrity to take a stand—or a knee—on issues while continuing to help others in their communities.

Sometimes what players do leads to controversy. The actions of some NFL players during the playing of the National Anthem—a hot-button issue if there ever was one—certainly fall into that category. At first Colin Kaepernick, and later scores of other players, knelt or linked arms as the anthem played to call attention to what they believed to be continued racial injustice in America. For many, their message was lost in translation; it seemed a disrespectful action toward both our flag and our country by spoiled, overpaid, and ungrateful athletes. You can debate fairly whether it was the right place and the right time to protest, but you can't debate these players' First Amendment right to demonstrate against things they believe are wrong. President Trump brought the players and owners together, however briefly and inadvertently, as they protested against his attack on the players' fundamental constitutional rights.

The real point is that players today have thrown off the shackles of the past and are empowered to speak their minds without fear of reprisal. Fans, like it or not, will just have to get used to it or stop watching.

In October 2016—the 40th anniversary of the *Robertson* antitrust settlement, which led to real free agency for the first time in professional sports—Oscar Robertson appeared in a Town Hall discussion cosponsored by ESPN's online sports and culture magazine, *Undefeated,* and the Smithsonian Institution's newly opened National

Museum of African American History and Culture in Washington, DC. The day prior, he published a first-person article on *Undefeated*, in which he wrote the following:

> As the longest-serving President of the NBPA from 1965 to my retirement in 1974, the basketball union's newfound direction makes me proud. I am also proud of the fact that 2016–17 Season will be the 40th Anniversary played under the Oscar Robertson Agreement, which was enacted following a court settlement in April 1976 and led to NBA Players becoming the first professional athletes to achieve free agency. I consider the Oscar Robertson Agreement as important to my legacy as anything I did on the basketball court.
>
> The *Oscar Robertson* lawsuit was also a civil rights issue. Bound to their teams by the reserve clause, and actively discouraged from exercising their First Amendment rights, the growing contingent of black players in the 1960s NBA was nowhere near as vocal during the civil rights era as they wanted to be. Once free agency became a reality, the shackles were broken.

Practically every player already lends his name, time, and money to one or more foundations or causes. Many are focused on hometown issues, which are important. We are just starting to see the potential as these organizations proliferate and link up with one another to achieve critical change on a broader scale.

Today's players owe an enormous debt to those who came before them and who were willing to stand up and fight, even at the risk of their careers. The roster is long and storied: Oscar Robertson, Bob Lanier, Paul Silas, and Junior Bridgeman (basketball); John Mackey, Marvin Powell, Freeman McNeil, and Gene Upshaw (football); Curt Flood, Andy Messersmith, Catfish Hunter, and Dave McNally (baseball); and Dale McCourt and Gerry Cheevers (hockey). It took real courage for these players to stand up to their "owners." They were putting their careers and their very livelihoods on the line, as their bosses were not known to be tolerant of "troublemakers."

Then there were the labor leaders: Fleisher, Miller, Fehr, Goodenow, and Upshaw (again), who led these players and others in battles with the owners in each of the leagues. Their zealous belief in the rule of law, common decency, and a sense of fairness created the structures that have benefited not just the players but also the leagues and the sports owners themselves. Together these individuals proved that while the arc of the moral universe may be long, it does bend toward justice.

Among owners and league officials, there were many pioneers who foresaw the future and embraced it. Pete Rozelle's concept of revenue sharing among NFL owners and his belief in network television made the NFL the unmatched success that it is today. Lamar Hunt's vision created the AFL and ultimately the Super Bowl. Paul Tagliabue and owners like Dan Rooney and Wellington Mara recognized that endlessly fighting with their players was bad for the sport and bad for business. They each played critical roles in the landmark *White* settlement, which combined free agency with revenue sharing.

Tagliabue, perhaps sports' most underrated commissioner, not only recognized how critical labor peace would be for football but also negotiated a series of television contracts, which hugely expanded NFL coverage and filled the pockets of the 32 NFL owners with more gold than even they could handle. For some reason, Tagliabue remains unappreciated by his own side.

David Stern, a.k.a. "King David," the kid from Teaneck, New Jersey, turned out to be a marketing genius. He recognized that the way to promote the NBA was through its players—particularly through superstars like Magic Johnson, Larry Bird, and later, Michael Jordan and LeBron James. He took a league that was deeply troubled in the early 1980s and, through his creativity and in particular the idea of a salary cap tied to a revenue-sharing formula, turned it into a powerhouse. Stern also recognized the enormous potential for popularizing the NBA on an international scale, both in Europe and, more importantly, in China, which has become the league's second-largest market. Russ Granik, a highly intelligent and decent man, deserves credit for forging some of those initiatives and for putting up with Stern for more than two decades.

In baseball, Bud Selig, for all his faults, ultimately realized that endless squabbles with the baseball union were injurious to the game. Working particularly through Selig's deputy commissioner Bob DuPuy, baseball ultimately created a structure with its players that has maintained labor peace for more than two decades. Rob Manfred, the latest commissioner, appears to be following along the same lines.

And Gary Bettman deserves at least some credit for his sheer perseverance in keeping the NHL afloat and expanding its revenue base over the last quarter-century. For that he gets a quasi-honorable mention, notwithstanding his penchant for lockouts.

I should mention NFL general counsel Jeff Pash, at whom I've taken some shots along the way. I received a handwritten note from him a few weeks after I left the Weil firm in 2017 to start a new adventure in mediation—trying to settle disputes instead of causing them. Pash wrote, in part, "Your impact on all of sports will be lasting and deep. You should be very proud of what you have accomplished and of the leadership role you've played in so many fields. My warmest wishes to you for much success and happiness in your new role as peacemaker."

And that from a worthy adversary of three decades. I guess he ain't so bad after all. Thanks, Jeff.

Of course, there were many Neanderthals along the way who did everything they could to keep players "in their place," a doomed strategy that actually hurt the growth of the very games they sought to protect. This rogues' gallery includes men like Bowie Kuhn, Charlie Finley, and Calvin Griffith, among others, who sought to prevent players from being represented by a strong union and later fought bitterly to bar any form of baseball free agency. Luckily, they lost, and the sport has thrived ever since.

In hockey, there was Alan Eagleson, who conspired with the likes of Bill Wirtz and John Ziegler to keep his own players down. Eagleson would eventually go to jail for that.

In football, there was a long list of rogues, starting back in the 1970s with men like Tex Schramm, Hugh Culverhouse, and Jack Donlan, who sought to "keep the cattle down on the range." They too would fail. It was only an enlightened man like Paul Tagliabue who realized that in the modern era, NFL players had to be free.

Later, men like Roger Goodell and Jerry Richardson would try to turn back the clock and, through arrogance and greed, try to squeeze every penny they could from the battered bodies of NFL players. Indeed, Richardson would eventually be forced to sell his team when he went from abusing players to allegedly abusing women.

Basketball too had its share of goats and racists, men like Ted Stepien and, more recently, Donald Sterling. David Stern back in the day and Adam Silver more recently were able to right that ship quickly and get owners like that out of the NBA.

While the games themselves have barely changed, the business of sports has—radically. Thanks largely to free agency, minimum salaries have risen, average salaries have risen, guaranteed contracts are now the norm in three of the four major sports, and the players' share of revenues, in terms of gross dollars, has gone up dramatically. And who has benefited most? The team owners. There has been an extraordinary explosion in the size of the major team sports' revenue pie. Prior to 1970, it was less than $1 billion; now, it's approaching a combined $35 billion. Franchise valuations in all sports except hockey average more than $1 billion per team, with the NFL averaging close to $2 billion. Even hockey hovers around half a billion—still 50 times the value of a hockey franchise back in 1970. The combined total franchise value in all four sports is nearly $250 billion. Indeed, the sheer amount of money to be shared among owners and players, particularly with the injection of new television and other revenue sources, has recently led the players and owners in at least two sports, baseball and basketball, to resolve their collective bargaining issues without the need for lawsuits or lockouts. This is likely to be the future of collective bargaining in sports.

This is real progress. It could only have been achieved because a group of young men, many of them black, who battled each other ferociously on the court and on the field, came together for a higher purpose. They came together to establish their fundamental rights and to ensure that they and future players would be treated with respect and dignity. It also could not have been achieved unless men on both sides were willing to compromise. Throughout the fight, legal battles were won and lost, sports law evolved, and leverage shifted from one side to the other with each new lawsuit and each new legal theory. That uncertainty led to compromise—a concept that many of our current politicians might do well to reinsert into today's political environment of gridlock and rancor.

Not everything is candy and roses among the major sports. Hockey continues to struggle financially, with too many franchises and not enough US national interest in the sport. The NFL lives under the shadow of concussions and injuries, which may in the long run have an impact on its continued growth, at least at today's rate.

There continue to be issues regarding performance-enhancing drugs in all four sports, which can only be dealt with through continued vigilance and testing. So far that issue has not dimmed fans' enthusiasm for the games. The NFL also worries that increased technology, with giant home movie screens and many other ways to watch games outside the stadium, may have an impact on stadium revenues. This is a phenomenon that will be carefully monitored in the future.

Baseball's big problem is demographic; the sport continues to skew toward older, whiter fans. The MLB has lost touch with many African American fans, though its Latino fan base is vital and growing. Only the NBA seems to have no current worries, as new superstars continue to emerge and the international market flourishes. There is growing competition out there from new hybrids of sports and entertainment, including mixed martial arts, gaming, and fantasy sports of all types. It is hard to know what kind of impact all this will have on the interest of younger fans in traditional sports. There are no guarantees.

For now, professional sports have more meaning and cultural power than ever. In a country that is so widely divided politically, economically, racially, and in many other ways, athletic contests seem to be the one thing that pulls people of all stripes—rich or poor, black or white, Muslim or Christian—together. Democrats and Republicans alike, the far left and the far right, collectively root for and against Bill Belichick, Robert Kraft, Tom Brady, and the New England Patriots. Whether you are from a red state or a blue state, you can still enjoy the Super Bowl, the World Series, the Stanley Cup, or the NBA Finals.

Regardless of how you voted in November 2016 or will vote in future elections, you can still turn on the television and watch these magnificent athletes battle each other to win a championship. That is something we all share, whatever happens in Washington or anywhere else. Together we revel in the simple joy of watching the players play the game.

Acknowledgments

WHEN I FIRST CONVINCED MYSELF THAT WRITING this book was actually something worth doing, I had no idea what I was getting myself into. I had spent a career writing legal briefs, pleadings, and arguments on everything from nuclear power plants to cartoon characters, with some sports stuff in between. But writing a book was about to be a whole new ball game. Luckily, I had a lot of help along the way.

From the outset, friends and colleagues who had heard some of these stories and knew of my involvement in sports urged me to write a book about my experiences. Little did I know it would take five years and at times become all-consuming as I continued my legal career and launched a new chapter after leaving Weil, Gotshal & Manges a couple of years back. A special thanks goes to my close friend and now law partner, David Berg. Through his experience as the author of several books, David gave me excellent guidance and endless encouragement filtered through his raucous and sometimes annoying sense of humor.

He also lent me his agent, David McCormick, who was instrumental in giving me great feedback on both the original concept and the drafts as we went along. He also found me a trio of terrific editors, who took my misshapen efforts at storytelling and turned them into a real narrative that someone might actually want to read. At the start, Jamie Malinowski took my initial drafts chapter by chapter and through painstaking editing and insightful comments shaped my work into an actual book. Along the way, he taught me whatever I now know about real writing in contrast to spewing out legal mumbo jumbo. Thankfully, Jamie is also a font of sports trivia, which helped enormously in framing the narrative with interesting tidbits of sports arcana.

Next came Jane Fransson, whose insight and gentle persuasion convinced me to discard some of my favorite stories because she told me they were either boring or otherwise standing directly in the way of the narrative force of the book. Thanks, Jane.

I also owe an enormous debt of gratitude to the talents of Hugh Lundgren, who took what I thought was the final product and punched up the prose, rewrote whole sections to make them more readable for those not steeped in legal bullshit, and insightfully suggested a new and now final title, noting that those words pretty much summed up the whole purpose of the book. Also, honorable mention goes to Michael O'Daniel, whose timely suggestions and last-minute edits corrected some errors and made the book a better one.

Of course, this book simply could not have been written at all without the extraordinary aid of my many assistants, starting with Angela Evans and Brenda Young at Weil and followed by Lusia Lee, Betty Lam, and Tiffany Stokes at Berg & Androphy. They took my awkward dictation, turned it into the beginnings of a manuscript, and then patiently typed my edits and reedits until the words were actually readable and understandable. Angela was there at the beginning and stuck it through to the end. And thanks also go to Mark Fretz and Evan Phail at Diversion Publishing / Radius Book Group, who got all these efforts over the finish line. Stuart Tink was helpful in this regard as well.

And finally, a special and loving thanks to my wife, Katy, who put up with me through this ordeal and for the 50 years or so that preceded it.

Notes

1 Steve Aschburner, "The All-Star Game That Nearly Wasn't," NBA.com, February 13, 2014.

2 Ibid.

3 Ibid.

4 Ibid.

5 *New York Times* obituary, May 5, 1989.

6 Ibid.

7 *Los Angeles Times* article, November 2, 2002.

8 Bruce Berman, "Can the NBA Save Itself," *Sports Illustrated*, November 1, 1982.

9 Ibid.

10 Ibid.

11 *Sports Illustrated*, November 1, 1982.

12 *Newsweek*, April 4, 1983.

13 Sam Goldaper, "The Sublime and the Ridiculous," *New York Times*, March 4, 1982.

14 "Cavs a Disaster," *Cleveland Plain Dealer*, April 2, 1982.

15 *Sports Illustrated*, November 1, 1982.

16 Ibid.

17 Sam Goldaper, "Rumors of Salary Cap," *New York Times*, May 25, 1982.

18 Sam Goldaper, "Fight Looms over Salary Cap," *New York Times*, June 26, 1982.

19 Ibid.

20 *Sports Business Journal*, March 16, 2015.

21 Ira Berkow, "The NBA Money Game," *New York Times*, March 4, 1983.

22 *Sports Business Journal*, March 16, 2015.

23 Sam Goldaper, "NBA Strike Averted with Accord on 4-Year Pact," *New York Times*, April 1, 1983.

24 *Los Angeles Times*, April 1, 1983.

25 *New York Times*, April 1, 1983.

26 Ibid.

27 Ibid.

28 Sam Goldaper, "Quick but Expensive Trip to London," *New York Times*, November 1, 1985.

29 Sam Goldaper, "Knicks Upheld in Effort to Acquire Albert King," *New York Times*, November 5, 1985.

30 Ibid.

31 *New York Times*, November 8, 1982.

32 Joe Nocera, "Donald Trump's Less-Than-Artful Failure in Pro Football," *New York Times*, February 19, 2016.

33 *Wall Street Journal*, November 16, 1984.

34 USFL v. NFL Trial Transcript.

35 Ibid.

36 *Los Angeles Times*, July 30, 1986.

37 USFL v. NFL Trial Transcript.

38 *Los Angeles Times*, October 30, 1986.

39 *Washington Post*, November 8, 1986.

40 "Union Seeks to Disband," *Orlando Sentinel*, November 8, 1989.

41 Ibid.

42 Charles Bricher, "Rival Group Campaigning to Represent NFL Players," *Florida Sun Sentinel*, December 16, 1990.

43 *USA Today*, June 15, 1990.

44 *Washington Post*, May 24, 1991.

45 *San Francisco Chronicle*, January 30, 1992.

46 *New York Times*, February 2, 1992.

47 *USA Today*, March 6, 1992.

48 All testimony quotes are taken directly from the McNeil v. NFL Trial Transcript.

49 Paul Domowitch, *Philadelphia Daily News*, June 17, 1992.

50 Paul McEnroe, "NFL Players Just Gotta Be Free Agents," *National Law Journal*, July 20, 1992.

51 Thomas George, "Jury Sacks NFL's Plan B," *New York Times*, September 11, 1992.

52 Ibid.

53 Ibid.

54 "NFL Plan B Found Illegal," *Minneapolis Tribune*, September 11, 1992.

55 "Thoughts Turn to Future," *USA Today*, September 11, 1992.

56 *New York Times*, September 11, 1992.

57 Mike Freeman, "Plan B Is Dead," *Washington Post*, September 11, 1992.

58 *New York Times*, September 13, 1992.

59 Glen Macnow, "Players Prevailed in a Blowout," *Philadelphia Inquirer*, September 12, 1992.

60 Ibid.

61 *Pro Football Weekly*, October 25, 1992.

62 Ibid.

63 Larry Tye, *Boston Globe*, November 22, 1992.

64 Thomas George, "Football Talks Stall," *New York Times*, December 30, 1992.

65 Ibid.

66 *New York Times*, November 18, 1992.

67 "NHL Files Licensing Suit," *New York Times*, December 9, 1993.

68 Dave Caldwell, "NHL and Players Reach Deal to End Lockout," *New York Times*, July 13, 2005.

69 Wendy E. Lane, "NBA Makes a Deal with Players," *Arizona Desert News*, June 22, 1995.

70 Ibid.

71 Ibid.

72 Mike Jensen, "NBA Players to Vote on Keeping Union," *Philadelphia Inquirer*, July 27, 1995.

73 Ibid.

74 Wendy E. Lane, *Arizona Desert News*, July 27, 1995.

75 Scott Howard-Cooper, "NBA Players Chose Union by a Landslide," *Los Angeles Times*, September 13, 1995.

76 *Spokane Spokesman* review, September 13, 1995.

77 Phil Taylor, "State of the NBA Union," *Sports Illustrated*, November 2, 1998.

78 Mike Wise, "NBA's Final Proposal," *New York Times,* January 1, 1999.

79 *New York Times,* January 9, 1999.

80 Michael Heistand, "Quinn Earns an Eleventh Hour Assist," *USA Today,* January 19, 1999.

81 Mark Maske, "NFLPA's Upshaw Will Stay for Now," *Washington Post,* April 10, 2008.

82 Ibid.

83 "NFL Retirees in Dispute with Union," *New York Times,* March 2, 2008.

84 *Washington Post,* March 14, 2012.

85 Charles P. Pierce, "Grantland, Patriot Games," ESPN.com, August 3, 2015.

86 ESPN.com, September 13, 2011.

87 Howard Beck, "NBA Union Signals a Shift," *New York Times,* November 8, 2011.

88 Joanne C. Gerstner, "Players Express Frustration," *New York Times,* November 15, 2011.

89 "NHL and Players Settle," *New York Times,* January 6, 2013.

90 Ibid.